New York
e>>guide

New York
e>>guide

In style • In the know • Online

www.enewyork.dk.com

LONDON, NEW YORK,
MELBOURNE, MUNICH AND DELHI
www.dk.com

Produced by Blue Island Publishing

Contributors
Dahlia Devkota, Rachel F. Freeman, Jonathan Schultz

Photographers
Susan Sayler, Andrew Holigan

Reproduced in Singapore by Colourscan
Printed and bound in Singapore by Tien Wah Press

First published in Great Britain in 2005
by Dorling Kindersley Limited
80 Strand, London WC2R 0RL

A CIP catalogue record is available from the British Library.

ISBN 1 4053 0616 5

The information in this e>>guide is checked annually.

This guide is supported by a dedicated website which provides the very latest information for visitors to
New York; please see page 7 for the web address and password. Some information, however, is liable to
change, and the publishers cannot accept responsibility for any consequences arising from the use of this
book, nor for any material on third party websites, and cannot guarantee that any website address in this
book will be a suitable source of travel information.

We value the views and suggestions of our readers very highly. Please write to:
Publisher, DK Eyewitness Travel Guides,
Dorling Kindersley, 80 Strand, London WC2R 0RL, Great Britain.

Contents

The only guidebook that's always up-to-date

Written by people who know the city inside out, this guide provides in-depth information and reviews of the best the city has to offer. Listings are packed with great ideas and accompanied by stylish photographs, for a tantalizing foretaste of what's in store. Detailed practical information for each entry – including map references to the Street Finder at the back of the guide – take you directly to the heart of the action. So, whether you live in New York or are just visiting, to experience the real soul and pace of the city, you need this guide. Now visit the website...

top choice

- Spend the morning at a department store or museum

- Stroll in Central Park and other havens

- Browse New York's clothes shops for new ideas

- Discover cutting-edge performance and innovative arts

- Gain a new perspective on the classic tours and sights

- Find a bar to match your mood, be it mellow or loud

- Take your pick of restaurants, from pizzerias to Japanese

features

The one-stop website for all the city has to offer

Click on to enewyork.dk.com for the latest, most complete news from and about places listed in the guide, plus travelers' reviews, features on hot topics and an up-to-the-minute shortlist of New York's most useful service providers, from the visitors bureau to ticket agents. The website is only available to purchasers of e>>guide New York (the unique password given below allows you access). And it's constantly updated. Every time you visit, you bring your guidebook bang up to date!

• Get the latest travel news and miss the crowds

• Check out the weather forecast and catch a cheap flight

• Book a hotel room that suits your budget and style

• Tap into what's on downtown and who's in at the Guggenheim

• Browse reviews of the latest productions and secure tickets online

• Reserve a top table or seek out the best cheap eats

• Plan your shopping trip online

reviews

 password for access to website: **newyork59263**

top choices

Against a backdrop of thrusting skyscrapers, New York is a city that buzzes with energy, its adrenaline-fueled, 24-hour lifestyle always charged with excitement. This is also a city of diverse cultures, which come together to offer some of the most talked-about shops, bars, restaurants, and clubs in the world. This guide leads you to New York's latest and best, opening with the top choices of what to do through the year and 24/7.

TOP CHOICES – *the year*

Whatever the season, there's always something going on in New York. Spring's arrival recharges New Yorkers, sending everyone outdoors to explore their city. Many venture to Brooklyn's Botanic Garden to witness the brief, energizing display of cherry blossoms. Summer, hot and sultry, offers the greatest number of cultural events for visitors, with outdoor concerts, parades, and neighborhood festivals, and the famous Museum Mile celebration. The metamorphosis of Central Park into a sea of bright yellow, rusty red, and mellow orange foliage heralds the Fall, when the Marathon snakes through the city's five boroughs. Winter might bring record snows one month and mild days the next. Yet not even the weather's mercurial nature can detract from the pageantry and fairytale spirit of the holidays.

SPRING

Cherry Blossom at Brooklyn Botanic Garden
www.bbg.org; first weekend in May
Blooming on 220 trees adjacent to the world-renowned Japanese Hill and Pond Garden, the cherry blossoms are celebrated for one precious weekend. Traditional Japanese dances are performed, music is played, and there are origami workshops, Japanese animated films ("anime"), and samurai sword demonstrations. **May**

Tribeca Film Festival
www.tribecafilmfestival.org; late Apr–early May
Since it began in 2002, the Tribeca Film Festival has attracted hundreds of thousands of cineastes eager to view, debut, and discuss films of all scales and styles. Every year the festival attracts more attention, so check the website's booking page as early as possible if you want tickets to the hottest premieres. Everything from one of the *Star Wars* prequels to 10-minute, student-produced animated shorts have featured. The festival box office is at 20 Harrison Street (Map 1 C1), and events take place in venues as diverse as the Tribeca Film Center and Prada's SoHo store. **Apr–May**

SUMMER

Outdoor Concerts
www.summerstage.org; www.celebratebrooklyn.org/celebrate
Central Park's eclectic SummerStage outdoor concert series might host superstar DJ Paul Van Dyke one night and the New York Philharmonic the next. Meanwhile, across the East River in Prospect Park, Celebrate Brooklyn has more of a neighborhood flavor, with jazz, indie pop, and plenty of Latin salsa. **Jun–Aug**

Museum Mile Festival
www.museummilefestival.org; 6–9pm second Tue in Jun
For one June evening, the stretch of Fifth Avenue known as the Museum Mile (82nd to 105th streets) closes to traffic, and its venerable art museums waive admission charges. However, three hours to rush around the Met or the Guggenheim is a little tight, and it's better to

For more events and festivals throughout the year, see ➤➤ www.enewyork.dk.com

simply soak up the vibrant street scene on Fifth Avenue. Noted local artists lead art workshops, while musicians, dancers, and jugglers perform. **Jun**

Parades

Puerto Rican Day: 2nd Sun in Jun;
Gay Pride (www.hopinc.org): last Sun in Jun
The Puerto Rican Day Parade takes over Fifth Avenue from 44th to 86th streets, and ranks among the city's largest and most festive celebrations, with over 100,000 marchers and 3 million spectators. The Gay Pride March (check website for current route) commemorates the 1969 Stonewall riots in West Village, a galvanizing moment in the Gay Pride movement. The parties and club nights built around Gay Pride are legendary. **Jun**

FALL

Feast of San Gennaro

www.sangennaro.org
Get a taste of old Little Italy during the grandest festival on the calendar for Italian New Yorkers. For 11 days, the spiritual heart of the neighborhood – Mulberry Street between Canal and East Houston streets – teems with vendors selling sausage-and-pepper, fruit ice, and Italian pastries. Processions featuring effigies of San Gennaro take place throughout the festivities. **Mid-Sep**

New York Marathon

www.ingnycmarathon.org;
first Sunday of November
Attracting 35,000 athletes and over two million spectators, the marathon weaves through all five boroughs before a victor crosses the finish line. Celebrity competitors have recently included local hip-hop impresario Sean "P. Diddy" Combs, who ran modeling a mohawk – and a pack of bodyguards. Check the website for the race route map. Most spectators congregate along Central Park; head to an outer borough to get a closer look at the action. **Nov**

WINTER

Carnegie Hall & Lincoln Center Holiday Performances

www.carnegiehall.org; www.lincolncenter.org;
www.nycballet.com
Come December, Carnegie Hall turns its attention to seasonal favorites, with performances by the Vienna Boys Choir and Musica Sacra. The New York City Ballet's staging of George Balanchine's *The Nutcracker* at Lincoln Center is a hallowed holiday tradition. Evening and weekend performances sell out quickly, but off-peak tickets are far more readily available. **Dec/Jan**

Restaurant Weeks

Check nycvisit.com for participating restaurants and dates
What began as an effort to attract local diners to their neighborhood restaurants has evolved into one of the city's most hotly anticipated events. For selected weeks in winter (and also in summer), Manhattan's most acclaimed restaurants offer three-course, prix-fixe lunch and dinner menus that rarely venture above $20 and $30 respectively. **Nov–Jan**

Hot Chocolate Festival at City Bakery

www.hot-chocolate-festival.com, throughout Feb
As if the original hot chocolate at City Bakery *(see p39)* were not cause enough for celebration, more than 20 novel varieties join the menu during February to melt away the city's winter doldrums. Visitors can perk up with a regular or espresso hot chocolate until 11am, after which the day's specially prepared flavor is featured. Some unlikely successes include chili pepper, beer, and banana peel varieties. **Feb**

The start to any day in the city-that-never-sleeps is filled with anticipation. Take a stroll around Manhattan in the early morning light and you may see fruit vendors setting out produce on a midtown corner, oblivious to suited professionals hustling by, or Upper East Side dog-walkers, with four leashes to a hand, shepherding overeager purebreds through Central Park. Though the subways are thronged with commuters, there is a less harried side to New York mornings, offering pleasures that even many locals are oblivious to. Workers in Herald Square may never know the simple enjoyment of watching chess in Chinatown, or of sampling fresh-baked muffins at the Union Square Farmer's Market. So, take advantage of the early hours to best experience snippets of the city as it rouses itself for the day ahead.

Jog or Walk on Brooklyn Bridge

For the virtuous early riser, no activity in New York suggests "morning" so emphatically as a jog across Brooklyn Bridge. To best appreciate the early rays, take the A train to High Street/Brooklyn Bridge, and walk or run with the commuter traffic toward Lower Manhattan. The sun glows pink against the bridge's arches and gradually illuminates the city's towering columns of glass, steel, and stone. Below, the East River shimmers gold.

Wall Street at the Start of Trading

The New York Stock Exchange, founded in 1792, is America's most hallowed temple of money-making. At around 9:15am, just before the opening bell tolls at 11 Wall Street, glimpse traders scurrying between the granite columns of the Broad Street entrance. Watching their hustle might give you an appetite, so grab a fortifying gourmet muffin and coffee from Dean & DeLuca Café at Borders (100 Broadway). *(See also p160.)*

Sunday Mass at St. Patrick's Cathedral
50th Street and 5th Avenue (Map 6 E1)

Even for travelers who have seen Europe's most dazzling Gothic cathedrals, St. Patrick's is still an awesome spectacle. It is the country's largest Gothic church – at 405 ft (123 m) long and with spires reaching skyward some 330 ft (100 m). Every Sunday, the cathedral fills with hundreds of parishioners and visitors for Mass. Should you not wish to participate directly in the service, watch proceedings from a pew near the Fifth Avenue entrance.

The Early Boat to Liberty Island
Ferry: www.statueoflibertyferry.com
Statue of Liberty: www.statuereservations.com

After nearly three years of closure following the 9/11 terrorist attacks, the Statue of Liberty reopened to the public. Once again, visitors can experience the sweeping panorama of New York Harbor from the feet of Lady Liberty. It is, of course, a perennially popular attraction, but you can avoid the heaviest crowds by catching the 9am Circle Line ferry from Battery Park's Castle Clinton (ticket windows open at 8:30am).

Union Square Farmer's Market

E. 17th St. and Bdwy (Map 3 D1), 8am–6pm Mon, Wed, Fri & Sat
For four days each week, the lot adjoining Union Square West fills with farmers from all over the region, eager to show off and sell the season's bounty. Besides the unmatched quality of the produce, the market provides a direct link between growers and consumers. Drink a little cider, and chat to the farmer about the orchards where his apples grow.

Brunch in the West Village

Paris Commune, 411 Bleecker Street (Map 3 B3); Deborah, 43 Carmine Street (Map 3 C4); Florent (see p38)
Around 10am, on virtually every West Village block, slate signs spring up outside the neighborhood's bistros, proclaiming "Brunch!" in bright pastel chalk. At the most

popular restaurants, you may have to queue for a table, but with mimosas, juices, and Bloody Marys often included free of charge, the value and quality of a West Village brunch is worth the wait. Try the French toast at Paris Commune, the fluffy, vegetable-studded omelets at cozy Deborah, or the old favorite Florent.

Dress Racks in the Garment District

The grit and pace of workaday New York is on vibrant display in this historic district. Roughly bounded north and south by 34th and 40th streets, and east and west by 9th and 7th avenues, the Garment District hosts a colorful fashion show every morning as clothing and fabric wholesalers of Hasidic Jewish, West Indian, Pakistani, Chinese, and Indian backgrounds push bulging dress racks from delivery trucks to storefronts. Buy a bagel and coffee from a vendor's cart, and try to avoid encounters between dress-rack wheels and your toes.

Pastries at Dean & DeLuca

560 Broadway (see p65)
The nation's pre-eminent purveyor of gourmet groceries traces its origin to the corner of Broadway and Prince Street, in the heart of SoHo. Morning customers can find formidable temptations among Dean & DeLuca's renowned pastries and cakes, as well as superior coffee and fine teas. The in-house grocer selects muffins, Danishes, doughnuts, and scones from the city's top bakeries, so customers can choose from a cross-section of the best baked goods leaving New York ovens. The coffee counter is designed with commuters in mind – drinks are sold to go.

A Stroll through Columbus Park

Mei Lai Wah Coffeeshop, 64 Bayard Street (Map 2 E1)
Over 100 years ago, this pleasant Chinatown park was the heart of the violent Little Five Points neighborhood, dramatically depicted in Martin Scorcese's film *Gangs of New York*. Though times have clearly changed, tempers do still flare when elderly Chinese men battle it out over chessboards at the park's many picnic tables. Close to the park's gates, palm readers and cobblers solicit business from Chinese-speaking passersby. Buy a roast pork bun and coffee from the Mei Lai Wah Coffeeshop, and take in the charming scene.

Dim Sum in Chinatown

Golden Unicorn (see p25); HSF, 46 Bowery (Map 2 E1)
Be it a fishmonger tying crab claws shut or a woman weighing a sack of lychee nuts, Chinatown offers a feast for the eyes. And during late morning, the feast moves into the neighborhood's grand dim sum dining rooms. Steaming carts filled with roast pork buns, lotus leaf-wrapped rice, veget-able dumplings, and dessert custards circulate between communal tables. Indicate to the server which plates intrigue you (note that most servers speak very little English, so pointing is the accepted vocabulary), and start eating. Two of the best dim-sum restaurants are Golden Unicorn and HSF.

TOP CHOICES – *afternoon*

New York hits its stride in the afternoon. Save for the nightclubs and a few bars and restaurants, the entire city is open for business and the shopping streets are at their most bustling. Of course, even commerce takes a lunch break, and, when it does, there is no better place to be on a sunny day than midtown's picturesque Bryant Park. Here, in one of the city's most treasured green spaces, you can enjoy unrivaled people-watching. If you're feeling energetic after lunch, you might opt for a walk or bike ride through Central Park, art gallery browsing in Chelsea, or some retail therapy in SoHo's chic boutiques. Afternoons are for taking things at your own pace, even if that means simply sipping an espresso and reading a first-edition classic in a cozy armchair.

Boutique-Browsing in SoHo

Moss *(see p64)*; Chanel, 139 Spring St. (Map 3 B5); Helmut Lang *(see p62)*; Dolce & Gabbana, 434 West Broadway (Map 1 C2)
Shoppers who stray from the big, brash emporiums on Broadway's SoHo stretch are duly rewarded on the neighborhood's quaint side streets, where designer boutiques abound. Fans of sleek, modernist furnishings should stop at Moss. European-fashion mavens can take their pick from Chanel, Helmut Lang, and Dolce & Gabbana.

Gallery-Hopping in Chelsea

Pace Wildenstein, 34 W. 25th St.; Mary Boone Gallery, 541 W. 24th St.; Gagosian Chelsea, 555 W. 24th St. (All Map 5 D5)
Chelsea has some of the world's most prestigious commercial art galleries, including Pace Wildenstein and Mary Boone, who has built on her success with 1980s art stars Julian Schnabel and Jean-Michel Basquiat. Larry Gagosian is one of the biggest international dealers, with galleries in the Upper East Side, Beverly Hills, and London. Exhibitions at his Chelsea outpost are among the most hotly anticipated in New York. *(See also p96.)*

Open-Air Swimming

Astoria, 19th Street & 23rd Drive, Queens; Hamilton Fish Pool, 128 Pitt Street, Manhattan (Map 4 G4); www.nycgovparks.org
Many New Yorkers themselves are not aware that the city's park service maintains over 20 outdoor swimming pools, let alone that the facilities are free of charge. This inexplicable oversight by the locals is the visitor's gain, however. Of all the city's pools, the jewel in the crown is the Astoria in Queens (use the Astoria Boulevard stop on the N or W subway trains). This giant of a pool hosted the U.S. team's swimming trials for the 1936 Olympics. Portions are sectioned off and designated for lap swimming or for general use. In Manhattan, check out the Hamilton Fish Pool in Alphabet City, which has pleasant shady areas around the pool. Note that there is no admittance without proper bathing attire, and you need to take a padlock for your locker.

An Invigorating Massage

Graceful Services, 2nd Floor, 1047 2nd Avenue (Map 8 G5), 212 593 9904, www.gracefulservices.com
Should sightseeing leave your muscles tight and achy, Graceful Services holds the remedy: deep tissue massage, practised according to the age-old techniques of the East. Refreshingly bereft of rose petals, scented candles, and other frivolous spa accoutrements, the private rooms at Graceful Services appear somewhat clinical. But as your blocked chi, or life energy, is released by the deft hands and fingers of a licensed masseur, you will not want for anything more. It's popular with midtown workers and diplomats from the nearby U.N. headquarters, so you'll need to book.

Biking & Boating in Central Park
Loeb Boat House, between 74th & 75th streets (Map 8 E2), 212 517 2233; open 10am–5:30pm; roads closed to vehicular traffic 10am–3pm Mon–Fri, 7–10pm Sat & Sun

Comprising 843 acres of ponds, meadows, hills, and forest, Central Park is an urban oasis like no other, but its sheer scale presents a challenge for those with limited time. Luckily, you can hire a bicycle and helmet by the hour at the Loeb Boat House. Note that cycling teams practice in the park, and etiquette requires recreational riders to move toward the curb to let them pass. Alternatively, take to the water in a rowing boat or gondola.

Picnicking at Bryant Park
42nd Street (Map 6 E2), www.bryantpark.org

At the first sign of fair weather, beautifully maintained Bryant Park transforms into the alfresco lunch room for

hundreds of midtown professionals. Garden furniture is plentiful, and the public restrooms are uncommonly clean. There's also a "reading room," where visitors can borrow current issues of popular magazines, while music and dance performances take place on the sprawling lawn. Above all, the park is a prime spot for people-watching. Buy a sandwich at Pret a Manger (11 W. 42nd St.), take a seat, and indulge.

Reading a Book
Housing Works Used Book Café, 126 Crosby Street (Map 3 D5), 212 334 3324, www.housingworksubc.com

Browse books, sip cappuccino, nibble cookies, and support a good cause – all at the same time. Housing Works provides job training, health care, and housing advocacy for the city's homeless who have HIV and AIDS, via profits from its used books and coffee. This bookstore-café, housed in a former warehouse, has high ceilings, mahogany paneling, and spiral staircases that impart an airy richness to the ambience. Make your purchases, find a comfortable armchair, and while away the afternoon with an out-of-print classic.

Markets and Shops of East Harlem
East 116th Street between Park & 3rd avenues (Map 12 F5)

Spanish Harlem was populated almost entirely by Puerto Rican New Yorkers until the 1980s, but now it also has many Mexican, Chinese, and other Caribbean residents. On East 116th Street, the waft from a Mexican bakery is just as likely to seize your attention as the candles burning inside a Haitian *santería* (shop selling mystical goods), or the elderly Dominican gentleman pushing his tropical fruit ice cart and shouting out the day's flavors in Spanish. Score authentic Mexican sweets and restorative *horchata* drinks at Don Paco López Panadería (2129 3rd Ave.).

A Tour of Penn Station
4th Mon of every month; meet at 34th St. Tourist Info Kiosk, Penn Station Rotunda (Map 5 D4), 212 719 3434

New York lost a treasure when this Neo-Classical station was destroyed by thoughtless planners in 1964. However, traces of the 1910 structure do survive, and well-informed guides illuminate these details, and describe the grandeur that was lost.

TOP CHOICES – *evening*

Evening's arrival might signal the end of the working day, but to board the homebound train immediately after leaving the office is an alien concept for most New Yorkers. With so many happy-hour specials at the city's myriad bars, a dining scene unmatched in its diversity and quality, free cultural events, and top-quality sports games, it is not difficult to understand the reluctance to go straight home. Such choice can be overwhelming, even for locals – should you be racked with indecision, concentrate on the area below 14th Street, where Manhattan's restaurants and bars are most densely packed. It never hurts to call ahead and reserve a table for dinner, especially on weekends. But, unless you plan to dine at the most exclusive restaurants *(see pp22 & 38)*, getting a table on the day is usually easy.

"Vicious" Cocktails at the Algonquin
59 W. 44th Street (Map 6 E2), www.algonquinhotel.com
In the 1920s, when the acerbic Dorothy Parker wrote for *Vanity Fair*, she would meet with other writers (including novelist F. Scott Fitzgerald) for cocktails and gossip at the Algonquin Hotel. Their group was known as the Vicious Circle, as no celebrity was spared their sharp-tongued critiques. Soak up the sophisticated atmosphere in the hotel's Blue Bar, where witty cartoons by *New Yorker* veteran Al Hirschfeld adorn the walls.

Museum Deals
Cooper-Hewitt *(see p105)*; Jewish Museum *(see p105)*; Guggenheim *(see p104)*; Whitney *(see p101)*; BMA *(see p108)*
Several museums operate a "pay what you wish" policy in the evening: the Cooper-Hewitt (5–9pm Tue); the Jewish Museum (5–9pm Thu); the Guggenheim

(6–8pm Fri); and the Whitney (6–9pm Fri). At the Brooklyn Museum of Art, admissions are waived all day (until 11pm) on the first Saturday of the month, when bands, dance troupes, and a cash bar create a party atmosphere.

Latin American and Yiddish Theater Peformances
El Repertorio Español, 138 E. 27th St. (Map 6 F4), www. repertorio.org; Folksbiene Yiddish Theater at the Manhattan JCC, 334 Amsterdam Avenue (Map 7 B1), www.folksbiene.org
El Repertorio Español stages productions adapted from Spanish literature as well as original pieces from emerging Latin playwrights. Performances are in Spanish, with simultaneous translation through headphones. The Folksbiene's repertory recalls early 20th-century New York, when scores of Yiddish theaters dotted the downtown area. Productions (in Yiddish, with English supertitles) are heavy on songs and slapstick humor.

A Sunset Ferry to Staten Island
Whitehall Ferry Terminal (Map 2 E5), www.siferry.com
Sunset adds immeasurable ambience to an already spectacular ferry trip across the Hudson River. The free 25-minute journey offers views of Lower Manhattan's skyscrapers and bridges, plus Liberty, Ellis and Governor's islands. Ferries depart every 15 to 20 minutes between 5 and 8pm.

Shooting Pool
SoHo Billiards, 289 Mulberry Street (Map 4 E4); Fat Cat Billiards, 75 Christopher Street (Map 3 B3)
A pool player's pool hall, SoHo Billiards dispenses with the brass fixtures and high polish of uptown parlors and

simply provides 20 pool tables in excellent condition, and reasonable hourly rates. It doesn't have a bar though – if you want a beer with your Eight-ball, head over to the subterranean world of Fat Cat.

Happy Hour at McSorley's
15 East 7th Street *(see p142)*
Around 5pm on weekday evenings, a mix of intellectuals, edgy East Village types, and hard-drinking regulars congregate at this old bar for discounted rounds of ales. More convivial than on busy weekends, weeknight happy hours allow you to relax at a communal wood table, or press the bartender for obscure McSorley's history.

Catch the Knicks at Madison Square Garden
2 Pennsylvania Plaza (Map 6 E5), 212 465 5867, www.nba.com
Although the Knicks are one of the most popular basketball teams, visitors to Madison Square Garden can nearly always obtain tickets – even when the game is officially sold out. The Garden box office withholds the release of hundreds of tickets until game day, so spontaneous travelers with a sudden desire to scream in unison with a 20,000-strong crowd should phone the ticket line or go down to the box office. Check the team's website for occasional discount-ticket promotions.

Poetry Slams in the East Village
Nuyorican Poets Café, 236 East 3rd Street *(see p119)*
The Nuyorican Poets Café was founded in 1973 with the specific aim of providing a forum for Puerto Rican-New Yorker writers – a group that included poet and award-winning playwright Miguel Piñero. The intimate space has a much wider remit these days, and is renowned for its raucous, informal poetry-recital competitions – known as

"slams" – and collaborations between musicians and vocal artists. Performances often blur the line between hip-hop lyricism and spoken-word poetry. Respected hip-hop personalities Mos Def, Company Flow, and Rahzel occasionally stop by for impromptu sessions.

Outdoor Movies in Bryant Park
Map 6 E2, www.bryantpark.org
Enchanting at any time of the day *(see also p15)*, Bryant Park acquires a communal, festive mood on warm summer evenings. Every Monday throughout July and August, the Park organizes free screenings of classic movies on the lawn, which begin as soon as the sun sets – with luck, you might see it dip below the horizon while gazing down West 40th Street. Go early, take a picnic meal, and enjoy the show. Also during summer, jazz musicians play free concerts by the park's terrace; most performances have a groovy, Latin flair.

The View from Top of the Tower
Top of the Tower @ Beekman Tower Hotel *(see p172)*
This cocktail lounge and restaurant offers some of the best seating in New York to watch the spectacle of the city's buildings lighting up at night. Book a window terrace table (off the main room), and ideally arrive at dusk to enjoy the subtle transformation of the skyline. Once night has fallen, you can turn your attention to the well-mixed cocktails and menu of American cuisine.

TOP CHOICES – *night*

On weekends in Chelsea and the East and West Villages, and spilling over into adjacent neighborhoods, sidewalks teem with as many pedestrians at 2am as at 8pm. New York, in this regard, feels more akin to European cultural capitals than to any other American urban center. The pulsing nightclubs of New York attract the world's top DJs, lured instinctively to the city that nurtured jazz in its infancy and gave birth to hip-hop and rap. The city is also famous for producing sharp-witted comedians, who supply laughs nightly in the many comedy clubs. It is difficult not to love such a place, even if you prefer more subdued diversions, such as ogling New York's incomparable skyline from the top of its most fabled building, or swapping stories with friends over a few glasses of wine at Rhône.

Stargazing at the Hayden Sphere

Rose Center for Earth and Space, American Museum of Natural History (Map 7 C1), 212 769 5200, www.amnh.org/rose
Housed in a glass box, the 87-ft (27-m) diameter Hayden Sphere is the world's largest virtual reality simulator. Its striking form, luminescent at night, has endeared it to New Yorkers since the Rose Center opened in 2000. Come on a Friday, when it stays open until 8:45pm, for a mesmeric journey through the cosmos.

Improv at the Upright Citizens Brigade Theatre

307 W. 26th St. (Map 5 B5), www.ucbtheatre.com
New York's boldest, most irreverent comedians ply their trade on this Chelsea stage. Any given night sees performances by sketch and improvisational comedy troupes, plus stand-up comics. Tuesday's "Harold Night," which generally offers the most reliable laughs of the week, pits the city's best long-form improv comedy troupes against each other.

Nighttime Views from the Roof of New York

Empire State Building Observatory (Map 6 E3), 212 736 3100, www.esbnyc.com (last elevator up at 11:15pm)
On a clear night, the scene from the 86th floor of the Empire State Building is breathtakingly beautiful. Southward views show the Flatiron Building cleaving downtown traffic into two luminous veins: one bound for further travel down Fifth Avenue, the other for Broadway. Surrounding you are the twinkling icons of the Art Deco era *(see p99)*, including the Chrysler, Chanin, and General Electric buildings. No visit to the city is complete without this experience.

Bar-Hopping in East Village

If you're in the mood for a sleek, intimate wine bar, an authentic Irish pub, a hard-rocking dive, or any combination thereof, make the East Village your destination. Second Avenue has the neighborhood's greatest concentration of bars, and high-quality drinks and diversions abound off this principal nightlife thoroughfare. The scene below St. Mark's Place is fun, but can become rowdy after midnight. Try Swift Hibernian Lounge *(see p142)* for traditional Irish cheer and well-drawn pints. Bar Veloce *(see p144)* is good for reasonably priced Italian wines. Should you find yourself craving cheap beer, loud rock and 1970s living-room kitsch, then put Welcome to the Johnson's *(see p140)* on your itinerary.

Check the latest clubs on the scene at ▶▶ www.enewyork.dk.com

Wine-Sipping at Rhône

63 Gansevoort Street *(see p148)*

Following a long day at the office, New York's stylish set migrates to this cavernous wine bar in the Meatpacking District. Rhône is a reflection of everything the area has become: pricey, chic, and trend-setting. It has a lofty ceiling, painstakingly modern furnishings, and mammoth windows. The knowledgeable bartenders can assist you in choosing one of the 30 reds available by the glass.

A Midnight Movie at the Sunshine Cinema

143 East Houston Street (Map 4 E4), 212 330 8182, www.landmarktheatres.com

Each weekend brings a different cult classic for a midnight screening at this immaculately restored, late 19th-century former vaudeville theater. Favorites include Mel Brooks's *Blazing Saddles* (1974), while Steven Spielberg's *The Goonies* (1985) is popular with NYU students hooked on 80s nostalgia. The screenings are social events; some audience members even arrive in costume and shout out classic lines along with film.

Music on the River

Barge Music, Fulton Ferry Landing, Brooklyn *(see p130)*

Ships on the East River, when sounding their baritone airhorns, impart a salty maritime character to the city. But could they share the river air with, of all things, the dulcet harmonies of chamber music? Barge Music, docked at the eastern end of Brooklyn Bridge, believes so. This gorgeously renovated barge provides the city's most rarified environment for hearing classical music. And for a backdrop, the 125-seat auditorium has the entire glittering spectacle of nighttime Manhattan.

Club-Hopping in Chelsea

Style is paramount in Chelsea – a neighborhood of design studios, art galleries, and architecture firms. And where aesthetically minded people work, nightclubs tend to follow. Witness Avalon *(see p149)*, a world-class dance club housed in a former church. Spirit *(p150)* is unrelenting in its pursuit of sensory stimulation: multiple rooms offer a panoply of sounds, light shows, and performance arts. Hiro *(p150)* feels like a modern speakeasy hiding in the bowels of an exclusive Tokyo hotel, while Roxy *(p149)* caters to the most colorful clubbers in the city.

Jazz at the Village Vanguard

Village Vanguard, 178 7th Avenue South *(see p116)*

The Vanguard inspires almost religious levels of veneration, and a glance at the roster since it was founded in 1935 explains why. Miles Davis, John Coltrane, Dizzy Gillespie, and Wynton Marsalis have all performed (and sometimes recorded albums) in this intimate West Village space. The award-winning Vanguard Jazz Orchestra plays on Mondays; saxophone master Joe Lovano and jazz-rock fusion artists The Bad Plus are other regulars.

Late-Night Quick Bites

New York caters well to nocturnal appetites. Wherever there is a large concentration of bars, there is also a choice of eateries that are open late. The East Village has the Turkish cafeteria Bereket *(see p27)*, the inexpensive Yaffa Cafe *(p30)*, and the bright, historic Ukrainian café Vaselka *(see p223)*, which prepares a wondrous borscht. West Village night owls congregate outside Joe's Pizza *(see p222)* for some of the best slices in Manhattan.

restaurants

New York is one of the world's finest cities for dining out, whether you aspire to a table at one of the most fashionable restaurants, or simply want to pick up something cheap and tasty from a café or from a street vendor. Myriad restaurants cover every cuisine imaginable, the food served up on anything from banana leaves to porcelain plates. The following pages provide a snapshot of NY's dining scene.

TABLES	ROMANTIC SETTINGS	WORLD CUISINES
~~B~~abbo **110 Waverly Place** One of celebrated Italian chef Mario Batali's first restaurants – tables here need to be booked two weeks in advance. *(See p34)*		**Aquavit** **13 West 54th Street** Succulent herrings, seafood stews, and other Scandinavian delectables are served in an atrium with its own running waterfall. *(See p45)*
66 **241 Church Street** The combination of Chinese fusion cuisine, sleek furnishings, killer cocktails, and a fashionable crowd makes 66 a hot Tribeca ticket. *(See p24)*		**Tomoe Sushi** **172 Thompson Street** New Yorkers are prepared to line up outside this small, simple space in order to sample ultra-fresh and tender sushi. *(See p33)*
Atlantic Grill **1341 3rd Avenue** This seafood restaurant is a perennial favorite with discerning Upper East Siders. Book in advance or be prepared to wait. *(See p48)*	**New Leaf Café** **Fort Tryon Park** Beautiful Fort Tryon Park provides a delightful backdrop – take a stroll before settling into the café. *(See p51)*	**Tamarind** **41–3 East 22nd Street** Here you'll find spices and Indian flavors with an individual twist, as in Tamarind's signature tandoori scallops. *(See p41)*
≫ *If you register on the www.iseatz.com website, you can do your restaurant booking online, using a credit card.*		**Sobaya** **229 East 9th Street** Noodles in broth never tasted so good as at this hip East Village Japanese dining room. There's a great range of sake too. *(See p32)*
	i Trulli **122 East 27th Street** Excellent Italian cuisine enhanced by first-rate Chianti. Cozy up by the fire in winter; enjoy the garden in summer. *(See p42)*	
	The River Café **1 Water Street** The ultimate mix of top-quality cuisine and divine views of the Manhattan skyline, rising up from the East River. *(See p52)*	

SWEET TOOTH	DINERS	BARGAIN BITES

Mezzaluna
1295 3rd Avenue
The pasta and brick-oven-baked pizza may be delicious, but the tiramisu is *divine* in this Upper East Side Italian joint. *(See p47)*

NY Dosas
West 4th Street & Sullivan Street
A vendor cart in Washington Square is renowned for sublime South Indian crêpes filled with finely spiced vegetables. *(See p37)*

Ouest
2315 Broadway
Ouest's generous helpings of panna cotta are heavenly – so long as you have room after meat loaf or braised lamb shank. *(See p49)*

Daily Chow
2 East 2nd Street
Creative pan-Asian bites include marinated chicken skewers, Mongolian barbecue bowls, and luscious, exotic fruit juices. *(See p30)*

Balthazar
80 Spring Street
Balthazar is known throughout town for brunches and sweet pastries. The home-made donuts are perfect for dipping into a coffee. *(See p25)*

Paul's Palace
131 2nd Avenue
Monstrous hamburgers, fries, and milkshakes team up well with the salty personalities of Paul's endearingly gruff waitresses. *(See p31)*

Joya
215 Court Street, Brooklyn
Joya's ultra-modern, hip dining room belies a menu rich in absurdly affordable, delicious Thai standards. *(See p52)*

>> *Remember that tipping the waitstaff is de rigueur in New York, regardless of whether the service is great or indifferent – the accepted rate is 15–20%.*

Relish
225 Wythe Avenue, Brooklyn
This Williamsburg destination serves robust, inventive American bistro cuisine in a classic diner setting. *(See p55)*

Sandwich Planet
534 9th Avenue
A tiny shop that scores with almost limitless combinations of fillings, and fresh breads. *(See p43)*

Tartine
253 West 11th Street
This bijoux West Village bistro has a tempting array of fresh fruit tarts and mousses. It also does a wonderful crème brûlée. *(See p38)*

2nd Avenue Deli
156 2nd Avenue
More than 50 years of tradition go into huge sandwiches, thick soups, smoked fish, and other Jewish classics. *(See p33)*

Restaurants

241 Church Street • 212 925 0202
» www.jean-georges.com
Open lunch & dinner daily (to midnight Mon–Thu,
to 1am Fri & Sat, to 10:30pm Sun)

A restaurant in the empire of prestigiously gifted chef
Jean-Georges Vongerichten, 66 has a chic, minimalist
interior, immersed in shades of white, silver grays,
and black. The lofty space, with a view to the kitchen
above a row of fish tanks, attracts style slaves and
foodies alike. Dishes draw on Chinese influences, and
are produced with the customary Jean-Georges flair –
specialties include Peking duck, the 66 sesame
noodles, sweet and sour two-flavored shrimp, steamed
cod, Vietnamese coffee-flavored sorbet, and five-spice
vanilla ice cream. The evening is when 66 is at its
liveliest best – if you haven't reserved, imaginative
cocktails ease the wait for a table. Lunch is cheaper,
with a reasonable prix-fixe menu. The check is accompanied by light, green-tea fortune cookies. **Expensive**

Montrachet *quality food and wine* `1 C1`
239 West Broadway • 212 219 2777
Open lunch & dinner Mon–Fri, dinner only Sat

With one of the best cellars in the country,
Montrachet has a wine selection to match its *haute
cuisine*. A sommelier will provide information and
advice without a trace of condescension, should the
list seem daunting. The three-room dining space is
relaxed and comfortable. **Expensive**

Acappella *gourmets and grappa* `1 C2`
1 Hudson Street • 212 240 0163
» www.acappella-restaurant.com
Open lunch & dinner Mon–Fri, dinner only Sat

This ever-popular New York haunt produces deliciously
authentic northern Italian food. Along with seasonal
variations, the menu boasts well-prepared lamb and
fish as well as superb pasta and pesto. And the
indulgent waitstaff provide free grappa. **Expensive**

Peking Duck House *perfect poultry* `2 E1`
28 Mott Street • 212 227 1810
Open all day from 11:30am daily

Chinatown's bustle carries into this restaurant on busy nights, and the Peking duck leaves little wonder why: crisp skin and succulent meat are served with sliced cucumber, scallions, and tangy-sweet sauce. Service can be brusque, and other dishes are fairly standard, but the bird is transcendent. **Moderate**

Golden Unicorn *a beacon in Chinatown* `2 F1`
18 East Broadway • 212 941 0911
Open all day from 9am daily; dim sum 9am–3:30pm

Deep in Chinatown lies this shrine to the indulgent Cantonese tradition of dim sum. Late on Sunday mornings, the 1,000 seats of a pleasantly appointed dining room fill with families eager to sample petite plates of shrimp dumplings, roast pork buns, and sweet egg custards. Dinner is a quieter affair. **Cheap**

Balthazar *timeless brasserie* `3 D5`
80 Spring Street • 212 965 1785
≫ www.balthazarny.com Open from 7:30am daily (to 1am Mon–Thu, to 2am Fri & Sat, to midnight Sun)

Parisian in style, Balthazar has retained its popularity through consistently good bistro fare. The menu changes throughout the day, catering for breakfast, lunch, dinner, and through to after hours. Sublime desserts, and weekend brunch is a winner. **Moderate**

Mercer Kitchen *hip French/American* `3 D4`
99 Prince Street • 212 966 5454
≫ www.jean-georges.com Open breakfast: 7–11am; lunch: noon–2:45pm; dinner: from 6pm daily

The Mercer is all about keeping things simple and chic. The SoHo location attracts the trendsetters; the menu attracts the foodies. Its setting is casual, with tables, banquettes, and bar seating surrounding an open-plan kitchen. **Moderate**

Restaurants

L'Ecole *gastronomy defined*
3 D5

462 Broadway • 212 219 3300
>> www.frenchculinary.com/lecole
Open lunch & dinner Mon–Fri, dinner only Sat

A restaurant that ticks all the right boxes: set in a prime location, it has a bright, airy interior with huge windows, serves excellent food, and offers bargain prices. L'Ecole is indeed a school, and the students of the French Culinary Institute use the patrons as their willing and hungry guinea pigs. It's a wonderful arrangement – diners indulge on three- and five-course meals without having to sell off the family silver, while students have a chance to hone their skills. You can order à la carte, but the prix fixe is excellent value.

These students are potentially star chefs, and the menu reflects that ambition by offering dishes rooted in both traditional and contemporary French cuisine. Creations such as poached sole with shrimp and mussels in a cider cream sauce, eggplant and red pepper terrine, and tea flan served with madeleines demonstrate the challenging nature of the cooking. If you prefer simpler fare, omelet with shoestring potatoes won't disappoint. Even the delectable bread is made on the premises. The menu changes every six weeks.

You'll be hard-pressed elsewhere to find such a winning combination of bright atmosphere and first-rate cooking at these prices. **Cheap–Moderate**

Jane *creative American fare*
3 D4

100 West Houston Street • 212 254 7000
>> www.janerestaurant.com
Open all day from 11am daily

Jane takes the food you may already know and adds special touches, subtly reinventing but not disguising the main ingredients. Meat and salmon burgers reign supreme, though the juicy fruit-purée cocktails give them a run for their money. **Moderate**

Cafe Gitane *North African spices*   4 E4
242 Mott Street • 212 334 9552
Open all day from 9am daily

French/North African offerings such as fragrant cous cous and spicy mergüez sausages draw the area's fashionable youth. In summer, the sidewalk tables are hotter commodities than the designer sandals in the neighboring boutiques, but the cozy dining room holds plenty of charm too. **Cheap**

Cafe Habana *Cuban/Mexican café*   4 E4
229 Elizabeth Street • 212 625 2001
Open all day from 9am daily

Flavorful specialties from this bustling corner café inspire devotion among Nolita's beautiful people, who eye one another over delicious Cuban pork sandwiches, huevos rancheros, and corn on the cob. Quench your thirst with a *chelada*: Mexican lager with lime juice and salt. **Cheap**

Bereket *late-night Turkish belly-filler*   4 F4
187 East Houston Street • 212 475 7700
Open 24 hours daily

Rare is the downtown resident who, after a night of barhopping, hasn't relished the succulent lamb shawarma sandwich, fresh hummus or tangy, stuffed vine leaves at this East Houston institution. For what is essentially a Turkish fast-food restaurant, Bereket offers surprisingly subtle, authentic eats. **Cheap**

The Elephant *French/Thai fusion*   4 F4
58 East 1st Street • 212 505 7739
>> www.elephantrestaurant.com
Open lunch & dinner Mon–Sat, dinner only Sun

Reds and golds dominate the whimsical, evocatively lit dining room, where couples sip luscious Elephant Martinis – vodka, cassis, and pineapple. Don't miss Sticky Rice – chicken and pork steamed with rice and vegetables in lotus leaf wrapping. **Moderate**

>> *For a listing of restaurants by cuisine, see pp220–23*

Restaurants

'inoteca *great small plates*
4 F4
98 Rivington Street • 212 614 0473
Open noon–3am daily

A happening corner wine bar/restaurant, 'inoteca is perfect for a few glasses while you munch on a selection of snacks, known as "small plates." These include cheeses, a generous helping of sliced meats, panini, and salads. Weather permitting, you can sit outside for high-caliber people-watching. **Moderate**

WD-50 *adventurous American*
4 G4
50 Clinton Street • 212 477 2900
≫ www.wd-50.com Open dinner daily

Chef Wylie Dufresne built his reputation on taking risks in the kitchen, and you can try some of his daring and delicious experiments in this simple, clean restaurant. Rabbit sausage with avocado, snapper with juniper berries, or lamb with hibiscus-date purée are typical attention-grabbers. **Expensive**

Cube 63 *unique sushi in a stylish setting*
4 G4
63 Clinton Street • 212 228 6751
Open lunch & dinner Mon–Fri, dinner only Sat & Sun

Having worked in New York's top sushi kitchens, brothers Ken and Ben Lau carry priceless expertise into their sleek restaurant. Mellow green light illuminates the sushi counter, while votives cast sexy shadows on young professionals sharing *omakase*: a sampler platter of the Laus' wildly creative rolls. **Moderate**

Alias *deceiving appearance; convincing menu*
4 G4
76 Clinton Street • 212 505 5011
Mon–Thu 6–11pm, Fri & Sat 6–11:30pm, Sun 5–9pm

Don't let the kitsch signage mislead you; there's no spam on the menu. Alias serves imaginative dishes, including lamb spare ribs, duck confit, and candied avocado. It's one of the places that has made the Lower East Side a destination for eclectic dining. The prix-fixe Sunday menu is a bargain. **Moderate**

Check New York's best places for global food on ≫ www.enewyork.dk.com

Le Souk *North African dining* `4 G3`
47 Avenue B • 212 777 5454
>> www.lesoukny.com Open dinner daily

With the arrival of trendy restaurants, boutiques, and
bars in recent years, Alphabet City (easternmost part
of the East Village) has seen its profile rise considerably. But the neighborhood conceals some of its best
assets behind a gritty urban cloak. Le Souk is a fine
example of this – a fantastic North African restaurant
that, externally, does little to distinguish itself from
the surrounding neighborhood grocers and bars. An
unassuming shell, however, belies a sultan's treasure
trove of African textures, tones, and delicacies within.
Fashionable groups dine shoulder to shoulder on
plush banquettes, while the adjacent bar area has low,
Moorish tables, floor pillows, and softly lit iron lanterns. Meze plates serve as a prelude to the arrival of
ceramic tajines filled with aromatic cous cous, tangy
mergüez sausages, and garlicky mussels. After 9pm,
belly dancers gyrate between the tables. **Moderate**

Bao *modern design meets Vietnamese cooking* `4 G3`
111 Avenue C • 212 254 7773
>> www.bao111.com Open dinner daily

Architect/chef Michael Huynh prepares brilliant
Vietnamese cuisine in this sleek space of his own
design. Diners – many of them artists and fashion
models – rest on crimson banquettes sipping fragrant
pho soup or browsing Bao's eclectic dessert menu.
Black sesame ice cream, anyone? **Cheap**

Le Tableau *French/Mediterranean cuisine* `4 F3`
511 East 5th Street • 212 260 1333
>> www.letableaunyc.com Open dinner daily

Wonderful French food in a button-sized hot spot.
The menu changes often, but the produce is
consistently flavorful, with dishes such as pork loin
with maple yam purée, gorgonzola, and porto
reduction. Try the early evening prix-fixe three-course
menu for super savings. **Moderate**

Restaurants

Pylos *taverna in Alphabet City* `4 F3`
128 East 7th Street • 212 473 0220
>> www.pylosrestaurant.com
Open dinner Mon–Sat, brunch Wed–Sun

Many worlds lie within eight blocks of the 2nd Avenue subway station: the Orthodox Jewish Lower East Side, Ukrainian East Village, and Chinatown, for example. Most surprising of all, however, is the spirit of the Aegean that hides amid Alphabet City's hard-rocking bars. Pylos is a handsome Greek taverna, with stucco walls, blue shutters, and earthenware jugs hanging from the beams. Gastronomes from all over the city worship the *dolmathes* (stuffed vine leaves) here. Another popular dish is *arnaki yiovetsi* – stewed lamb chunks redolent of clove, oregano, and tomato, served on toothsome *orzo* grains. Knowledgeable staff help you navigate the encyclopedic Greek wine list. Save room for the *galaktobaureko* – these flaky, custard-filled phyllo triangles covered in warm honey are perhaps Pylos's greatest temptation. **Moderate**

Yaffa Cafe *pita stop* `4 F3`
97 St. Mark's Place • 212 505 7739
Open 24 hours daily

Day and night, punk rockers and poets flock to this offbeat eatery on St. Mark's. After last call at the neighborhood's bars, Yaffa's leafy, festively lit back patio fills with hungry revelers eager to curb their impending hangovers with home-made pita, hummus, and other tasty Middle Eastern fare. **Cheap**

Daily Chow *casual pan-Asian dining* `4 E3`
2 East 2nd Street • 212 254 7887
Open dinner daily

Smart dining areas and huge windows overlooking the Bowery ensure that there's not a bad seat in the house. The decor has a subtle Polynesian theme, while the menu stretches from the Pacific to mainland Asia. Luscious coconut-flecked chicken skewers and creamy Thai iced coffee make fantastic starters. **Cheap**

Paul's Palace *huge hamburgers* `4 E3`
131 2nd Avenue • 212 529 3033
Open all day daily

The quintessential American hamburger experience. From the linoleum countertop and checkerboard tablecloths, to the cheeky burger descriptions posted above the well-seasoned grill, Paul's is a greasy charmer. Go in for peerless 1/2 pound burgers and extra thick milkshakes. **Cheap**

Mermaid Inn *seafood, New England style* `4 E3`
96 2nd Avenue • 212 674 5870
»www.themermaidnyc.com Open dinner daily

With its framed nautical charts, ship diagrams, cabin lamps, and rustic tables, this classic fish house would seem more suited to the Maine Coast. But the modern rock soundtrack and style-conscious local clientele anchor the proceedings in urban bohemia. When restaurant mogul Jimmy Bradley unveiled this oddity on edgy Second Avenue in 2003, it was an instant hit.

The inn is extremely popular, and you'll generally have to wait for your table at the weekend. This is when the seafood bar comes into its own, providing Nova Scotia oysters on the half shell. Once seated, you can continue with roasted mussels or feather-light clam fritters before considering the mains. Depending on the season, these might range from classic grilled salmon through tender pan-fried skate wing to the popular lobster salad sandwich. Complimentary cups of lemon pudding cap the meal. **Moderate**

Morning Coffee and Afternoon Tea
New York's plentiful "coffee shops" are great for cheap food and people-watching, but, ironically, not for coffee. For a real, European-style coffee, you need to seek out the city's best cafés. For excellent cappuccinos, go to **Via Quadronno** *(see p221)*, and if you want to pick up a quick espresso, stop at the orange mobile **Mud Truck** (on Union Square) or the **Mud Spot** (permanently parked on 9th St.). **Joe** *(see p220)*, in the West Village, also does great coffee.

The **Palm Court at the Plaza Hotel** serves a formal afternoon tea. **Tea & Sympathy** is cozy and casual, offering freshly made scones and perfectly brewed tea in mismatched china. **Lady Mendl's Tea Room** is rather upmarket, but their scones are divine. *(For all, see p222.)* For something funkier, try **Teany** *(see p70)*.

»» *For a full list of recommended cafés, see pp220–21; for tearooms, see p222*

Angelica Kitchen *incredible vegetables* `4 E2`
300 East 12th Street • 212 228 2909
Open all day daily

A vegan pioneer since 1976, Angelica earns high marks for cooking with extremely fresh ingredients grown using sustainable methods. This would be reason enough to lure environmentally aware citizens to the charming, Tuscan farmhouse-inspired dining room. Yet Angelica's greatest asset is perhaps the chef's ability to coax dazzling flavors out of the most basic ingredients. Omnivores will be hard pressed to note the absence of cream in a rich butternut squash soup, or bemoan the missing corned beef in a warm tempeh (a soybean preparation) Reuben sandwich.

Vegan approximations of American classics are on the menu alongside such exotica as *hiziki* and *kombu* (Japanese seaweeds), and *daikon* (a root), which bolster the Kinpira salad. Service is friendly and, should you be ignorant of the virtues of *edame* (salted soybeans), refreshingly non-condescending. **Cheap**

Sobaya *noodle seduction* `4 E2`
229 East 9th Street • 212 533 6966
≫ **www.ticakean.com/restaurant.html**
Open lunch & dinner daily

The menu explains that soba buckwheat noodles contain vitamins and protein, and are especially good to eat after drinking alcohol. Well, if that doesn't explain the crowds, then it must be the authentic Japanese flavors. Big bowls of stomach-pleasing noodle soup are the main focus, served with fresh scallions and your choice of extras, such as vegetables, duck, tempura, and yam. Appetizers include fried mushroom with shrimp paste, spinach with sesame sauce, and selected sushi-style dishes. A comprehensive sake menu offers a guide to the level of fullness and flavor of each type.

The decor is typically Japanese in its simplicity and sense of order. The friendly waitstaff are generally hip Japanese transplants sporting navy samurai bandanas on their heads. **Cheap–Moderate**

2nd Avenue Deli *kosher delicatessen* `4 E2`
156 2nd Avenue • 212 677 0606
 www.2ndavedeli.com Open 7am–midnight

King of Manhattan's Jewish-style delis, 2nd Avenue has been stuffing New York bellies with towering pastrami sandwiches, hearty matzo ball soup, and complimentary pickled vegetables since 1954. It's always crowded, but lines move surprisingly fast. Tables are communal. **Moderate**

Blue Ribbon Sushi *the freshest fish* `3 C4`
119 Sullivan Street • 212 343 0404
Open noon–2am daily

Like its West Village brother *(see below)*, the SoHo outpost of Blue Ribbon obsesses over the freshness of ingredients. Here, the main ingredient is raw fish. Try sitting at the sushi counter rather than the popular back room, where waits can seem interminable. And don't overlook the vast sake selection. **Moderate**

Blue Ribbon Bakery *Old World delights* `3 C4`
33 Downing Street • 212 337 0404
Open lunchtime to 2am daily (to midnight Sun)

Inside this cozy space, Village sophisticates crowd windowside tables for European indulgences such as foie gras, antipasti, and crusty home-made breads. Ask to be seated downstairs in the wine cellar-like space where diners can watch freshly baked breads come out of the oven. **Cheap–Expensive**

Tomoe Sushi *Japanese-style delectables* `3 C4`
172 Thompson Street • 212 777 9346
Open all day Wed–Sat, dinner Mon (cash or Amex only)

Tomoe presents New Yorkers with some of the freshest fish available in the city. That is why, despite a lack of atmosphere in this small sushi joint, people will line up for as much as an hour, just to get a taste of the "real thing." If the weather's nice, the wait is worth it. **Moderate**

Otto Enoteca & Pizzeria *huge snacks* `3 D3`
No. 1 5th Avenue • 212 995 9559
>> www.ottopizzeria.com Open all day daily

Throngs gather nightly to taste celebrity chef Mario Batali's hearty Italian snack foods. The thin pizzas are grilled (not baked) and topped with a diverse range of ingredients – anything from meatballs to fried duck eggs. Save room for the unique, savory *gelati* (ice creams). **Moderate**

La Palapa Rockola *authentic Mexican* `3 C3`
359 6th Avenue • 212 243 6871
>> www.lapalapa.com Open all day daily

This place debunks the myth that New York lacks credible Mexican cuisine. The interior evokes Mexico's colonial heartland and cinematic Golden Age, providing a festive backdrop for the robust dishes. Pair fish tacos with a frosty Negra Modelo beer and say "Hola" to heaven. **Moderate**

Babbo *the sophistication of northern Italy* `3 C3`
110 Waverly Place • 212 777 0303
>> www.babbonyc.com Open dinner daily

Babbo's reputation as one of New York's top Italian restaurants is due to the quality of its menu, devised by Mario Batali *(see also Otto, above)*. You will need to reserve early or ask about last-minute cancellations.

If your party agrees on a pricier meal, try the culinary adventure of either the traditional or pasta tasting menus. However, the main menu, offering dishes such as beef cheek ravioli and fennel-dusted sweetbreads, is also daring and justly lauded. Take time to peruse the wine menu or discuss the options with the knowledgable sommelier. The Italian selections are extensive and expertly chosen.

Despite the price tag, there's no need to dress up – the bi-level converted carriage house, with a skylight and elegant floral arrangements, provides the panache. Your only responsibility is to leave just enough room for a dessert and *digestivo*. **Expensive**

John's of
Bleecker Street *profound pizza*   `3 C3`
278 Bleecker Street • 212 243 6871
» www.johnsofbleeckerstreet.com
Open all day to 12:30am daily (cash only)

In this city, pizzeria comparisons are a hot topic and frequently dissolve into shouting matches. Even politicians dare not state their position on pizza, for fear of alienating potential voters. Out of the din, however, one name emerges that inspires more emotion than any other: John's of Bleecker Street.

John's likes to shout about its time-honored credentials: "Est. 1929" is writ large in white letters on its burgundy awning, and rapturous restaurant reviews are plastered to the window. For some New Yorkers, who believe a great pizzeria should be unknown to all but the savviest subway riders, John's very accessibility and fame are sufficient reasons to eliminate it from any discussion of the city's best.

Yet free from that illogical mindset, visitors to John's are in for a supremely satisfying meal.

The restaurant's popularity means that weekend lunch and dinner lines extend to the next storefront, but they move quickly. Once you're inside and seated at a weathered wooden booth, your olfactory nerves will soon react to the unmistakable, heady waft of garlic and romano cheese. To quiet your stomach, start with fresh antipasti and a frosty Peroni lager.

Purists should then opt for the basic cheese and tomato pie, fresh from John's coal-fired oven. What they will be presented with is a thin, smoky, lightly charred crust covered with a bright, slightly acidic sauce, full-cream mozzarella and vibrant spices. Non-purists can choose from garlicky meatballs and other tempting home-made toppings. Once you've chomped your way through a pie, you'll be able to establish your own position in a debate on New York's explosive topic. **Cheap**

Cones *superior ices*

272 Bleecker Street • 212 414 1795
Open 1–11pm Sun–Thu, 1pm–1am Fri & Sat

What compels a man to drive two hours from Upstate New York to the Village with an empty portable freezer plugged into his car's dash, only to drive straight home again after filling it? Simply this: hand-packed quarts of the best ice cream in the state. True story.

Looking at Cones, there is little to indicate what might stir such passion. It's a tidy parlor, with a few tables and photos of unremarkable sundaes on the walls. But the real show is in the freezer: 32 steel bins brimming with kaleidoscopically colored creams and sorbets, in the tradition of authentic Italian *gelaterias*. *Dulce de leche* and coffee mocha are deliciously rich, whereas tangy fruit sorbets and dairy-free ices present a lighter antidote to the summer swelter. This is why Cones' acclaim stretches from New York to its owners' native Argentina. Still undecided? Brothers Raul and Oscar readily offer tastings. **Cheap**

BB Sandwich Bar *cheesesteak perfected*

120 West 3rd Street • 212 473 7500
Open 10am–10pm daily

Gary Thompson claims he prepares the best cheesesteak in the city, and the length of the lunch line at his small, upstairs sandwich counter confirms this is no mere boast. Thinly sliced steak is placed on a puffy Kaiser roll, then topped with marinated onions, spicy tomato relish and white American cheese. **Cheap**

Food on the Hoof

Many downtown snack stops cater to people with bite-sized budgets and a desire to keep moving. Irresistible pork and vegetarian wontons can be had in the Lower East Side's **Fried Dumpling**. West Villagers swear by **Mamoun's** fresh, crispy falafel and tangy hummus, and **Pepe Rosso's** bright, delicious Italian specialties. Eat them while watching life's rich pageant in Washington Square Park. For late-night barhoppers, **Crif Dogs** offers sustenance in the form of Chihuahua hot dogs (wrapped in bacon and topped with avocado and sour cream). Or draw a barrage of envious glances on Second Avenue with a paper funnel full of fries from **Pommes Frites**, topped with any of their 25 tasty sauces. For all addresses, *see pp210–11*.

NY Dosas *cheap veggie manna* `3 C3`

West 4th Street & Sullivan Street • 917 710 2092
Open 11am–5pm Mon–Sat

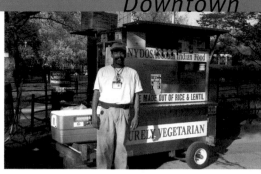

Even on blustery winter days, NYU students line up at this vending cart at the southwest corner of Washington Square for heavenly vegetarian dosas. The south Indian crêpes are filled with root vegetables, chickpeas, and spices, resulting in something far too delicate to be classified merely as "street food." **Cheap**

Mary's Fish Camp *chowder heaven* `3 B3`

64 Charles Street • 646 486 2185
>> www.marysfishcamp.com
Open lunch & dinner Mon–Sat

Mary's seafood chowder, and lobster and clam rolls are equal to the best of any New England oceanside restaurant. Add to this the atmosphere of rustic charm, and you see why customers are lured to this tiny space, if necessary waiting outside for tables. **Moderate**

Wallse *august Austrian fare* `3 A3`

344 West 11th Street • 212 352 2300
>> www.wallse.com Open lunch & dinner Mon–Fri, dinner only Sat, brunch & dinner Sun

Opened by chef Kurt Gutenbrunner in 2000, Wallse has developed a devoted following. The two-room restaurant has a restful feel, with white linen tablecloths, pale walls, and carefully chosen art work. Many of the clientele are regulars, giving the place an easy-going West Village vibe.

In accordance with Austria's gastronomic traditions, Gutenbrunner produces richly flavored dishes. Besides his famed Wiener schnitzel, other notable dishes include beef goulash with herbed *spaetzle* (a noodle side dish), apple strudel, and *rosti* (a potato and onion side dish) with lobster.

Wallse also attracts a die-hard band of smokers too, due to its policy of lending all puffing customers beautifully tailored, bright red capes to wear during their stint outside in the cool night air. **Expensive**

>> *Wallse's sister establishment, Café Sabarsky at 86th and 5th Avenue, serves excellent coffee and cakes* `37`

Restaurants

Florent *24/7 camp* `3 A2`
69 Gansevoort Street • 212 989 5779
>> www.restaurantflorent.com Open 24 hours daily

There's no better place than this for *moules frites* at
3am. In addition, Florent offers great home-made
soups and a superb weekend brunch. The clientele
ranges from daytime workers to outrageously dressed
clubbers. Regularly changing messages placed over
the bar provide an amusing distraction. **Moderate**

Sumile *great fish – raw and cooked* `3 C2`
154 West 13th Street • 212 989 7699
>> www.sumile.com
Open dinner Tue–Sun

A chic Japanese joint. Chef Josh DeChellis creates
innovative dishes, such as tea-smoked eel and black
sesame paste with raspberries. The cocktails are
fruity and fun, and the menu changes seasonally.
There's not a grain of rice in the house! **Expensive**

Tartine *bijou bistro* `3 B2`
253 West 11th Street • 212 229 2611
Open lunch & dinner Tue–Sat, dinner only Sun,
brunch Sat & Sun (cash only)

On a prime corner location that's great for people-
watching, Tartine serves consistently delicious light
French fare. Croissants are super-buttery, the savory
tarts are divine, and the weekend brunch is one of the
best deals in town. There's a BYOB policy. **Moderate**

Dining Institutions

Whether for food, tradition, location, or ambience,
some classic restaurants in New York just can't be
ignored. **Nobu** is renowned for celebrity-spotting
and the chef's tasting menu of creative sushi. **The
Four Seasons** has been serving Continental cuisine
to those with deep pockets since 1959. The space
was designed by Mies van der Rohe and Philip
Johnson and features Lichtenstein lithographs.
Chanterelle in Tribeca has been offering classic
French and innovative Franco-American cuisine since
1979. For a more casual feel, with first-rate food to
boot, **Gramercy Tavern** is another favorite, serving
New American cuisine in relaxed surroundings.
Finally, **Tavern on the Green** does great brunches.
For individual restaurant details, *see pp220–22*.

City Bakery *pastries & chocolate* `3 C1`
3 West 18th Street • 212 366 1414
Open 7am–7:30pm Mon–Fri, 7am–6:30pm Sat, 9am–6pm Sun

City Bakery leaves every customer contented. Its salad bar is arguably New York's best, and it also has a huge selection of flaky breakfast pastries, tarts, and decadent tortes. Linger over one of their superb hot chocolates – irresistible with a big home-made marshmallow floating in the froth. **Cheap**

Union Square Café *NY favorite* `3 D1`
21 East 16th Street • 212 243 4020
Open lunch and dinner daily

Perennially rated as one of New York's favorite restaurants, USC delivers New American cuisine in a relaxed atmosphere. The crowds never seem to abate, so reserve a table early or try for a space at the bar. Fresh flowers and a spacious feel give the café a relaxed air. Go for the daily specials. **Expensive**

Red Cat *creative cuisine in a funky place* `5 B5`
227 10th Avenue • 212 242 1122
>> www.theredcat.com
Open dinner daily

Red Cat's funky decor, fabulous food, and seamless service round off perfectly an afternoon spent gallery-hopping. Creative dishes might include chicken with sugarplum and sweet onion sauce, or risotto fritters with blueberry compote. **Moderate**

Grand Sichuan `5 C5`
International *bad decor, great food*
229 9th Avenue • 212 620 5200
Open all day daily

In style-obsessed Chelsea, this rarity attracts a loyal crowd on the merits of its food alone. For while the decor is stark, the Chinese cuisine is excellent. Try whole fried fish, garlicky sautéed spinach, and addictive pork and vegetable dumplings. **Cheap**

Biltmore Room *plush atmosphere*   5 C5
290 8th Avenue • 212 807 0111
>> www.thebiltmoreroom.com Open dinner daily

An entrance through thick velvet curtains adds an air of exclusivity to the Biltmore Room. Beyond the threshold lies a swanky bar and stylish dining room. The bar has its own scene, and people often come just to sip signature cocktails such as the Gin Blossom (infused with basil and combined with elderflower syrup). In the dining area – a mixture of gentlemen's-club tradition and something far more chic – chandeliers hang from the high ceiling and mirrors amplify the grandeur. Subtle lighting and funky music create a warm mood, and orchids add color.

The attentive staff serve dishes with Asian and Middle Eastern influences, including Algerian spiced lamb, miso-marinated Alaskan cod, and giant prawns wrapped in crispy noodles with avocado and tomato salad and mango salsa. The warm chocolate tart is not to be missed. **Expensive**

Bolo *more than paella*   6 E5
23 East 22nd Street • 212 228 2200
>> www.bolorestaurant.com Open lunch Mon–Fri, dinner daily

Bolo creates modern interpretations of some of the best traditional Spanish dishes. The menu features inventive tapas, such as a 12-layer potato dish with caramelized onions, black squid ink risotto, and egg tortilla with goat cheese. There's a bar, and the atmosphere is upbeat. Good lunch deals. **Expensive**

Tabla *Indian fusion*   6 E5
11 Madison Avenue • 212 889 0667
Open all day Mon–Sat

Fusing New American and Indian cuisine, Tabla presents dishes such as Goan spiced crab cake and tandoori breads using inventive flavors. A striking staircase divides the colorful formal upstairs dining room from the downstairs Bread Bar, which offers a less formal, slightly cheaper dining option. **Expensive**

Tamarind *epicurean spices*
6 F5

41–3 East 22nd Street • 212 674 7400
» www.tamarinde22.com Open lunch & dinner daily

Large glass windows, an unfussy modern interior, and cut flowers on each table set the tone. Tamarind has earned several prestigious culinary accolades, and its two proud owners are often seen milling about with diners, basking in positive feedback, no doubt. Such openness also extends to the kitchens, which are surrounded by glass, so you can watch the food being prepared without getting a noseful of every dish.

House specialties include a signature dish of tandoori scallops presented in a fried potato lattice cup, *bhagerey baignan* (eggplant with coconut, sesame, and peanut sauce), Tamarind's chutneys, and a home-made cheese. Lamb and lobster feature prominently on the menu too.

The Tearoom offers sandwiches, a vast array of teas, and desserts in a more casual, intimate environment. **Moderate**

Dos Caminos *trendy Mexican*
6 F5

373 Park Avenue South • 212 294 1000
» www.brguestrestaurants.com
Open lunch & dinner Mon–Fri, brunch & dinner Sat & Sun

Hugely popular with a regular crowd of young professionals, this large restaurant and bar is a vibrant place in which to indulge in margaritas and great Mexican fare. The famed guacamole is prepared at your table, so you can dictate the spice factor. **Moderate**

Blue Smoke *upscale American barbecue*
6 F4

116 East 27th Street • 212 447 7733
» www.bluesmoke.com Open lunch & dinner daily

Chef Ken Callaghan smokes spareribs, beef brisket, organic chicken, and sausages over hickory and apple woods, keeping meats flavorful without sacrificing succulence. The handsome, modern dining room fills with boisterous Manhattanites every night. Excellent beer selection, and live jazz downstairs. **Moderate**

i Trulli *wine & pasta in a warm atmosphere* `6 F4`
122 East 27th Street • 212 481 7372
>> www.itrulli.com Open lunch & dinner Mon–Fri, dinner Sat

i Trulli's delectable cuisine is true to its roots, which lie in the Italian region of Puglia. Specialties here include the *panelle* (chickpea fritters with goat cheese) and home-made pastas. Try a "flight of wine" (a selection of three to taste from a vast list), and sample cheeses, olives, and cured meats. **Moderate**

Mandoo Bar *Top-notch Korean cooking* `6 E4`
2 West 32nd Street • 212 279 3075
>> www.mandoobar.com Open all day daily

Uniformed cooks bustle about near the window preparing plump little *mandoo* – delicate dumplings stuffed with vegetables, fish, or meat. The salads and seafood dishes are also superb. Avoid weekday lunchtimes, though, when this informal restaurant is packed with local business people. **Cheap**

Artisanal *cheese, please* `6 F4`
2 Park Avenue (entrance on 32nd Street) • 212 725 8585
Open all day daily (brunch served 11am–3pm Sat & Sun)

The revived tradition of fondue-sharing creates a social buzz in the high-ceilinged dining room of this bistro and fromagerie. Various fondues are available, prepared with different cheeses, herbs and oil infusions. Some are traditional recipes, others experimental. Cheese is also the focus of salads, and appetizers such as a three-cheese onion soup. A tarte tatin in a cheddar crust continues the theme into dessert. There are non-cheese selections – *cassoulet* (bean stew), or chicken roasted "under the brick" – but choose at least one course devoted to the star ingredient.

A requisite cheese plate takes on new meaning as the *fromagier* guides you through 200-plus selections. For a five-cheese platter, choose from goat, cow, sheep, blue, and cheddar varieties. You can also order a "cheese and wine flight" at the bar (three choices of each), and buy cheese from the shop. **Moderate**

Cho Dang Gol *Korean creations* `6 E3`
55 West 35th Street • 212 695 8222
Open all day daily

Located in the heart of "Koreatown," this establishment is unusual in catering equally to meat-eaters, vegans, and vegetarians. The authentic yet accessible dishes form a perfect introduction to Korean cuisine.

Gop dol bim bap is a good one to try. With this, a heated stone bowl is filled with rice, vegetables (or meat), broth, spicy red paste, and an egg. You mix the ingredients and let some of the rice crisp at the bottom. You can also expect to receive the *ban chan* – little plates of appetizers that come with any meal and include *kim chi* (spicy pickled cabbage).

Cho Dang Gol is also known for its superb leek pancakes and melt-in-your-mouth tofu (bean curd), which is made on the premises, as is an alcoholic drink called Makkuli. The dishes vary in spiciness – ask the waitstaff for guidance if necessary. The lunchtime specials are great deals. **Moderate**

Sandwich Planet *sliced bread sensation* `5 C2`
534 9th Avenue • 212 273 9768
>> www.sandwichplanet.com Open 10:30am–8:30pm daily

Despite its closet-like dimensions, this pitstop offers a seemingly limitless choice of custom-made sandwiches. Should one of the five tables be available, linger over a signature creation like the Armani: thin prosciutto, fresh mozzarella, artichoke hearts, and rocket pressed between toasted foccacia. **Cheap**

Mi Nidito *surprisingly good Mexican* `5 C1`
852 8th Avenue • 212 265 0022
Open all day daily

With its gaudy signage hawking dozens of margarita varieties, this unassuming Hell's Kitchen eatery is not the most obvious place to find some of the city's best Mexican food. But the roasted chicken is irresistible – crisp, succulent, and studded with garlic – and the mango margaritas justify all the hoopla. **Moderate**

Churrascaria Plataforma *Brazilian BBQ* `5 C1`
316 West 49th Street • 212 245 0505
» www.churrascariaplataforma.com Open all day daily

Catering mainly to a post-theater crowd, this Brazilian *churrascaria* is a novel and lively fixed-price barbecue. Guests are led to tables in the capacious, elegant dining room and each given a round disk – one face red, the other green. After trips to the salad bar, the crowd settles in for the impending meat extravaganza.

When the disk's green side is displayed, gracious uniformed servers approach, wielding skewers of top-quality roasted meats – sirloin steaks, sausages, prime rib, chicken, and baby lamb chops – and fish such as salmon. When your plate is sufficiently full, flip the disk to red. When you've emptied it, flip again to green, and repeat the performance until your belly attains the desired level of distension.

Plataforma's perfect *caipirinha* is a refreshing, albeit potent, palette cleanser of cachaça rum, sugar, and mint over cracked ice. **Moderate**

Ess-a-Bagel *classic snacks* `6 F1`
831 3rd Avenue • 212 260 2252
» www.ess-a-bagel.com Open 6:30am–9pm daily (to 5 Sun)

This spacious midtown bagel shop bakes arguably the city's best example of the dense, rotund breakfast bread. Feel free to linger over any of 14 bagel varieties, coupled with award-winning whitefish salad, Nova Scotia smoked salmon, eggplant salad, or a classic spread of cream cheese. **Cheap**

Genki Sushi *sushi on the roll* `6 E1`
9 East 46th Street • 212 983 5018
Open 11:30am–8:30pm Mon–Fri, noon–5pm Sat

A metal conveyor belt stocked with midtown's freshest fish revolves through the colorful dining area. Take your pick from plates (color-coded according to price) of whimsically assembled rolls and succulent sashimi. Lunchtimes are busy, so come in the early evening if you can. **Cheap**

Acqua Pazza *fresh pasta, seafood & fish* `8 E5`

36 West 52nd Street • 212 582 6900
» www.acquapazzanyc.com
Open lunch & dinner Mon–Fri, dinner only Sat

Acqua Pazza – "crazy water" – belies its name with serious Italian food. Octopus, crab, and whole baked fish are typical items on the menu. Pasta infused with espresso is an unusual dish, harking back to the days when coffee was used as a preservative. **Expensive**

Aquavit *Swedish sensation* `8 E5`

13 West 54th Street • 212 307 7311
» www.aquavit.org Open lunch & dinner Mon–Fri, brunch Sun

Swedish chef Marcus Samuelsson, who won a prestigious "Best Chef in New York City" award in 2003, has taken the Scandinavian cuisine at this restaurant to new levels of gastronomic genius. A visit's not cheap, but worth the price, especially if you sit in the main dining room, which is in an atrium that features an indoor waterfall.

The eponymous aquavit is a potent Scandinavian spirit, double distilled, with flavors added in the second distillation. This and glasses of Carlsberg beer are served alongside house specialties such as herrings. Other favorites include seafood stew in a delicious dill sauce, brioche-wrapped salmon, and Kobe beef ravioli. The restaurant also prepares a beguiling gravlax and tandoori smoked salmon.

Three tasting menus, including a vegetarian option, offer seven-course "Aquavit Bite" meals. Another way to sample many of these flavors at a little less expense is to eat upstairs in the Aquavit Café. The café's kitchen is separate from the restaurant's, but both are overseen by the executive chef, so there's a decent amount of overlap. However, Swedish meatballs are available only in the café.

To uphold the restaurant's name, several house-made and unusual aquavits are available; flavors may include black pepper and vanilla, and pear and cloudberry. **Expensive**

» *Marcus Samuelsson also oversees the AQ Café at Scandinavia House, 58 Park Avenue, near 37th Street*

Restaurants

Town *sophistication & pizzazz* 8 E5
Chambers Hotel, 15 West 56th Street • 212 582 4445
>>www.townnyc.com
Open breakfast, lunch & dinner daily, brunch Sun

A fashionable restaurant, where a fanciful interior is matched by creative Euro-American cuisine. The menu changes seasonally, but signature dishes include, in spring, white asparagus with a blood-orange reduction, and, in summer, soft-shell crab. **Expensive**

Norma's *a perfect start to the day* 7 D5
At Le Parker Meridien Hotel, 118 W. 57th St. • 212 708 7460
>>www.parkermeridien.com/normas
Open breakfast & lunch daily

Norma's is a swish place, offering one of the most luxurious breakfasts in town. Between sips of freshly squeezed juice, dig into mango and papaya with cinnamon crêpes, mammoth omelets, and decadent French brioche toast. **Moderate**

Geisha *stylish Japanese-American joint* 8 E4
33 East 61st Street • 212 813 1112
Open lunch & dinner Mon–Sat, dinner only Sun

Don your best black outfit and blend in with the crowd sipping cocktails while waiting for tables. The menu focuses on seafood with Japanese flavors, such as lobster served with asparagus and mushroom *udon* noodles. Downstairs is hip and fun; upstairs is a bit more subdued. There's a sushi bar too. **Expensive**

Diner Etiquette

Diners – known as "coffee shops" within New York City limits – are part of the quintessential NY experience. They are social levelers, where a poor poet and a business mogul can rub elbows at the counter over omelets. Diner food is comfort food – all-day breakfast fare, including eggs any style, as well as burgers, French fries, and grilled cheese sandwiches. Prices don't dictate the quality of a diner; location, longevity, menu, and staff do. Your server should be courteous, but don't get offended if he/she rushes you during a busy period when tables need to be turned over. Coffee is rarely strong but should always be limitless. Kitchen lingo is part of the tradition: eggs are "sunny-side up" or "(easy) over"; rye toast is placed "whiskey down."

Serendipity 3 *American staples* `8 F4`
225 East 60th Street • 212 838 3531
≫ www.serendipity3.com Open lunch & dinner daily

A favorite with Upper East Side families, Serendipity 3 is loved for its mammoth portions of American comfort food. The chicken pot pies, juicy burgers, thick soups, and bright salads are, however, mere preambles to dessert: the frozen hot chocolate surely ranks among New York's finest creations. **Cheap**

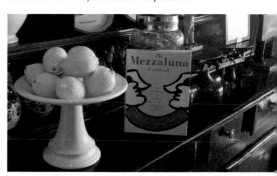

March *quiet elegance, gourmet food* `8 G4`
405 East 58th Street • 212 754 6272
≫ www.marchrestaurant.com Open dinner daily

Superbly presented food in a romantic renovated townhouse. The gourmet food takes in a wide range of influences, but there is a discernible Asian accent in the use of raw fish, soy, sesame, and dishes such as shrimp and wild mushroom tempura. You can dine outdoors from May to October. **Expensive**

Mezzaluna *heart-melting tiramisu* `8 F2`
1295 3rd Avenue • 212 535 9600
Open lunch & dinner daily (cash or Amex only)

A lively and intimate spot for northern Italian cuisine, Mezzaluna excels in freshly made pastas, fish dishes, and brick-oven-baked pizzas. The creamy, light tiramisu is one of the best you'll find in New York. Artistic depictions of half-moons *(mezzaluna)* adorn the walls. Staff are very friendly. **Moderate**

Annie's *hearty brunches* `8 F1`
1381 3rd Avenue • 212 327 4853
Open 8am–11:30pm daily (to midnight Fri & Sat)

An excellent Sunday brunch (served until 4pm) packs young families into this warm, classic New York bistro. Wicked Bloody Marys and generous portions are *de rigueur*; omelets could accommodate two appetites. Annie's is also a pancake lover's dream: wholewheat, apple, banana, mixed berry ... take your pick. **Cheap**

Restaurants

Atlantic Grill *fresh fish, fresh atmosphere* 8 F1

1341 3rd Avenue • 212 988 9200
>> www.brguestrestaurants.com
Open lunch & dinner Mon–Sat, brunch & dinner Sun

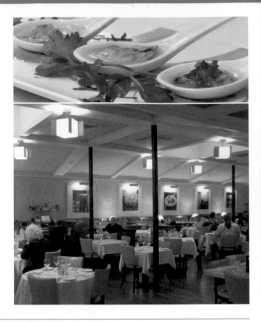

To please the finicky Upper East Side inhabitants, food, service, and atmosphere have to be of a high order in any establishment here. So the long-standing popularity of the Atlantic Grill attests to its culinary credentials. The restaurant excels at well-prepared, very fresh fish, accompanied by a good wine list, and waitstaff who are both competent and efficient.

A sense of refined informality pervades the spacious dining area, spread throughout two rooms. Additional sidewalk seating is available when weather permits. Specialties include oysters, crabcakes, lightly fried sesame-crusted lobster roll, and barbecued *mahi mahi* (a particularly succulent, slightly sweet fish). There are also daily specials, and you can order small plates from a sushi bar. Book ahead to reserve a table or be prepared to wait – it's worth it. **Moderate**

Candle 79 *fine meat-free dining* 8 F1

154 East 79th Street • 212 537 7179
>> www.candlecafe.com Open lunch & dinner daily

An upscale restaurant offering wonderful vegetarian and vegan masterpieces, Candle 79 pushes the limit of what you might expect from a meatless menu. Many a dedicated carnivore is won over by the flavors and textures experienced here. Inventive dishes include squash and wild mushroom risotto, and porcini-crusted *seitan* (a meaty wheat protein concoction) with garlicky greens and a wild mushroom red wine sauce.

In addition to organic wine, sake, and beer, the list of non-alcoholic juices and tonics is enough to make one giddy. Options such as an elderberry extract with apple and lemon, and an orange juice, coconut cream, and banana smoothie are divine. The less formal, sister establishment, Candle Café (1307 3rd Avenue; 212 472 0970), also offers creative green food, focusing on tasty salads, wraps, and soups, and has a juice bar at the front. **Moderate**

Sushi of Gari *inspiring sushi* 8 G1

402 East 78th Street • 212 517 5340
Open dinner Tue–Sun

The tasting menu here allows innovative sushi chef Masatoshi Gari Sugio and his staff to demonstrate their mastery over fish and seafood. An à-la-carte menu is available, but the principal reason for dining at this small, simply decorated treasure is to allow the chefs to surprise and delight. **Expensive**

Ouest *first-rate New American fare* 9 B5

2315 Broadway • 212 580 8700
>> www.ouestny.com Open dinner daily, brunch Sun

Ouest is about panache in just about every detail. The bar area is the first thing you'll notice, with its wood-paneled walls, shades of deep red, and old-fashioned fans hanging from the ceiling. Beyond this is a corridor that passes a glazed wine cellar and leads to the main dining area. Stylish round, red-leather booths take up most of the room, with square tables along the periphery. There's balcony seating too, though this is a bit cramped and best avoided. The bright kitchen is open for all to see, and the music adds to the atmosphere, tending toward 20s–40s jazz.

Owner/chef Tom Valenti has been much lauded for pleasing the palate and delighting the eye, here and at other top New York restaurants. Highly sophisticated dishes emerge from his kitchen, such as the intriguingly named "truffled omelet soufflé" with mousselline sauce, or lobster ravioli with a herb salad. Well-sourced game and other roast meats are typical offerings. Specials include braised lamb shanks on Mondays and Tuesdays, and the legendary meat loaf on a Sunday. Allow time to peruse the globe-trotting wine list, which has won awards, or ask for advice if the selection proves overwhelming. By contrast, the dessert selection is short and sweet, and includes a panna cotta that can't be beaten.

Ouest's superior brunch menu also wins plaudits by offering refined breakfast food such as scrambled egg with house-smoked sturgeon. **Expensive**

Restaurants

Picholine *traditional excellence*

7 C3

35 West 64th Street • 212 724 8585
Open lunch Sat, dinner Sun–Fri

The eponymous picholine (green olive) theme adorns the plates and is evident in some dishes, such as caramelized ribs with an olive sauce. But Picholine is equally renowned for its formidable cheese cart. Jackets are required in the main dining room, but less formal seating is available at the front bar. **Expensive**

Pasha *high-class Turkish*

7 C2

70 West 71st Street • 212 579 8751
Open dinner daily

A sumptuous eatery fit for Ottoman royalty. The luxurious, deep-red and yellow dining area is hung with vibrant tapestries. Kebabs, stuffed vine leaves, and dozens of other richly seasoned Turkish delights are presented in copper tureens by charming waitstaff. Pasha offers great pre-theater deals. **Moderate**

El Malecón II *Caribbean specialties*

9 B3

764 Amsterdam Avenue • 212 864 5648
Open dinner daily

Given New York's sizeable Dominican population, perhaps it is not surprising that some of the best Dominican cooking north of Miami is found here. While the cuisine's staples do not differ greatly from those used in other Caribbean and many Central American kitchens, nuances make all the difference. Few restaurants get the alchemy quite so right as El Malecón II, younger brother of the Washington Heights original.

Diners familiar with the restaurant's namesake – the pulsating seaside boulevard in Santo Domingo – might raise an eyebrow at the modest dining room. But one look at the spice-encrusted, brown skins of chickens turning on rotisseries will quell doubts. A mixed crowd of ex-pat families and students sit down to *mofongo* (sweet plantains mashed with stewed pork), *asopao con longaniza* (rice in broth with spicy Spanish sausage), and seafood paella. **Cheap**

Aix *inspiration from France* `9 B4`
2398 Broadway • 212 874 7400
>> www.aixnyc.com Open dinner daily, brunch Sun

The bright oranges and sky blues in this restaurant evoke the colors of Provence. Rather than focusing on traditional Provençal dishes, however, Chef Didier Virot's menu offers a wider range of creative French fare. The star dish is halibut in a garlic cream with oatmeal porcini cake and walnut sauce. **Expensive**

Symposium *genuine Greek* `11 B5`
544 West 113th Street • 212 865 1011
Open all day daily

Symposium has been serving stuffed vine leaves and mousaka for over 20 years to its regulars, who come largely from the Hellenic community. Sit in the cozy taverna or walk through the kitchen to the enclosed back garden. The Symposium Salad provides a little taste of many dishes on the menu. **Moderate**

New Leaf Café *urban renewal enterprise*
Fort Tryon Park • 212 568 5323 • Ⓜ "A" train to 190th Street
>> www.nyrp.org/newleaf
Open lunch & dinner Tue–Sat, brunch & dinner Sun

All net proceeds from this café, which is set in a converted stone house in Fort Tryon Park, go to the restoration and maintenance of the park. Organic salad leaves and wild salmon feature on the menu. Try to catch the Thursday evening Jazz Night. **Moderate**

Noodle Pudding *consistently tasty Italian* `13 B3`
38 Henry Street, Brooklyn • 718 625 3737
Open dinner Tue–Sun (cash only)

Don't let the name deceive you: Noodle Pudding refers to a pasta dish, not Asian food here. *Osso buco* (veal knuckle), *penne arrabiata*, real mozzarella, and panna cotta feature among the Italian staples. Locals show their appreciation by packing this casually stylish restaurant nightly. **Moderate**

The River Café · *enchanting views & food* · 13 A3

1 Water Street • 718 522 5200

>> www.therivercafe.com · Open dinner daily, lunch Mon–Sat, brunch Sun (formal dress required in evening)

The River Café began serving sublime food in 1977 and hasn't had time to look back. In a superb setting directly on the waterfront, with a stunning view of the Manhattan skyline and Brooklyn Bridge, this is probably one of the most romantic dining places in the world. Much of the seating allows couples to gaze out at the scene together.

The reputable kitchen tends to gravitate toward unusual meats and seafood. Foie gras, rabbit, suckling pig, and caviar might all feature on the menu, with a token dish for vegetarians. The Maine Lobster is a regular favorite. For novelty value, order the Chocolate Marquise Brooklyn Bridge – a model in fine chocolate.

Lunch is slightly cheaper than dinner. If, however, you just want to savor the atmosphere, go for wine and appetizers in the Terrace Room. **Expensive**

The Grocery · *a neighborhood star* · 13 B4

288 Smith Street • 718 596 3335

Open dinner Mon–Sat

The petite Grocery offers New American fare and has long been a favorite with locals. It is praised equally for its use of ultra-fresh ingredients and the warmth of its service. Dishes tend to be simple, allowing the flavors of the produce to sing out, as in the juicy and healthily trimmed grilled lamb. **Moderate**

Joya · *Thai spice* · 13 B4

215 Court Street • 718 222 3484

Open dinner daily

With its industrial-chic interior imparting a level of SoHo sophistication to the quaint Boerum Hill/Carroll Gardens neighborhood, Joya lures discerning Manhattanites across the river. Young professionals flock here for the ambience and the deftly executed Thai dishes that rarely venture above $10. **Cheap**

Park Slope Chip Shop *comfort food* `13 C4`
383 5th Avenue • 718 832 7701
>> www.chipshopnyc.com Open all day daily

One of Park Slope's most cheerful eateries is inspired by a British phenomenon in dining. Young families and ex-pat students pining for familiar comfort food relish generous platters of chips, fried haddock, crisps, curries, and fishcakes. Dessert? Fried chocolate candy, of course. **Cheap**

Al Di La *Venetian trattoria* `13 C4`
248 5th Avenue • 718 783 4565
>> www.aldilatrattoria.com Open dinner daily except Tue

First-rate food served in a romantic, candlelit setting ensures Al Di La's devoted following. Specials include polenta, gnocchi with fried sage, and grilled sardines. The restaurant doesn't take reservations, so be prepared to have a drink at a neighboring bar while you wait for a table, or go off-peak. **Moderate**

Convivium Osteria *splendid bistro* `13 C4`
68 5th Avenue • 718 857 1833
Open dinner Tue–Sun

Dim lighting and dark furnishings are a brooding contrast to the bright, bold flavors of the Mediterranean at this little bistro. Pair a reasonably priced wine with braised artichoke hearts, salt cod filets, or roasted rack of lamb. Few people outside the neighborhood know of this gem ... yet. **Moderate**

LouLou *a taste of Brittany* `13 C5`
222 DeKalb Avenue • 718 246 0633
Open dinner daily (except Tue), brunch Sat & Sun

Cozy LouLou is a great stop before or after a visit to the Brooklyn Academy of Music *(see p129)*. Fish, seafood, and scrumptious crêpes are the mainstays of a menu that focuses on the Brittany region of France. Try dining in the lovely back garden; you'll forget that you're in a metropolis. **Moderate**

>> *For advice on tipping in restaurants, see p233*

i-Shebeen Madiba *South African eaterie* `13 C3`

195 DeKalb Avenue, Fort Greene • 718 855 9190

>> www.madibaweb.com Open all day daily (to 1am Fri & Sat)

Part Zulu trinket shop, part rustic-style bistro, this place holds boundless intrigue. Cosmopolitan neighborhood residents come for authentic *bobotie* (a curried mince bake) and *potjie bredie* (fragrant meat stew served in a cast iron pot). There's outdoor seating and live music, weather permitting. **Moderate**

Butta'Cup Lounge *Southern-style food* `13 C3`

271 Adelphi Street • 718 522 1669

>> www.buttacuplounge.com

Open all day daily (to 2am Fri & Sat)

Sip a signature Applejack cocktail at the bar, then relax in a leopard print-upholstered booth. Notable main dishes include classic fried chicken and a piquant salmon Japonaise. On weekends, the upstairs lounge is good for DJ-spun soul and hip-hop. **Moderate**

DiFara Pizzeria *Neapolitan pizzas*

1424 Avenue J • 718 258 1367 • Ⓜ Subway Q to Avenue J

Open all day daily

The thin, round pizza of Naples – arguably New Yorkers' most beloved culinary import – is elevated to an art form at this tiny pizzeria in the predominantly Hasidic Jewish neighborhood of Midwood. Producing these transcendent pies behind a cracked linoleum countertop since 1964 is Domenico DeMarco, a master *pizzaiolo* with an obsessive commitment to fresh ingredients and the precise assembly (one blob of creamy mozzarella at a time) of just about perfect pizzas. Translation: you must wait for your food.

Patience is duly rewarded with the first bite. The robust, basil-laced tomato sauce, crisp crust, light olive oil, and tangy parmigiano reggiano cheese should conspire to put words like "the best" on your lips. They should also distract you from the smoke-stained ceiling, yellowing prints of Naples, and awkwardly arranged tables – just six altogether. **Cheap**

Relish *classic diner* `13 D2`
225 Wythe Avenue • 718 963 4546
Open all day daily (to 1am Fri & Sat)

Archetypal diners like this usually serve greasy, griddle-fried fare. But Josh Cohen's seasonally revised menus feature eclectic American bistro cuisine at diner-friendly prices: think chili-rubbed smoked ribs and tomato soup with chèvre croutons. Locals in the know fill the 1950s-style booths. **Moderate**

Planet Thailand *affordable specialties* `13 C2`
133 North 7th Street • 718 599 5758
Open all day daily to 1am (to 2am Fri & Sat)

The dining room here is cavernous, with towering windows and gray, industrial walls hung with sweeping paintings by Williamsburg artists. Within the space, venturesome Manhattanites and stylish Brooklynites nibble Thai papaya salads and Japanese *nigiri* sushi between sips of iced coffee or warm sake. **Cheap**

Peter Luger Steak House *sizzlers* `13 B2`
178 Broadway • 718 387 7400
» www.peterluger.com
Open all day to 9:45pm daily (to 10:45pm Fri & Sat); cash only

Renowned as one of the top meat purveyors in the country, Peter Luger has been in business since 1887, and the generations of experience show. The decor is no-frills, and the menu is simple. Steak — particularly the Porterhouse – rules. **Expensive**

Bamonte's *old-school Italian* `13 C1`
32 Withers Street • 718 384 8831
Open all day to 10:30pm; closed Tue

Home-made pastas and rich red sauces reign supreme at this establishment, which has been in business for more than 100 years. Bamonte's harks back to the past with wonderful photographs on the walls and a wait-staff who look like they've been around almost as long as the restaurant – all part of its charm. **Moderate**

shopping

New York is a famously fabulous place to shop. Rich pickings are to be had across the board – in the time-honored department stores of midtown, the designer flagships of Fifth Avenue, and the latest little gem to spring up in buzzing Williamsburg. Follow the lead of New Yorkers and shop where the locals shop – the great delis, bookstores and music outlets downtown, and the funky fashion boutiques in Harlem and Brooklyn.

DEPARTMENT STORES	FOOD	HIGH FASHION
Bergdorf Goodman 754 5th Avenue A bastion of understated style. Come here for high-end fashions and health treatments in the day spa. *(See p81)*	**Dean & DeLuca** 560 Broadway The first stop for foodies. Dean & DeLuca is a delicatessen par excellence, with the largest selection of gourmet foods in NY. *(See p65)*	**Miu Miu** 100 Prince Street A label that's adored for girly fashions: sensuous materials, beautifully cut dresses, and sexy underwear. *(See p63)*
>> *www.NYSale.com will give you the lowdown on up-and-coming designer sample sales.*	**Dylan's Candy Bar** 1011 3rd Avenue A two-story shop that's choc-a-bloc with sweets and confectionery of all kinds. Cute packaging too. *(See p82)*	**Marc by Marc Jacobs** 403–405 Bleecker Street With men's and women's stores next door to each other, this is perfect for couples to get kitted out in Jacobs' effortlessly cool look. *(See p72)*
Barney's New York 660 Madison Avenue On a more modest scale than New York's really big stores, Barney's is one of the least daunting places for browsing designer clothes. *(See p82)*	**Zabar's** 2245 Broadway A family-run New York institution, Zabar's stock includes mouth-watering cheeses, cured meats, and smoked fish. *(See p85)*	**INA** 21 Prince Street A treasure-house for girls who want top-end fashions but lack the funds. INA stocks barely worn second-hand designer clothes. *(See p67)*
Century 21 22 Cortlandt Street A bargain-hunter's dream – despite sometimes surly service – Century 21 is packed with heavily discounted designer clothes. *(See p60)*	**Magnolia Bakery** 401 Bleecker Street An irresistible hoard of cakes, muffins, and pastries is prepared daily at this Village bakery. *(See p71)*	**Costume National** 108 Wooster Street Typically fine Italian tailoring and a timeless sense of elegance are the hallmarks of the men's and women's clothing at this store. *(See p63)*
Jeffrey 449 West 14th Street The lion's share of this popular store is given over to shoes – from Prada to Puma. The clothes are top-range and expensive. *(See p74)*		

VINTAGE & RETRO	SHOES & ACCESSORIES	COOL STORES

Housing Works Thrift Shop
306 Columbus Avenue
The stock is donated by the most stylish New Yorkers, so you can find cheap design classics here. Profits go to an AIDS charity. *(See p85)*

Felissimo
10 West 56th Street
Felissimo treats household objects as works of art, exhibiting them in a five-floor shop-cum-gallery. *(See p80)*

Mini Minimarket
218 Bedford Avenue
Taking its stylistic lead from 70s and 80s leisurewear, Mini Minimarket is full of funky little numbers for the girl about town. *(See p88)*

Rafe
1 Bleecker Street
Candy-colored sandals with polka-dot insoles, strappy evening shoes, and soft, "ballet shoe" flats – Rafe's collections are fun. *(See p68)*

Takashimaya
693 5th Avenue
Asian influences are strong through-out Takashimaya's seductive store, which sells a mix of vintage furniture and high-tech gadgets. *(See p79)*

ALife Rivington Club
158 Rivington Street
This is *the* place to come for vintage trainers – Nike Air Wovens, old-school Adidas, etc. *(See p69)*

Manolo Blahnik
31 West 54th Street
The doyen of high-end, super sexy footwear, Manolo Blahnik designs shoes that are very desirable, and extremely expensive. *(See p78)*

>> www.lazarshopping.com *provides profiles of the city's fashion designers, along with all manner of shopping advice and information, including a list of sales happening each month.*

Christian Louboutin
941 Madison Avenue
A beautiful, Parisian-style shop, with a selection of elegant shoes for wealthy Upper East Siders. *(See p83)*

Flight 001
96 Greenwich Avenue
Be the coolest person on the plane with your own in-flight travel kit and maybe a mobile spice rack to liven up the airline food. *(See p72)*

Blades Board & Skate
120 West 72nd Street
If you want to get around Central Park with more speed and style, get your inline skates here. *(See p84)*

Isa
88 North 6th Street, Brooklyn
Street fashions are mixed with funky beats supplied by DJs. This is a place to hang out, chill out, and buy some cool duds. *(See p89)*

Century 21 *discount designer duds* `1 D3`

22 Cortlandt Street • 212 227 9092
>> www.c21stores.com
Open 7:45am–8pm Mon–Fri (to 8:30 Thu), 10–8 Sat, 11–7 Sun

This is a goldmine of a department store, so don't let the aggressive crowds scare you away. The discounted designer men's and women's clothes, shoes, make-up, and linens on offer will make the occasional elbow in the ribs well worth the hassle.

The women's shoe department tends to be the busiest and most chaotic, due to weekly shipments from the likes of Costume National, Dolce & Gabbana, and Marc Jacobs. The top floor is the jewel in the crown, though: it stocks the collections of designers such as Armani, Missoni, and Ralph Lauren, but at a fraction of the price you'd pay at the Madison Avenue flagship stores. The only downside to this heavenly situation is the service (often brusque), long lines, and communal dressing rooms – be prepared to undress in front of 25 other shoppers.

Kate Spade Travel *stylish accessories* `3 C5`

59 Thompson Street • 212 965 8654
>> www.katespade.com Open 11am–7pm Tue–Sat, 12–6 Sun

Luxury coupled with whimsy are the key ingredients of Kate Spade Travel. Nylon and leather weekend bags, personalized stationery, and vintage travel books from the 1960s make browsing a delight. (How the beautifully crafted luggage will cope with an airport check-in is another matter.)

Hotel Venus by Patricia Field *Cirque du Soleil meets S&M clothing* `3 D5`

382 West Broadway • 212 966 4066
>> www.patriciafield.com Open 11am–8pm daily (to 9pm Sat)

Patricia Field – costume designer for the HBO sitcom *Sex and the City* – has designed this SoHo store to give free rein to her eccentric fantasies. Hip girls, transvestites, and circus performers will all find something here to make them smile.

Keiko *bikinis & maillots* `3 D5`

62 Greene Street • 212 226 6051
>> www.keikonewyork.com
Open 11am–6pm Mon–Fri, noon–6pm Sat, 1–6pm Sun

Take some of the anxiety away from swimsuit shopping with Keiko's wide choice of colors and styles, which ranges from boy-shorts to string bikinis. The assistants will help you find the perfect fit and ensure you'll be a head-turner at the beach.

Pearl River Mart *Far Eastern treasures* `3 D5`

477 Broadway • 212 431 4770
>> www.pearlriver.com Open 10am–7:30pm daily

It has never been easier or more fun to get lost in a store. This three-story shrine to everything Asian feels like a cross between a flea market (yes, the prices are that good) and an exotic department store. The elegant Chinese robes, traditional Mandarin dresses, slippers, embroidered bags, and purses would be triple the price in a more conventional store. The simple ceramic bowls and delicate Japanese tea sets are also the same as those found in pricey boutiques.

The kitchen department offers everything you need to prepare an authentic Asian meal: teas, spices, and sauces are available in bewildering quantities. Among the bathroom products are herbal remedies and beauty treats galore. Many of the exquisite Chinese wedding items make stunning accessories or gifts. There's also a selection of cute and colorful kids' clothes, shoes, and toys.

Gifts and novelty items range from funky alarm clocks and butterfly-shaped kites to windchimes, and there's a selection of fascinating traditional musical instruments. This is not to mention the lanterns, the stationery, the bedding, the homewares, and thousands of other items that will make you suddenly feel as if you've developed adult attention deficit disorder. A word to the wise: if time is of the essence, get here early before the crowds, and keep an eye on the clock – one could easily while away an entire day at the Pearl River Mart and barely notice.

Helmut Lang *luxurious minimalist clothes* `3 D5`
80 Greene Street • 212 925 7214
>> www.helmutlang.com Open 11–7 Mon–Sat, 12–6 Sun

Splashing out on an outfit from Helmut Lang will reward you for years to come, as the clothes are perennially stylish. This designer epitomizes the world's image of New York chic: basic blacks, whites, and neutrals, in designs that work equally well for a SoHo art opening or a downtown club.

Le Corset by Selima *luxe lingerie* `3 C5`
80 Thompson Street • 212 334 4936
Open 11am–7pm Mon–Fri, 11am–8pm Sat, noon–7pm Sun

The great and the good, from Yoko Ono to Sir Ben Kingsley, have been spotted inside this closet-sized lingerie store. Underwear by Roberto Cavalli and kimonos (new and vintage) will tempt the temptress in you. The hand-dyed corsets are so beautiful that many buyers use them as outerwear.

Barney's CO-OP *hipster clothing* `3 D4`
116 Wooster Street • 212 965 9964
Open 11am–7pm Mon–Sat, noon–6pm Sun

If no-brainer shopping is what you're after, then look no further than this wild-child of Barney's New York *(see p82)*, the city's bastion of good style and taste. The CO-OP's eclectic mix of trendy clothes for young-ish shoppers takes the Barney's brand in a hipper direction. A vast stockpile of jeans (from Seven to Levi's) for men and women guarantees that you'll find the perfect fit. Other lines – such as Theory, Marc by Marc Jacobs, and Prada Sport – mingle with upscale labels and 1970s-inspired athletic gear from the likes of Puma and Adidas. The handmade hats, funky watches, jewelry, and shoes are quirky enough to warrant more than a second glance – in fact, it's almost impossible to make a bad purchase here. What's more, wearing clothes from Barney's CO-OP is sure to increase your likelihood of getting through the velvet ropes at New York's hot night spots.

Clio *whimsical home accessories* `3 C4`
92 Thompson Street • 212 966 8991
» www.clio-home.com Open 11am–7pm Mon–Sat, noon–6 Sun

Not one to focus on mass brands, Clio concentrates on up-and-coming homeware designers from around the world. Unique pieces, such as a walnut cheese board with turquoise inlay, can be found alongside hand-blown glassware. Look for the stunning Rehabilitated Dinnerware line of revamped vintage serving platters.

Costume National *sleek clothes* `3 D4`
108 Wooster Street • 212 431 1530
» www.costumenational.com Open 11–7 Mon–Sat, noon–6 Sun

Ennio Capasa's collection of streamlined clothes for men and women includes pieces you'll want in your closet forever because of their enduring style. The Italian designer's perfectly tailored jackets and skirts appear edgy yet elegant, and each season's shoe collection offers sexy heels and urban-style flats.

Kirna Zabate *wearable avant-garde* `3 D4`
96 Greene Street • 212 941 9656
» www.kirnazabete.com Open 11–7 Mon–Sat, noon–6 Sun

Every item here seems to be letting you in on a fashion secret, hinting at what is absolutely "of-the-moment." The two-story boutique is a hot spot for industry insiders, who love the drama of finding Jean Paul Gaultier next to unknown indie labels. Accessories for babies and dogs make the store even more delightful.

Miu Miu *off-beat elegance* `3 D4`
100 Prince Street • 212 334 5156
» www.miumiu.com Open 11–7 Mon-Fri, noon–6 Sat & Sun

This flagship store has major browse appeal due to its energetic and flirty designs. While the craftsmanship of parent company Prada can be seen in the details, a let-your-hair-down attitude gives the clothes verve. Miu Miu's fashions may not be cheap, but wearing a shirt that makes you feel happy is priceless.

Moss *museum-worthy designs* `3 D4`
146 Greene Street • 212 204 7100
>> www.mossonline.com Open 11–7 Mon–Sat, noon–6 Sun

This store pleases die-hard design fans as well as those who just love pretty things. Step into a world of modern furniture, retro lighting, and Moser crystal. While many of the items are ludicrously expensive, others, like the range of Lomo cameras and stuffed cartoon animals, are both fun and reasonably priced.

Marc Jacobs *fashion's golden boy* `3 D4`
163 Mercer Street • 212 343 1490
>> www.marcjacobs.com Open 11–7 Mon–Sat, noon–6 Sun

Given that writer/film director Sophia Coppola is Jacobs' muse, it's not surprising that every item in his store has an air of effortless, super-cool style. From this designer's much-coveted leather bags to his retro-style dresses, jackets, and shoes, there is little that won't please the eye.

Prada *vast flagship store* `3 D4`
575 Broadway • 212 334 8888
>> www.prada.com Open 11am–7pm, noon–6pm Sun

Prada's 24,000-sq-ft flagship in the heart of SoHo may have become as overexposed as a pop princess's midriff, but that doesn't mean we won't keep looking. The elegantly futuristic store, designed by Dutch architect Rem Koolhaas, retains the flavor of an art space (the building used to be the downtown arm of the Guggenheim Museum), and will entice travelers to visit just to witness architectural history in the making. Koolhaas included so many technologically advanced gadgets that even science and technology magazines covered the store opening.

As for the clothes, they remain beautiful examples of elegance reinterpreted. For women, the designs do not slavishly follow fashions, but assuredly set their own trends. The men's shoes – with the signature red stripe on the sole of the Prada Sport line – are staples that never lose their popularity.

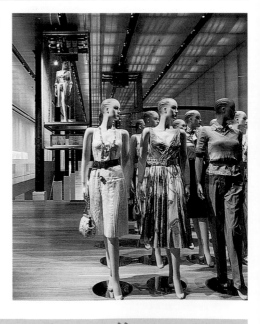

For tips on tax-free shopping, visit >> www.enewyork.dk.com

Scoop *high fashion* 3 D4
532 Broadway • 212 925 2886
>> www.scoopnyc.com Open 11am–8pm Mon–Sat, noon–7 Sun

The price tags may elicit a tiny (involuntary) gasp, but one piece will go a long way in building a great wardrobe. While the store caters mainly to sample-size fashionistas who don't balk at maxing out their credit cards for a poncho, it's a great place to come for the most sought-after pieces from each season.

Dean & DeLuca *a gourmet's mecca* 3 D4
560 Broadway • 212 226 6800
>> www.deandeluca.com Open 9am–8pm Mon–Sat, 10–7 Sun

Should there be a perfect way to stack mangoes, display passion fruit, and organize juice bottles according to the laws of color theory, then Dean & DeLuca will find it. This Aladdin's cave of a gourmet store carries top-quality produce, be it fresh, cured, made locally, or flown in from distant shores. All the produce looks wonderfully wholesome and good. Spices are clearly chosen with care, and the bottles of olive oil from Italy are almost too beautiful to open. And one of the best things about shopping here is that there are always free tasters to sample.

Each department carries delicacies from around the world. The cheese section stocks an ample selection of Goudas and Bries, as well as more exotic delights, such as Brillo de Treviso (a sweet cheese from Italy that is dipped in wine). There are also fine American cheeses, such as the creamy goat cheese Humbolt Fog. The seafood department carries sushi-grade tuna, and the bakery produces tasty numbers such as Portuguese corn bread – it's good enough to make you throw out the low-carb lifestyle for good.

Head to the back of the store for every type of kichen appliance you never knew you needed, from sushi trays and crème brûlée dishes to mixers, suede oven mitts, and cedar grilling planks (they keep food moist, apparently). And, lest you become over-whelmed by the choice of food on offer, there is an entire library of cookbooks to help sort things out.

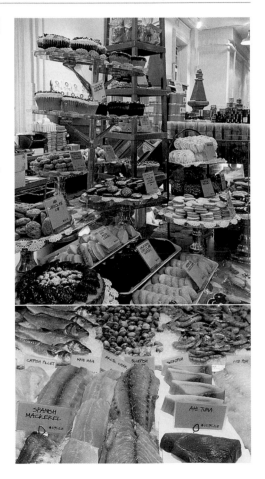

>> *Dean & DeLuca has a great in-store café for takeaway pastries and coffee (see p13)*

Kate's Paperie *stationery with panache* `3 D4`
561 Broadway • 212 941 9816
>> www.katespaperie.com Open 10–8 Mon–Sat, 11–7 Sun

Luddites who prefer the tactile pleasures of pen and paper to the ease of electronic mail should check out Kate's for all their stationery needs. Quirky thank-you cards, giant leather-bound photo albums, fountain pens, stamps, and tactile handmade paper sold by the sheet are here in abundance.

The Apartment *dream apartment loot* `3 D4`
101 Crosby Street • 212 219 3066
>> www.theapt.com Open Mon–Fri by appt only

Once you enter this experimental design studio set up to look like a real apartment, you may have difficulty returning to your own abode. Every aspect of The Apartment has been put together with an eye for what is both minimalist and sensuous. From the multicolored broom in the kitchen to the Philippe Starck fixtures in the bathroom to the Edith Mezard linens on the bed – everything exudes exemplary design. And, of course, everything you see is for sale: the clothes hanging in the closet, the toothpaste in the bathroom, even the food in the fridge.

The point of it all? To emphasize that by putting objects in a real, living, breathing space, design becomes more accessible. More than just a store, The Apartment hosts happenings and events, works with major corporations on brand development, and can be hired to re-style private and commercial spaces.

Rescue Nail Spa *velvet-rope nail spa* `4 E5`
21 Cleveland Place • 212 431 3805
Open 11am–8pm Mon–Fri, 10am–6pm Sat

Ji Baek – the super-stylish, Gucci-clad owner of Rescue – has put together NY's most hip beauty salon. As well as pedicures and manicures, Rescue offers many other treatments and all the lotions and potions associated with top-notch aromatherapy, massage, waxing, and brow-shaping.

SCO *customized skincare* `4 E4`
230 Mulberry Street • 866 966 7268
» www.scocare.com Open noon–7pm Tue–Sat, noon–6 Sun

Giant test tubes of pure infusions stand sentinel at the entrance to this tiny, bright, and crisply decorated skincare shop. SCO stands for Skin Care Options, and the products – which include facial cleansers, tonics and creams, a lip balm, body scrubs and polishes – are universal to all skin types. The infusions are used to customize them to each person's needs.

The consultant will ask you a series of health-related questions, then mix up a product appropriate to your requirements, choosing from more than 20 natural ingredients: caffeine for toning and tightening skin; vitamins A, C, and E for helping skin renewal; willow bark for its antiseptic properites; and mushroom for evening out skin tone. Products are packaged in elegant bottles and labelled with your name. Your prescription is filed for repeat orders, and any changes in skin condition can be accommodated.

INA *runway cast-offs* `4 E4`
21 Prince Street • 212 334 2210
Open noon–7pm daily (to 8pm Fri & Sat)

Ever longed for Prada heels but just couldn't afford them? Now you can find designer goods at a fraction of the original price at this store for girls with high-end tastes but low budgets. Many of the clothes are brand new, and legend has it that models occasionally bring in their just-off-the-catwalk items.

Calypso *hip hippy beachwear* `4 E4`
280 Mott Street • 212 965 0990
Open 11am–7pm Mon–Thu, 11am–8pm Fri & Sat, noon–7 Sun

This famously chic store carries clothes for the girl who spends half the year in Spain's Ibiza and the other half in the Caribbean's St. Barth's. Every item here oozes bohemian beach luxury. Flowing peasant skirts, colorful silk tops, and sandals can lend summer in the city a gloriously tropical appeal.

Hable Construction *beautiful interiors* `4 E4`
230 Elizabeth Street • 212 343 8555
>> www.hableconstruction.com Open 11–7 Mon–Sat, noon–5 Sun

The Hable sisters named their company after their grandfather's construction business. But rather than building houses, they design pretty, practical things for the home. The adorable canvas pillows, printed boxes, beach towels, and garden accessories will add color and a dash of fun to any home.

Mayle *dressing up for real life* `4 E4`
242 Elizabeth Street • 212 625 0406
Open noon–7pm Mon–Sat, noon–6pm Sun

Jane Mayle's vintage-style, super-sexy clothes are on every young Hollywood starlet's must-have list. Actress Kirsten Dunst (of *Spiderman* fame) is among the many fans of Mayle's slip dresses, girly blouses, and slouchy pants. The designer has recently extended her collection to include shoes, which have won rave reviews.

Rafe *eye-catching modern handbags* `4 E4`
1 Bleecker Street • 800 486 9544
>> www.rafe.com
Open 11am–7pm Tue–Thu, 11–8 Fri, noon–8 Sat, noon–7 Sun

Designer Ramon Felix creates glamorous bags and shoes that transport the imagination. His straw-and-leather Corsica bag looks like something Audrey Hepburn could have held, and the St. Germain clutch is pure Parisian chic. There are bags for men too.

Bond 07 by Selima *neo-bohemian looks* `3 D3`
7 Bond Street • 212 677 8487
>> www.selimaoptique.com Open 11–7 Mon–Sat, noon–7 Sun

Selima Salaun, known for her eye-catching optical wear, is behind this NoHo boutique, which caters women who favor unusual styles. An eclectic tion of shoes, bags, hats, lingerie, highly d dresses, and, of course, glasses is displayed rning customers.

LAFCO *highly coveted beauty products* `4 E3`
285 Lafayette Street • 212 925 0001
>> www.lafcony.com Open 11am–7pm Mon–Sat (to 8pm Thu),
noon–6pm Sun (closed on Sun in summer)

LAFCO sells a variety of exclusive beauty products,
including the creams and tonics of Lorenzo Villoresi.
This is also the NY base for Santa Maria Novella, a
coveted Italian skincare line. (LA and Florence are the
only other places where you'll find the entire range.)

TG-170 *clothes that epitomize downtown cool* `4 F4`
170 Ludlow Street • 212 995 8660
>> www.tg170.com Open noon–8pm daily

If you've ever wondered what the cutting-edge kids
wear to hip Lower East Side parties, TG-170 will let you
in on the secret. The shop stocks small quantities of
choice clothes and accessories that never seem to miss
the fashion bull's-eye. Owner Terri Gillis is often in the
shop to personally sort out shoppers' style dilemmas.

ALife Rivington Club *sneaker joint* `4 F4`
158 Rivington Street • 212 375 8128
>> http://rivingtonclub.com Open noon–7pm Tue–Sat

If an exquisite pair of retro trainers is what you're
after, you need to be willing to put up with a few
headaches. To begin with, ALife pretends not to want
to be found – there is no sign out front, and you must
ring a doorbell to enter. Such discretion may give you
the impression that you've intruded on a members-
only club – in fact, their business cards say
"members only." But this is all retail theater, and
once you're inside the wood-paneled shop any
misgivings you have will soon be forgotten.

The knockout shoes are individually displayed, each
allotted its own back-lit mahogany shelf space, like a
row of rare finds in a local museum. This is fitting, as
the items stocked here would be hard to track down
elsewhere. Vintage Air Jordans, Nike Air Wovens, and
old-school Adidas are just some of the lines available
that will grant you instant street credibility.

Shop *fun, feminine finds* `4 F4`
105 Stanton Street • 212 375 0304
Open noon–7pm daily

A rack of sexy dresses, lacy cover-ups for the beach, and cashmere sweaters makes Shop feel a little like an intimate dressing room for college sorority girls. The salespeople are extremely friendly too, treating you just like one of the girls. For more standard fare, there's an entire wall devoted to jeans.

Teany *Moby's tea shop* `4 F4`
90 Rivington Street • 212 475 9190
►► **www.teany.com** Open 9am–midnight daily

Electronica music maven Moby has created his own vision of what a teahouse should be (and very teeny it is indeed). The cozy interior is minimalist white, and the sound system reverberates with low-key club music, giving the shop a futuristic Zen-like ambience.

There are over 93 different teas to sample and buy, ranging from the exotic to the highly exotic. Try the Silver Needle (a white tea with a superior level of antioxidants), the Golden Nepal (just because the name is so cool), and the Earl Grey Creme (the unequivocal best-seller). Alongside metal canisters of leaf tea, the tiny retail section sells every accessory needed for the perfect brew, from the actual teapot – with the Teany logo – to cups, glasses, tea caddies, and milk jugs. Don't leave Teany without sampling the vegan and vegetarian menu, which features organic muffins, delicate sandwiches, and tofu scramble.

Chain Stores

New York has no shortage of chain stores offering reasonably priced fashion. There is a **Gap** on practically every corner – always good for basic T-shirts, jeans, khakis, and bookbags. Equally prevalent is Gap's more upscale sister store, **Banana Republic**. Popular with Wall Street yuppies, Banana offers clean-cut fashion. Prices can be a bit high for fashion with such little soul, but there is always a sale rack with bargains. The all-American, casual-preppy look of **J. Crew** is popular with all age groups, and can even make it into a fashionista's closet. For pseudo-punk flair, try **Urban Outfitters**, where you'll find the latest trends, such as Puma zip-ups, and funky household items like shower curtains and kitchenware. For individual contact details, *see p223–4*.

Subterranean Records *60s–7[...]*
5 Cornelia Street • 212 463 8900
>> www.recordsnyc.com Open noon–8pm daily

In the heart of the West Village, Subterranean Records is the kind of music store any die-hard rocker would be hard pressed to fault. Specializing in 70s-era NYC punk and 60s-era rock, the shop is crammed with 7-inch singles and LPs. There's soul, jazz, and blues, too, and plenty of CDs alongside the old-school vinyl.

Fat Beats *hip-hop & def sounds* `3 C2`
406 6th Avenue • 212 673 3883
>> www.fatbeats.com Open noon–9pm Mon–Sat, noon–6 Sun

Fat Beats caters to DJs and collectors of hip-hop vinyl. If you are a true connoisseur of underground hip-hop, you'll probably have the shop at the top of your NY itinerary. If, on the other hand, you're merely a dabbler in the music, at least go for the experience – especially the too-cool-for-school staff.

Fresh *decadent bath & body tonics* `3 B3`
388 Bleecker Street • 917 408 1850
>> www.fresh.com Open noon–8 Mon–Fri, 11–8 Sat, noon–6 Sun

The lotions and potions found here sound more like culinary ingredients than bathroom products. Sugar scrubs, sake bath gel, milk soaps, rice face washes, and soy hand cream are a few of the more exotic creations. All Fresh products are beautifully packaged, making them ideal gifts to take back home.

Magnolia Bakery *classic cupcakes* `3 B3`
401 Bleecker Street • 212 462 2572
Open noon–11:30pm Mon–Thu; 9am–12:30am Fri,
10am–12:30am Sat, 10am–11:30pm Sun

Instantly recognizable by the line of happy customers at the door, Magnolia is a Village institution, famed for its beautifully decorated and superb-tasting cupcakes. Don't be shy about guzzling one as soon as you've paid – everyone does.

>> *For a listing of the shops by category, see pp223–5*

Marc by Marc Jacobs *downtown cool*   `3 D4`
403–405 Bleecker Street • 212 343 1490
>> **www.marcjacobs.com** Open 11–7 Mon–Sat, noon–6 Sun

Ever wondered how models obtain that effortlessly chic, just-rolled-out-of-bed appearance? Step inside Marc's store, and you too can achieve that devil-may-care look, with a pair of 70s-inspired corduroys and a bomber jacket – the designer's perennial favorites. The men's and women's stores are next to each other.

Flight 001 *quirky accessories for jet-setters*   `3 B2`
96 Greenwich Avenue • 212 691 1001
>> **www.flight001.com** Open 11am–8pm Mon–Sat, noon–7 Sun

Ever thought you could do with a petal pink passport cover? You will be convinced you need more cool accessories and gadgets than 007 after visiting this West Village gem. A mobile spice rack to liven up airplane food, a cigarette lighter that will work in storm-force gales, and adorable laundry bags are among the essentials. For the transcontinental sophisticate, there are *New York Times* trivia games, airplane yoga books, travel candles, and Dr. Hauschka beauty products. This is also your chance to stock up on travel books locating the planet's hippest hotels. Walking-tour CDs of Brooklyn, Manhattan and the Bronx can be burnt on to your iPod, to ensure that you never get lost on the street. Still got money to burn? Then indulge in the silver, hardcase luggage, because nothing looks more dashing in an airport than a traveler who knows how to get there in style.

Bonsignour *coffee & beautiful people*   `3 B2`
35 Jane Street • 212 229 9700
Open 7:30am–10pm Mon–Sun

The reason why so many shoppers pack into this Lilliputian space is because it offers good coffee, even better baked goods, and has the friendliest vibe of any café/bakery in the West Village. The bench outside is arguably the best place in the neighborhood to sit and watch the world go by.

MXYPLYZYK *eclectic urban homeware* `3 B2`

125 Greenwich Avenue • 212 989 4300
» www.mxyplyzyk.com Open 11am–7pm Mon–Sat, noon–5 Sun

Keep your hands in your pockets at this unique store, as you're bound to want to touch, stroke, or squeeze *everything*. From puggy banks (pug-dog piggy banks – get it?) to purses resembling Bocce bowling balls, whimsy is the *raison d'être* of almost every item at MXYPLYZYK. (It's pronounced "mixyplitsick," by the way.) Vinyl bowls look like warped LPs, a shiny chrome toaster is suggestive of a prop in a 1950s sci-fi movie, and a nutcracker comes in the guise of a squirrel. Utilitarian products, such as cups and saucers, make the occasional appearance alongside a wealth of semi-useful stuff like salt and pepper dogs, psychedelic plates, wonky glasses, and rubber-bladed desk fans.

There are items for every corner of your home: modern measuring bowls and Japanese dishes for the kitchen, Korres skin care products and giant rubber ducks for the bathroom, a coffee table book of *Turkish Wrestling*, and sleek Martini shakers for your evening cocktails. The most sophisticated pieces (not outrageously priced considering the exclusive West-Village location) include office lamps and metal "industrial-style" jewelry. The point of this store is to bring a little humor and frivolity into the overly studious atmosphere that frequently surrounds contemporary design. Linking all the varied products in this fun store is the perennial question of what is functional design and what is art.

Stella McCartney *high chic/rocker chick* `3 A2`

429 West 14th Street • 212 255 1556
» www.stellamccartney.com Open 11–7 Mon–Sat, 12:30–6 Sun

Set in the newly fashionable Meatpacking District, Stella McCartney's store is a lesson in cool. Green stilettos with plastic cherries dangling off the straps epitomize her vision of elegance mixed with a little *joie de vivre*. The inlaid wood and mother-of-pearl dressing rooms are exquisite.

La Cafetiere *French-style homewares* `3 A1`
160 9th Avenue • 646 486 0667
Open 10am–7:30pm Tue–Sat, noon–6:30pm Sun

Francophiles and those who think a smattering of Provençal style might look good in their homes should head to this shop. While some of the rural-style tableware is pleasant but commonplace, the furniture – such as a weather-beaten armoire by Campagne Premiere – is exceptional.

Jeffrey *boutique department store* `3 A2`
449 West 14th Street • 212 206 1272
Open 10am–8pm Mon–Sat (to 9pm Thu, 7pm Sat), 12:30–6 Sun

A trailblazing store at the edge of the luxuriously gritty Meatpacking District *(see p161)*, Jeffrey is where beautiful people and celebrities shop (you'll often see tinted-glass limousines parked out front). While the store is not large, the stock is a discerning selection, and avant-garde labels such as Dries Van Noten and Balenciaga are much in evidence. This means that you won't have to spend hours digging around for the choicest outfits, but it also means that you won't find bargains either.

The women's shoe department – which takes up the entire center of the store – is quite possibly the best collection of footwear in New York. You'll find flirty sandals made in Capri, Prada flats, Yves Saint Laurent stilettos, Puma trainers, and a selection of other equally stylish brands. Adding to the enjoyment of shopping at Jeffrey are old-school touches, such as formal greeters at the doorway and an abundance of cheery salespeople at your beck and call.

Carapan Urban Spa & Store _city oasis_

`3 C1`

5 West 16th Street • 212 627 2265
>> www.carapan.com
Spa open 10am–9:45pm daily; store open 10am–8pm daily

Carapan's all-natural restorative products are made from plants, flowers, and minerals. Buy them here, or indulge fully at the on-site holistic spa, which offers some of the best massage and treatments in the city.

ABC Carpet and Home _beautiful, budget-breaking furniture_

`3 D1`

888 Broadway • 212 473 3000
>> www.abchome.com
Open 10am–8pm Mon–Fri, 10am–7pm Sat, 11am–6:30pm Sun

The six massive floors of ABC will be like the skies of heaven to many shoppers – there's a vision of unparalleled beauty wherever you look.

The first floor is an assortment of treasures, such as hand-blown Venetian glass chandeliers, vintage nursery furniture from France, and cast-iron Buddha heads. This level may look like a Parisian flea market, but don't expect flea market prices.

Walk upstairs to find modern furniture and retro 1960s-style chairs and light fixtures. The third floor stocks some of the world's finest linens, Frette and Pratesi among them. Head to floors five and six for Belle Époque French antiques. Many pieces – whether rustic cooking pots or formal chairs – would look at home in a museum.

Many native New Yorkers don't even know about the top-notch, top-floor restaurants at this extraordinary store. Le Pain Quotidien is a French-Belgian Bakery serving breads, pastries, gourmet sandwiches, and coffee. It's a popular place for brunch. There is also Pipa, a tapas restaurant, which has a lively atmosphere for larger parties. Lucy is a Mexican barbecue.

Without leaving the store, you can visit the Mudhoney Salon. This is a full-service luxury hair salon with a beguiling element of punk set amid the beauty of East Asian furniture.

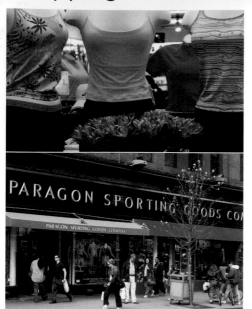

Paragon Sporting

Goods *clothes and equipment for the sporty*
867 Broadway • 800 961 3030
>> www.paragonsports.com
Open 10am–8pm Mon–Sat, 11:30am–7pm Sun

A three-floor megastore for your inner athlete, Paragon offers everything needed for just about any sport you care to mention. The basement is filled to the brim with trainers, including New Balance (the serious jogger's choice), Nike, and Puma. All manner of running paraphernalia is stocked: heart monitors, lap timers, even breathable underwear.

The first floor caters to the more genteel country club set, with tennis rackets, Lacoste shirts, and adorable tennis skirts. There's a wide selection of golf equipment too. Don't miss the large back room for swimwear (from delicate bikini sets made for lounging to serious one-piece Speedos for racing).

The top floor is the preserve of adventure sports: kayaking equipment, diving watches, and a full assortment of camping gear.

Department Stores

Manhattan's department stores are legendary, and visitors rarely feel a visit to New York is complete without venturing to at least one of the city's great shopping behemoths.

Macy's *(see p223)* is usually high on the list; this century-old icon spans a full city block and carries mostly moderately priced goods from homewares to fashion. You'll need to exercise patience, though, as Macy's is always crowded and easy to get lost in. But, if you have time to spare, you will uncover generous sale racks, with all-American brands such as DKNY, Tommy Hilfiger, and Polo.

If you're looking for a more upscale, less crowded variation, **Bloomingdale's** and **Saks Fifth Avenue** *(see p223 for both)* offer not only hundreds of every-day brands but also boutique labels and high-end designer showrooms. Chanel, Stella McCartney, and Yves Saint-Laurent are among the fashion houses represented at these department stores. During the amazing end-of-season sales, luxury items are reduced by as much as 50 per cent.

Henri Bendels *(see p223)* is much loved by New Yorkers and visitors alike because it feels deceptively more like a boutique than a large department store. This is due, in part, to its clever layout of split levels and winding staircases. Yet the selection here is vast, from hip make-up lines such as MAC and Laura Mercier to private label sweaters. There is a mini boutique of Diane Von Furstenburg wrap dresses and an impressive selection of evening frocks. Unlike the other department stores though, Bendels (as it's affectionately called by New Yorkers) does not sell everything from mixers to mattresses, but limits itself to cutting-edge designers and beauty products. *(See also **Bergdorf Goodman**, p81.)*

Kiehl's *world-famous for beauty products* `4 E2`

109 3rd Avenue • 800 543 4571

>> www.kiehls.com Open 10am–7pm Mon–Sat, noon–6 Sun

Conveniently located just steps away from the Third Avenue stop on the L train, this flagship store for Kiehl's has an awesome product line of plant-based beauty creams, tonics, powders, and soaps. In keeping with the simplicity of the products, the packaging is kept equally minimal.

Grab a basket upon entering and start walking down the rows of cucumber body washes, rose toners, coconut hair conditioners, and more. Friendly and well-informed staff are on hand to answer questions and offer suggestions. A few suggestions for your shopping list: Kiehl's Silk Groom (which does wonders for conditioning and styling hair); the excellent Lip Balm; and Kiehl's Original Musk Oil (which has been known to stop people in their tracks, so intoxicating is its aroma). Kiehl's is also very good at offering free samples of any item you are curious about.

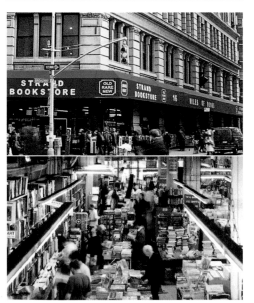

The Strand *the first and last word in books* `3 D1`

828 Broadway • 212 473 1452

Open 9:30am–10:30pm Mon–Sat, 11am–10:30pm Sun

The Strand is a downtown institution, and all visitors to the city should pay a visit here to participate in a New York rite of passage. This is not a bookstore with neatly arranged shelves and space to sit on sofas and sip lattes. And that is precisely why The Strand is so precious to bibliophiles. Books are its sole *raison d'être*; they seem to spill from every direction, and book-hunters duly crowd the store to scour the shelves for out-of-print books, first editions, and obscure tomes at greatly discounted prices.

A large collection of photography, architecture, and design books sits alongside shelf upon shelf of fiction, from pulp to literary classics. A treasure trove of children's books can be found downstairs. Outside, there are always hundreds of books stacked up, on sale for a dollar each. Whatever you're looking for, there are always astonishing discoveries to be made.

>> *A great place to eat on Broadway is L'Ecole, see p26*

St. Mark's Sounds *new & used CDs* `4 E3`
16 St. Mark's Place • 212 677 2727
Open noon–8pm Mon–Sun

This is no place in which to worry about surly service, dust collecting on the CD covers, or the absence of listening booths. However, it is the place to go wild about an amazing selection of used and new CDs of rock, jazz, new wave, soul, and more at prices that rarely go above double digits.

Jazz Record Center *hidden store of jazz jewels* `5 C5`
236 West 26th Street (8th floor) • 212 675 4480
» www.jazzrecordcenter.com
Open 10am–6pm Mon–Sat

A music store for those who know that jazz isn't just about Miles Davis, John Coltrane, and Dizzy Gillespie. The Jazz Record Center specializes in rare vinyl for true jazz fanatics. Auctions are held via the store's website, through which you can purchase books, magazines, jazz ephemera, and LPs, including coveted first pressings.

Jimmy Choo *shoes that pinch the wallet* `8 E5`
645 5th Avenue • 212 593 0800
» www.jimmychoo.com Open 10am–6pm Mon–Sat

If the shoe fits (or even if it hurts a bit), don't deny yourself the luxury of owning a pair of status-making Jimmy Choos. There is a style to match any aspect of your life (except maybe hiking): flat sandals for holidays, strappy stilettos for the evening, sporty pumps, and even a bridal collection.

Manolo Blahnik *shoe shrine* `8 E5`
31 West 54th Street • 212 582 3007
Open 10:30am–6pm Mon–Fri, 10:30am–5:30pm Sat

If shoes can be considered works of art, then Manolo Blahniks are masterpieces. Every pair is meticulously hand-crafted, and any woman who wears them gains instant sex appeal (that is, if she can master walking in such dainty heels). Plan on paying a hefty price though: such stylistic wizardry does not come cheap.

Takashimaya *hand-picked exotica* 8 E5

693 5th Avenue • 800 753 2038
Open 10am–7pm Mon–Sat, noon–5pm Sun

If you find yourself on the crowded streets of Fifth Avenue, duck into Takashimaya for some peace and tranquillity. A hushed quality fills this six-level store, and the objects therein form a refined selection of goods from around the world (many of them with an Asian influence). Comfort and luxury come in many forms: vintage furniture, state-of-the-art gadgetry, pamperingly soft bathrobes, lacquered bowls, handmade sweaters, and exotic flower arrangements.

The top floor carries deluxe beauty items, such as outrageously decadent silk Japanese slippers that release a perfume as you walk in them. This department also stocks the most coveted and hard-to-find beauty products and fragrances. You'll find ranges by Czech & Speake, Different Company perfumes, and Takashimaya's own T fragrance line.

The slick "lifestyle" floor sells everything from modern dishes to ancient-looking tables and wardrobes. If a one-of-a kind gift is what you're after, there is an endless selection of pretty little things, such as delicate Japanese writing paper and old-fashioned photo albums. Everything is displayed in a sparse Zen-like fashion, and every item is specially selected for its uniqueness and high quality.

The Tea Box Café on the bottom floor is the best place to rest tired feet and reinvigorate the tired shopper. It serves authentic Japanese green teas and bento boxes filled with healthy East-West fusion morsels to munch on.

Felissimo *half-gallery, half-boutique* `8 E5`
10 West 56th Street • 212 247 5656
>> www.felissimo.com
Open 11am–6pm Mon–Wed & Sat, 11am–8pm Fri

The five-story design house of Felissimo is unlike any other store you'll find in New York – or anywhere else, for that matter. It is a hybrid gallery/design boutique, filled with one-of-a kind products to contemplate and to buy. The owners of Felissimo (which means "beyond happy" in Italian) collaborate with designers from around the world to produce temporary exhibitions. The beautiful and often highly original objects on display may be prototypes for goods not yet mass-produced. Each exhibition has a theme, and aims to make the audience/customers question the effect of design on society. During 2004, for example, one of the exhibitions was called "White Out." All five floors were filled with white furniture, clothes, and objects for the duration of the show, which explored the perception of white.

If this all seems a little pretentious, take comfort in the fact that proceeds from the sale of many of the designs go to good causes. For example, a portion of the price of the Tribute Plates – ceramic plates individually designed by famous actors, designers, and artists – goes to the charity of the designer's choice, as well as UNESCO.

In the gift shop downstairs, you can view and buy more down-to-earth objects, such as modern steel tea pots, metal earrings, funky wrapping paper, T-shirts, and other eclectic but well-designed items.

Niketown *a Nike for everyone* `8 E5`
6 East 57th Street • 212 891 6453
>> www.niketown.com   Open 10am–8pm Mon–Sat, 11–7 Sun

Much as the name implies, this is, if not quite a town, then certainly a decent-sized village of Nike products. The newest trainers are on display alongside men's and women's workout clothes – cool enough for street wear. If you're less concerned about the latest craze, seek out the Clearance Department for great bargains.

Shop online at >> www.enewyork.dk.com

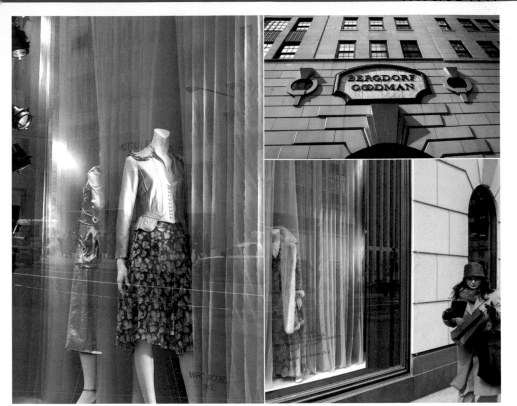

Bergdorf Goodman *old-school charm* `8 E4`
754 5th Avenue • 800 558 1855
>> www.bergdorfgoodman.com
Open 10am–7pm Mon–Sat (to 8pm Thu), noon–6pm Sun

Bergdorf's, as New Yorkers affectionately call this landmark department store, is almost as definitive a symbol of the city as the Statue of Liberty. Located near the Trump Tower and across the street from the Plaza Hotel *(see p183)*, this is where the well-heeled ladies who lunch choose to shop.

The basement level has been converted into the beauty floor. This bright and cheerful space showcases skincare brands, such as La Prairie, and make-up lines including Shu Umera. The Buff Spa is

a manicure/pedicure stand (no appointment necessary). More beauty needs can be fulfilled upstairs at the Susan Ciminelli Day Spa (which is known for its use of soothing, seaweed-based products) and the John Barett Salon.

As for fashion and accessories, everything you could ever need (and didn't even know you needed) is all under the same roof. There's a stunningly fine jewelry selection on the first floor, while a large collection of Marc Jacobs, Gucci, Prada, and Chanel jostles for space on the second floor. The very sophisticated clothes are all displayed as mini-boutiques, showcasing renowned design labels such as Moschino and Dolce & Gabbana.

>> *For a roundup of New York's other famous department stores,* see p76

Shopping

Dylan's Candy Bar *sugar-lover's dream* `8 F4`
1011 3rd Avenue • 646 735 0078
>> www.dylanscandybar.com Open 10am–9pm Mon–Thu,
10am–11pm Fri & Sat, 11am–8pm Sun

Dylan Lauren, daughter of American designer Ralph Lauren, offers a fantasy for both kids and adults: a two-story candy store. Not one to do anything run-of-the mill, she stocks hard-to-find candy in tins that you'll cherish long after the contents are eaten.

Barney's New York *hip versus classic* `8 E4`
660 Madison Avenue • 888 822 7639
>> www.barneys.com
Open 10am–8pm Mon–Fri, 10am–7pm Sat, 11am–6pm Sun

Too original to be called a department store and too large to be a boutique, Barney's is unique. Off-beat clothes by little-known designers are carried right next to heavy hitters, such as Marc Jacobs and Prada. The top-floor restaurant lures New York's power elite.

La Perla *luxurious lingerie* `8 E3`
777 Madison Avenue • 212 570 0050
>> www.laperla.com
Open 10am–6pm Mon–Sat, noon–5pm Sun

Bikinis and lingerie couldn't be sexier. Glamorous and risqué tulle-knit bathing suits play peek-a-boo with the body, while the lingerie selection goes from nice to naughty in no time at all. The sporty Studio and saucy La Perla Black collections are included.

Bra Smyth *tailored bras & underwear* `8 E2`
905 Madison Avenue • 212 772 9400
>> www.brasmyth.com Open 10am–6pm Mon–Sat, noon–5 Sun

Just as no two snowflakes are identical, neither are two breasts – a fact not lost on Bra Smyth. With more than 3,000 bras to choose from, and full-time seamstresses on board to customize each bra to fit perfectly, falling straps and poking underwire should never be an issue again.

Liliblue *feast of accessories for Europhiles* `8 E2`
955 Madison Avenue • 212 249 5356
Open 10am–6pm Mon–Sat, noon–6pm Sun

This French-owned boutique imports hats, scarves, purses, and other accessories from Italy and France. The reasonably priced jewelry comes mostly from two Parisian brands: Satellite and Poggi. Both are known for their bright, characterful costume jewelry and silver rings, set with semiprecious stones.

Clyde's *boutique pharmacy* `8 E2`
926 Madison Avenue • 800 792 5933
>> www.clydesonmadison.com
Open 9am–7pm Mon–Sun (to 8pm Thu)

Yes, Clyde's is a pharmacy in the sense that you can buy vitamins and cough syrup, but this popular neighborhood institution offers so much more. The store is stocked with high-end beauty and skincare products, candles, and imported bathroom goods.

Christian Louboutin *scarlet soles* `8 E2`
941 Madison Avenue • 212 396 1884
Open 10am–6pm Mon–Sat

The quirky designs and scarlet soles that mark every Louboutin shoe signify that you've arrived in the style-conscious world of Madison Avenue. Well-heeled fans include New York socialites and Hollywood A-listers. Even if you're not buying, drop by to admire the glorious, Parisian-style interior.

Diane B *clothes & shoes for uptown girls* `8 F2`
1414 3rd Avenue • 212 570 5360
Open 11–7:30 Mon–Fri, 10–6:30 Sat; closed Sun in summer

Situated in the lonely shopping territory of the far eastern Upper East Side, Diane B is a good stop for French and Italian women's clothing if you don't feel like venturing downtown. Finding a hot number isn't hard with brands such as Stephan Kelian and Vera Wang, but don't expect to find Prada and Gucci.

Shopping

ABH Designs *creature comforts* `8 H1`
401 East 76th Street • 212 249 2276
Open 11–6:30 Mon–Sat

Owner Aude Bronson-Howard's career as a Hollywood costume designer is evident in her eye for detail when choosing items for her store. Linen napkins with silk trim, Italian plates, down shawls, and faux-mink slippers are some of the items that will bring a touch of luxury to any home.

Searle *coats and cashmere tops* `10 E5`
1124 Madison Avenue • 212 988 7318
≫ www.searlenyc.com
Open 10–7 Mon–Fri, 10–6 Sat, noon–6 Sun

What began as a store focusing on stylish shearling coats has expanded to include the full gamut of delectable women's clothing. From TSE cashmere sweaters to casual lines such as Blue Dot, Trina Turk, and classic Lacoste, Searle provides a great mix of styles.

Intermix *must-have clothing* `7 C3`
210 Columbus Avenue • 212 769 9116
Open 11–7 Mon–Wed, 11–7:30 Thu–Sat, noon–6 Sun

Intermix is a beacon of style in the relative fashion desert of the Upper West Side, where pickings can be slim for trend-conscious shoppers. The staff can be less than helpful and the prices are high enough to leave you temporarily broke, but Intermix provides an irresistible selection of cool, slinky outfits.

Blades Board `7 B2`
& Skate *gear for movers and skaters*
120 West 72nd Street • 888 552 5233
≫ www.blades.com Open 10–9 Mon–Sat, 11–7 Sun

The name says it all. Kneepads, goggles, and helmets are among the essential equipment sold here for skateboarders, snowboarders, and inline skaters. Make your choice from an impressive array of skates then head across the street to Central Park.

Housing Works
Thrift Shop *treasures at bargain prices*

7 C2

306 Columbus Avenue • 212 579 7566
>> www.housingworks.org
Open 11–7 Mon–Fri, 10–6 Sat, noon–5 Sun

This is not just a thrift shop, but a store with heart. It was conceived in 1990 by Keith Cylar and other activists as a not-for-profit shop to help homeless New Yorkers living with AIDS. Housing Works has now become the largest community-based AIDS activist group in the U.S. Cylar passed away in April 2004 after a long AIDS-related illness, but the shop continues his work.

The soul and integrity of the project encourages New York's most stylish residents to donate anything from couches to lamps to coveted clothes. It's not uncommon to find rare and sought-after furniture, designer clothes, antiques, and even collectable art. Despite all this, prices remain rock bottom, in contrast to those found in other trendy thrift stores.

Super Runners *joggers paradise*

7 B1

360 Amsterdam Avenue • 212 787 7665
>> www.superrunnersshop.com Open 10–7 Mon–Fri
(to 9pm Thu), 10–6 Sat, 11–5 Sun

Even if you're not training for the New York marathon, this shop has a running shoe for every terrain, from the gym treadmill to Central Park nature trails. Stock is not restricted to trainers; you can also buy a watch for keeping a check on lap times.

Zabar's *top-notch deli*
2245 Broadway • 212 787 2000
>> www.zabars.com
Open 8–7:30 Mon–Fri, 8–8 Sat, 9–6 Sun

Were Zabar's to close, the city could well descend into chaos. Since the 1920s, New Yorkers have relied on this family-run business for all their gourmet kitchen needs, from fine cheeses to the best smoked fish. Don't leave without buying a famous Zabar's coffee.

Shopping

11 D4

Xukuma *cool lifestyle store*
183 Lenox Avenue • 212 222 0490
>> www.xukuma.com
Open noon–7 Wed–Sun, 10–6 Sat & Sun

Xukuma, pronounced "zoo-koo-ma," is a lifestyle store for hip city-dwellers. The shop-owners define Xukuma (a word they dreamed up) as "life the way you want it to be." Their vision encompasses homewares – groovy lamps, frames, clocks, etc. – and clothing lines that bank heavily on 1960s/70s-influenced "sista-soul" appeal.

You'll see the lanky, sexy silhouette of a black woman with an Afro (dubbed "X Girl") on everything from T-shirts to posters and cards. Her best cameo is on the tank top and panty sets emblazoned with phrases such as "obey me" and "please me." There's a range of men's underwear with "hustler," "dirty devil," and "bad boy" emblems. Xukuma also stocks gourmet food, teas, and Sia candles, as well as chandeliers and gift baskets.

12 G3

Demolition Depot *historic artifacts*
216 East 125th Street • 212 777 2900
>> www.demolitiondepot.com
Open 10–6 Mon–Fri, 11–5 Sat

Many a New Yorker can thank Demolition Depot for helping to spruce up a bland apartment with objects from a bygone era. At the four-story warehouse in Harlem, you'll uncover treasures such as 19th-century light fixtures, mirrors that once hung in American farmhouses, fireplace mantles, and oil paintings.

Owner and antiques dealer Evan Blum salvages most of his stock from homes and buildings that are about to be destroyed. Because of this, he can buy cheap and sell a beguiling range of architectural pieces – from plumbing fixtures and door furniture to stone sculptures, stained-glass windows, gates and railings – at far more reasonable prices than you'd expect to pay at an auction. Demolition Depot's smaller items include decorative tiles, clocks, old shop signs, and NYC subway signage.

Butter *current trends for women*   `2 C4`
389 Atlantic Avenue • 718 260 9033
Open noon–7 Mon–Sat, noon–6 Sun

Though not completely original by NYC standards, Butter has been a ground-breaking store for Brooklyn, being the first in the neighborhood to offer top-end women's clothing. With lines such as Dries Van Noten, Rick Owens, and Rogan jeans available here, Brooklyn girls no longer have to trek across the bridge.

Breukelen *one-of-a-kind gifts*   `13 B4`
369 Atlantic Avenue • 718 246 0024
>> www.breukelenny.com
Open noon–7 Tue–Sat, noon–6 Sun

"Lifestyle stores" are becoming something of a phenomenon in New York, and Breukelen is hailed as the first example of this genre in Brooklyn. In old-fashioned parlance, however, Breukelen is an interior design store, predominantly stocking contemporary pieces, such as Japanese glass, South African wooden bowls, and jewelry by local artists.

Because the selection offered at Breukelen is so unusual and distinctive, even Manhattanites are prepared to leave the island once in a while to visit it. Expensive kitchen supplies, such as coffee-makers, handmade ceramic dishes, and stainless steel mixers offer endless appeal. The wonderfully elegant, aromatic Diptyque candles are the store's most affordable and best-selling items, but this is not really the place for bargain-hunting.

Loom *groovy knick-knacks*   `7 C2`
115 7th Avenue, Brooklyn • 718 789 0061
Open 11–7 Mon–Sat, 11–6 Sun

Loom is a design store catering to the well-heeled, stroller-pushing crowd of Park Slope. Italian stationery, mod jewelry, and cute little *objets* make wonderful gifts for the friend who has everything. Come and agonize over the discerning selection of glass vases and hand-embroidered bed linen.

Nest *clutch of delectable home furnishings* `13 C5`
396a 7th Avenue, Brooklyn • 718 965 3491
Open noon–7 Mon, 11–7 Tue–Sat, noon–6 Sun

When graphic designer Jihan Kim and his wife decided to settle down together and have a baby, they decided to open a store that would combine this cozy time in their lives and their artistic backgrounds. Thus Nest was born (and their baby girl) to fill the niche in Park Slope for off-beat *objets* and furniture for starting a home.

Their range of products for a groovy home include sleek, handmade ceramic vases – made by Kim's aunt – and Japanese mugs with bold graphic prints. Nest also stocks hand-embroidered pillows and stylish window shades, tiny wooden children's chairs in bold colors (really adorable), and space-age Blue Dot desks, made of white Lucite. The perfect buy if space is tight in your suitcase are Nest's giant, adhesive dots, which come in bright colors and are designed to decorate walls, ceilings, and floors.

Mini Minimarket *ironic girly lifestyle store* `13 B2`
218 Bedford Avenue • 718 302 9337
➤➤ www.miniminimarket.com Open noon–8 daily

A hodgepodge of all things cool, this store has everything for the hipster Williamsburg girl: playful jewelry, fashions from Tokyo, sexy underwear, Gola trainers, and 1980s-inspired tops. The minimarket stocks only small quantities of each item, so it's un-likely you'll find anyone else wearing the same thing.

Spoonbill & Sugartown Booksellers *rare tomes* `13 B2`
218 Bedford Avenue • 718 387 7322 Open 11–9 daily

Books on painting, photography, architecture, and graphic design cater to Brooklyn's bohemians. At the back of the store, you'll find used books on everything from religion to geography. What you won't find at Spoonbill & Sugartown is anything off the current *New York Times* best-seller list.

Spacial *high-end crafts* `13 B2`
199 Bedford Avenue • 718 599 7962
»www.spacialetc.com 11–9 Mon–Sat, noon–8 Sun

Spacial (sic) feels simultaneously folksy and urban. In the window are handmade ponchos, clogs, and precious children's clothes. Step inside to find highly stylized lamps, jewelry, and bowls, as well as imported design journals and soaps. The only factor that unites all these items is their evident coolness.

Isa *trend-setting clothes* `13 B2`
88 North 6th Street • 718 387 3363
Open 1–9 Mon–Fri, noon–10 Sat, noon–8 Sun

Walking into Isa is like stumbling upon the closet of pop prince Justin Timberlake. An array of vintage-looking (but new) T-shirts adorn the wall, each bearing a dramatic or provocative slogan, such as "Hold On To Young Ideas," and "Dine At The Y." Another popular design is Jean-Michel Basquiat's image of Cassius Clay. The hip urban gear includes limited-edition Nikes, high-end Levi's, and a selection of expensive sweaters.

Beautiful people work the counter, and DJs spin the sounds to remind you what a very cool shop this is. But Isa is not just a great boutique selling of-the-moment clothes; it also functions as a gallery and "happening" space in the heart of Brooklyn's fast up-and-coming Williamsburg district. The owner, Isa, often moves the clothing racks to one side and turns the place into an all-night DJ dance party.

Beacon's Closet *vintage clothes trader* `13 B1`
88 North 11th Street • 718 486 0816
»www.beaconscloset.com
Open 12–9 Mon–Fri, 11–8 Sat & Sun

Sick of all your old clothes? Then take your suitcase to Beacon's Closet and either sell your garments for cash or trade them for in-store credit. In the shop, you'll find lots of second-hand clothing and accessories for men and women. There are also brand-new CDs.

Earwax *sounds to clean out your ears* `13 B2`
218 Bedford Avenue • 718 486 3771
Open noon–8pm Mon–Fri, 11am–9pm Sat & Sun

Earwax is the antithesis of record store chains: there is no adjoining coffee shop/bookstore and you can't pre-listen to CDs. But what you do get is a hand-picked selection of music that won't let you down. New CDs are biased towards indie rock, while the formidable second-hand section runs the full gamut of tastes.

Fortuna *boutique clothes store* `13 B2`
370 Metropolitan Avenue • 718 486 2682
Open 2–9pm Thu & Fri, 1–9pm Sat & Sun

It is very hard to visit this old-school style salon and leave empty handed. All the beautifully displayed vintage men's and women's clothes are carefully selected by the owner, who scours the country in her search. There are slips from the 1930s, wedge shoes from the 1970s, and even the occasional top hat.

MiniMall *alternative retail space* `13 B2`
218 Bedford Avenue
Stores at MiniMall have differing opening times, but most are open between 10am and 7pm daily

Located on Williamsburg's hippest boulevard *(see p165)*, the MiniMall is one of the best places for shopping and lounging in Brooklyn. This retail space-cum-club house takes up the entire ground floor of a loft building, and houses myriad stores.

Once inside the cavernous entryway (where computers and tables are set up for Internet perusal), you can venture into shops such as **The Girdle Factory,** in which vintage treasures can be found (a $30 Gucci wallet!). **Otte,** on the other hand, sells only what the uptown girl wants: Seven jeans and flirty dresses. **Go Yoga** offers some of the best yoga classes in the city, and the **Tibet Boutique** will help you look the part. One of the most popular stores is the **UVA Wine Shop.** There, you'll find young connoisseurs deliberating over their purchases.

Browse designer websites at ≫ www.enewyork.dk.com

Astroturf *vintage homewares* 13 B4
290 Smith Street • 718 522 6182
Open 11am–7pm Tue–Fri, 11am–5pm Sat & Sun

There is something comforting about setting foot into this Cobble Hill homewares and furniture store. It's almost as if you've just stepped into a really groovy grandmother's attic. Astroturf sells everything that was left carelessly behind from the 1950s and 60s: orange plastic bowl sets, curvy lamps, now-prized vintage lunchboxes, turquoise coffee thermoses, and Formica tables. Everything in this store yells – no, screams – kitsch!

If all the fun and funky appeal is too much for the pottery-barn aesthetic you have studiously cultivated in your home, take a sleekly sculpted ashtray or vase to add a dash of *Austin Powers* grooviness to your decor. There are shelves and shelves of knick-knacks, so the choices are practically endless. Best of all, prices are still pretty retro here, so you can afford to have fun with the cheap-and-chic look.

Two Jakes *period furniture* 13 B2
320 Wythe Avenue • 718 782 7780
▶▶ www.twojakes.com
Open 11am–7pm Tue–Sun

Head to this industrial-chic area of Williamsburg for used metal office furniture that would be triple the price if it were sold in SoHo. Two Jakes' massive warehouse space offers classic 20th-century office furniture in remarkably good condition.

Moon River Chattel *farmhouse furniture* 13 B2
62 Grand Street • 718 388 1121
Open noon–7pm Tue–Sat, noon–5pm Sun

In the urban jungle of Brooklyn sits a store that offers items more befitting a country cottage than a city pad. Light fixtures look as if they were taken from an early 20th-century soda shop, old clocks tick ponderously, wooden tables carry the burden of age, and appliances seem more artistic than purposeful.

art &
architecture

New York is the pre-eminent city for Modernist art and architecture, famously evident in its towering skyscrapers and in the unsurpassed collections of the Guggenheim and the Whitney. Along with great cultural icons, such as The Met and Brooklyn Museum of Art, New York also has a thriving contemporary art scene, split between Manhattan's galleries and a dynamic community of artists in Brooklyn.

Art & Architecture

U.S. Customs House *Beaux Arts affair* `1 D5`

1 Bowling Green
Open 10am–5pm daily (to 8pm Thu)

New York's grandest example of Beaux Arts architecture has figures representing the four continents incorporated into its facade. They were sculpted by Daniel Chester French, most famous for his work at the Lincoln Memorial in Washington. The National Museum of the American Indian is housed here.

St. Paul's Chapel *New York's oldest* `1 D3`

209 Broadway, between Fulton & Vesey streets
» www.saintpaulschapel.org

It has served the residents of Lower Manhattan for well over 200 years, but St. Paul's Chapel gained wider public attention in the wake of the 9/11 attack on the World Trade Center, when it acted as a steadfast beacon for New Yorkers.

Modelled on St-Martin-in-the-Fields in London, the church was completed in 1766, making it New York's oldest building in continuous use. George Washington worshipped here during the two-year period (1789–91) when New York served as the nation's capital. His pew is singled out, and above it hangs what is believed to be the first oil painting of the Great Seal of the United States – the image of the bald eagle, with a red-and-white striped shield, thirteen arrows, and an olive branch.

The chapel bore witness to another kind of history on September 11, 2001, as debris from the collapsing North Tower of the World Trade Center rained down, cloaking the building in pale ash. Within hours of the catastrophe, St. Paul's converted into a base for recovery squads. Firefighters, police officers, and medical personnel ate, slept, and grieved here, while volunteers ministered, the city's top chefs cooked, and students from the Julliard School of Music performed impromptu concerts.

The chapel has an exhibition of memorabilia and testimonies from 9/11 survivors called *Out of the Dust: A Year of Ministry at Ground Zero*.

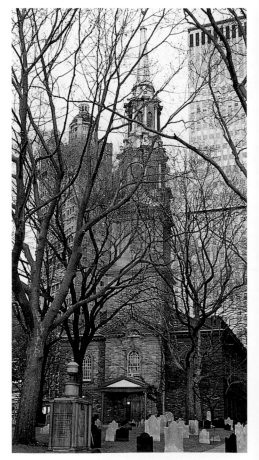

Check opening hours on » www.enewyork.dk.com

Ground Zero *poignant reconstruction site* `1 C3`

In 2002, the Lower Manhattan Development Corporation – in collaboration with families of victims, local business owners, and politicians – selected a master plan for Ground Zero: site of the former World Trade Center. The design was by Daniel Libeskind, an architect renowned for his ground-breaking Holocaust Museum in Germany. His scheme intended to retain the twin towers' footprints at 30 ft (9 m) below sidewalk level, creating a contemplative space for a memorial. But the most dramatic part of his design was an astonishing 1,776-ft (540-m) skyscraper, the Freedom Tower, its height echoing the date of the signing of the Declaration of Independence – 1776.

Libeskind's designs have undergone significant alterations, however, due to the commercial imperative to maximize office space. Until it is completed, visitors can view the site from a pedestrian platform at Vesey and West streets. The memorial is scheduled to open in 2006, with a museum to follow.

Skyscraper Museum *homage to height* `1 D5`

39 Battery Place • 212 968 1961
≫ www.skyscraper.org
Open noon–6pm Wed–Sun

After seven years bouncing from one office lobby to the next, the Skyscraper Museum finally found a home in 2004. One of the city's most ingeniously designed museums, it honors its soaring subjects through illusion and intriguing details. Freestanding white columns are vertically reflected between stainless steel floors and mirrored ceilings, creating the appearance of infinite height. Throughout this echoing space, architectural fragments from Manhattan's most notable skyscrapers are displayed. The museum contextualizes New York's 100 year-old obsession with building tall in terms of economic cycles, an interesting counterpoint to the apparent brashness of the form. The museum also mounts temporary exhibitions, and future shows are set to redress the current NY bias with more international subjects. **Adm**

Woolworth Building   *pinnacled tower*   `1 D2`

Gothic in style and topped off by a green turret, the Woolworth Building is utterly distinct from its clean-edged, Lower Manhattan neighbors. Erected in 1913 for the houseware-catalogue magnate Frank Woolworth, it was, at 55 stories, the tallest structure in New York until the 1930s, when the Chrysler Building was constructed. The nave-like lobby contains a statue depicting the thrifty Mr. Woolworth counting his dimes.

Broken Kilometer   *relative distance*   `3 D5`

393 West Broadway • 212 989 5566 (Dia offices)
>> www.brokenkilometer.org   Check website for opening times

In five parallel rows, 500 gleaming brass rods lie on a SoHo hardwood floor in Walter De Maria's 1979 installation. Lain end to end, the rods would measure exactly one kilometer. The seemingly straightforward arrangement plays subtly with perspective in a work loved by mathematicians, despised by real estate agents.

Earth Room   *deep, dark soil*   `3 D4`

141 Wooster Street • 212 989 5566 (Dia offices)
>> www.earthroom.org   Check website for opening times

Commissioned by the trailblazing Dia Art Foundation, Walter De Maria's *Earth Room* (1977) is a white-walled exhibition space, filled to a depth of about 2 ft (55 cm) with moist, dark soil. Viewers stand at the threshold to the space and quietly stare in. The third of De Maria's earth sculptures, it is the only one still in existence.

Contemporary Art Galleries

Some of the hottest galleries in the contemporary art world are grouped in Manhattan. The SoHo nexus, comprising Wooster, Grand, Greene, and Spring streets, boasts the highest concentration of galleries. **Deitch Projects** mounts some of the area's most highly anticipated shows, from paintings inspired by skateboard design to performances. Chelsea has welcomed defecting SoHo dealers for years. **Pace Wildenstein** and **Mary Boone** have Chelsea outposts as well as midtown locations, and **Larry Gagosian's** little empire, extending from Beverly Hills to London, mounts prestigious exhibitions at his large Chelsea space. Elsewhere, Chinatown's **Leo Koenig Gallery** deals in lively work from emerging artists. For individual contact details, *see p225*.

Lower East Side Tenement Museum *home of NY's early immigrants*

`4 F5`

90 & 97 Orchard Street • 212 431 0233
» www.tenement.org
Open for guided tours only: Sep–Jun Tue–Sun, Jul & Aug Mon

In the heart of the old garment district in the Lower East Side, the Tenement Museum offers an enlightening overview of how pioneering immigrants lived and worked in the late 19th and early 20th centuries. Guided tours explore an 1863 tenement, which was home to some 7,000 immigrants from 20 countries during its 72 years as a residential building.

Engaging tour guides lead visitors through the humble, virtually unchanged units, peppering biographical accounts of former tenants' lives with fascinating facts about the neighborhood's social organizations, businesses, sights, sounds, and smells. It is advisable to book a few days ahead. The museum also arranges historical walking tours of the Lower East Side. **Adm**

Merchant's House Museum *19th-century opulence*

`4 E3`

29 East 4th Street • 212 777 1089
» www.merchantshouse.com Open afternoons Thu–Mon

Between the Bowery's punk-rock bars and Broadway's name-brand shops rises a magnificent Federal-style house of around 1832. It is one of the last vestiges of a prosperous merchant-class suburbia that once thrived in downtown Manhattan. The hardware-importing Tredwell family lived here until 1933, resisting the late-19th century trend among Manhattan's elite to construct estates bordering Central Park.

Opened as a museum in 1936, the Merchant's House provides an unparalleled glimpse into how the high life was lived in mid-19th-century Manhattan. Tours (weekdays only) take visitors through a Greek Revival interior of Ionic columns, ornate plasterwork, and beautiful black-and-gold marble mantelpieces. The backyard garden is a delightful mix of arbors, perennials, and 19th-century iron furniture. **Adm**

Jefferson Market
Courthouse *architectural treasure*

3 C2

A building loved by West Villagers, the fairytale Venetian-Gothic courthouse was saved from the wrecking ball when local residents campaigned to have it converted into a public library. The former civic court is now the library's main reading room and the children's reading room occupies the police court; the reference section in the basement used to be the holding cell.

Forbes Magazine Gallery *toys/games*

3 D2

60 5th Avenue at West 12th Street • 212 206 5549
Open 10–4 Tue, Wed, Fri & Sat

The private art estate of publishing magnate Malcolm Forbes is displayed here. Although his unrivaled Fabergé egg collection recently sold for $100 million, visitors can still glimpse a frivolous side to the notoriously pragmatic Mr. Forbes in his vintage toy collection and staggering array of boardgames.

Block Beautiful *decorous abodes*

4 E1

Among Manhattan's most picturesque residential blocks is this fanciful melange of Tudor, late-Federal, and brownstone houses. Attractive paint schemes, varied door arch designs, and intricate wrought-iron gates distinguish each home from the next. In fair weather, the block enchants with window-mounted planter boxes brimful of color, and slender trees sprouting acid-green leaves.

Museum at the Fashion Institute
of Technology *past and future trends*

5 D4

7th Avenue at 27th Street • 212 217 5970
≫ www.fitnyc.suny.edu Open noon–8 Tue–Fri, 10–5 Sat

Do Andy Warhol's early footwear sketches bear hints of future greatness? Contemplate this question and scores of other fashion designs at F.I.T.'s free museum. Special exhibitions draw on the school's textile, illustration, and photography collections.

Find out about changing exhibitions at ≫ www.enewyork.dk.com

Midtown Deco *classic buildings* `6 F1–6 G2`

Evoking an age of tuxedoed jazz orchestras, jet-black limousines, high hems, and cocked fedoras, midtown's Art Deco skyscrapers are, for many, quintessential emblems of New York. Beyond the well-known destinations (most obviously the **Empire State Building**, *see p18*) rise equally impressive yet less-visited landmarks. The following buildings are not open to the public, but you can admire the exterior forms and nearly always venture into the foyers, which often contain the buildings' most elaborate designs. The **General Electric Building** (570 Lexington Ave.), for

example, has a rare, nickel-silver embellished lobby. Over on 42nd Street, look for the **Chanin Building's** intricately carved facade and doorway with elaborate, gold-plated convector grilles (122 E. 42nd St. at Lexington Ave.). Also on 42nd Street, you'll find a huge revolving globe and antiquated weather instrumentation in the lobby of the **New York Daily News Building** (220 E. 42nd St.). Though not exactly a hidden gem, the shimmering **Chrysler Building** (405 Lexington Ave.) is a revelation if you've never seen the lobby; mosaics, multicolored African marble, and whimsical automotive motifs make it a must-see.

Art & Architecture

International Center of Photography *massive photo archive*
5 D2

1133 Avenue of the Americas • 212 860 1777
≫ **www.icp.org** Open 10–5 Tue–Thu, 10–8 Fri, 10–6 Sat & Sun

Combining a school, an archive, and frequent exhibitions, the ICP is one of the world's biggest centers of photography. The subject of a show here might be historical – a 1920s French avant-gardist, perhaps – or contemporary, such as reportage from Iraq. **Adm**

Whitney Museum of American Art at Altria
6 F2

120 Park Avenue at 42nd Street • 917 663 2453
≫ www.whitney.org
Open 11am–6pm Mon–Fri; sculpture garden daily

The airy, bright lobby of Altria Group, Inc. serves as an exhibition space for cutting-edge contemporary art. There are two spaces, in fact – an intimate gallery and a glass-walled indoor sculpture court. The focus of the exhibition program is emerging contemporary artists. Recent shows put the spotlight on Mark Bradford, Louis Gispert, and Dario Robleto.

Rose Museum at Carnegie Hall *musical memorabilia*
7 D5

154 West 57th Street, 2nd Floor • 212 903 9629
≫ www.carnegiehall.org Open 11am–4:30pm daily

The Rose Museum gives an insight into the status of the prestigious Carnegie Hall *(see p125)* and is a treasure trove of intriguing memorabilia, from concert programs to vintage costumes. For tours of the concert hall (11:30am, 2pm, and 3pm, Sep–Jun) call 212 903 9765.

Icons

Ever since King Kong scaled the **Empire State Building** *(see p18)* in his 1933 film debut, the 86th-floor observatory has been a compulsory visitor destination. Eleven blocks south, the **Flatiron Building** was New York's first skyscraper (1902). In midtown, **Grand Central Terminal** (Map 6 F2) is a Beaux Arts sculpture brought to frenetic life each morning.

You can shop for souvenirs, buy fresh goods at the market, and count stars twinkling on the concourse ceiling. Nearby **Times Square** is site of dizzying neon lights and the world's most famous New Year's Eve celebration. Stately **Brooklyn Bridge** was one of the world's first steel-cable suspension bridges – walk across it for majestic views of Manhattan and glimpses of the **Statue of Liberty** *(see p12)*.

Museum of Modern Art *home at last*   `8 E5`
11 West 53rd Street • 212 708 9400
>> www.moma.org Open 10–5 Mon & Thu–Sun (to 7:45pm Fri)

After leading itinerant lives in cities around the world and in a temporary space in Queens, MoMA's most highly prized holdings have returned to their dramatically revamped six-story gallery back in Manhattan. Reopened in late 2004 after the most ambitious building project of the museum's 75-year history, MoMA has reaffirmed its status as the world's foremost modern art institution.

Yoshio Taniguchi's renovation has doubled the museum's exhibition capacity and restored one of its most beloved attributes, the Abby Aldrich Rockefeller Sculpture Garden. The redesign also incorporates a smart new restaurant. Set off by the refreshed gallery spaces, the collection continues to impress, with such delights as Vincent Van Gogh's *Starry Night*, Picasso's formidable *Les Demoiselles d'Avignon*, and Dalí's seminal *The Persistence of Memory*. **Adm**

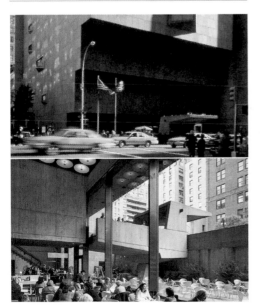

Whitney Museum   `8 E2`
of American Art *America's finest*
945 Madison Avenue • 800 944 8639
>> www.whitney.org Open 11–6 Wed, Thu, Sat & Sun, 1–9 Fri

As with Frank Lloyd Wright's Guggenheim building *(see p104)*, Marcel Breuer's cantilevered Whitney is more than just a home for an art collection, it is a statement of radical intent. Built in the mid-1960s, it is distinctive, powerful and Modernist, reflecting the strongest elements of the exclusively American art it holds. The permanent collection boasts works by Warhol, Pollock, and Jasper Johns, and by abstract sculptors David Smith and Alexander Calder. It also has an extensive collection of paintings by Georgia O'Keeffe and Edward Hopper.

The Whitney's program of temporary exhibitions is excellent, including one-person retrospectives (Philip Guston, for example) and themed shows, such as on film and video (shorts by John Baldessari and Ed Ruscha were shown in 2004). **Adm**

>> *The Whitney's famed biennial (next in 2006) showcases the best new and established American artists*   `101`

Art & Architecture

Frick Collection *art in a glorious setting* 8 E2

1 East 70th Street (at 5th Avenue) • 212 288 0700
>> **www.frick.org** Open 10am–6pm Tue–Sat (to 9pm Fri), 1–6 Sun

The family of steel tycoon Henry Clay Frick bequeathed their Fifth Avenue mansion to the city shortly after Henry's death in 1919. Included in the gift was one of the country's most spectacular collections of fine and decorative arts, spanning more than five centuries, from the Renaissance to the late 19th century.

Henry took incredible care over situating his most prized pieces in specific rooms and halls, a habit not forgotten by the collection's present directors, who may arrange entire floorpans in order to showcase one single piece. The Whistler portraits in the Oval Room, for example, are a mere backdrop to the room's main focal point, Houdon's life-size sculpture *Diana the Huntress*. The capacious West Gallery is more egalitarian with its hanging arrangements, granting Old Masters Rembrandt, Velásquez, Van Dyck, and Goya equal wallspace. On the rich, oak-paneled walls of the intimate Living Hall, at the heart of the residence, are major works by Titian, El Greco, and Bellini. Elsewhere are Jan van Eyck's *Virgin and Child with Saints and Donor*, El Greco's fearsome *The Purification of the Temple*, and Holbein's luminous portrait of *Sir Thomas More*.

However, it's the house itself that makes a visit so unforgettable. Furnishings range from Louis XVI opulence to 19th-century English restraint. Plant-filled atriums and a charming outdoor garden, with graceful magnolia trees and views of Central Park, also add extra dimensions to the Frick experience. **Adm**

Metropolitan Museum of Art *cultural behemoth*

1000 5th Ave • 212 535 7710
>> www.metmuseum.org 9:30–5:30 Tue–Sun (to 9pm Fri & Sat)

The Met's two million objects form one of the world's largest museum collections. Among the myriad galleries of the hulking Beaux Arts structure are estimable collections of Egyptian artifacts, Islamic art, and European paintings. Among the paintings are works by Renaissance giants Botticelli and Leonardo, and canvases by Rembrandt, Cézanne, and Monet.

If the prospect of such a vast museum seems daunting, consider attending an informal gallery talk. More in-depth than the museum highlight tours, they are led by art historians and offer the opportunity to learn more about specific works. Check the Met's website for the talks calendar. Also note the Met's highly varied program of temporary exhibitions, which range from ancient Chinese art to the photographs of Diane Arbus and a Max Ernst retrospective in 2005. **Adm**

Museum of Television and Radio *classic footage & recordings*

25 West 52nd Street • 212 621 6000/6800
>> www.mtr.org Open noon–6pm Tue–Sun (to 8pm Thu)

Yearning to revisit a classic *Muppets* episode? The Museum of Television and Radio exists for just such desires, with its constant streams of vintage newsreel, landmark radio broadcasts, and classic comedy shows. There's a huge searchable archive too. **Adm**

Asia Society *Asian arts*

725 Park Avenue at 70th Street • 212 288 6400
>> www.asiasociety.org Open 11am–6pm Tue–Sun (to 9pm Fri)

The superb Asian art collection of American philanthropist John D. Rockefeller III is housed in this bright, modern building. Japanese screens and bronze Buddhist deities are among the exhibits spread throughout a series of galleries. Shows by contemporary Asian and Asian-American artists are often staged, and the building acts as a venue for performances of Asian music and dance. **Adm**

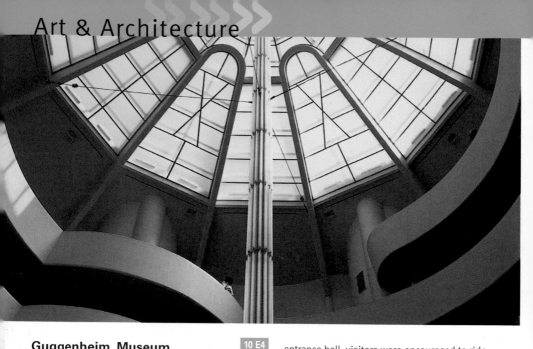

Guggenheim Museum

10 E4

1071 5th Avenue (at 89th Street) • 212 423 3500
>> www.guggenheim.org
Open 10am–5:45pm Sat–Wed, 10am–8pm Fri

With museums now bearing the name in Las Vegas, Venice, Berlin, New York, and Bilbao in Spain, "Guggenheim" has penetrated the world's cultural vocabulary. But before becoming the art-world juggernaut that it is today, Guggenheim was simply the surname of Solomon, a private collector who wanted to publicly exhibit his collection of abstract art.

In the minds of Guggenheim and his advisor, the painter and curator Hilla Rebay, the collection required a new kind of gallery space – one that complemented the pioneering, iconoclastic form of the paintings in his collection. What resulted was one of the world's most instantly recognizable buildings. Designed by American Modernist architect Frank Lloyd Wright, the building shattered notions of rectilinear exhibition space. Rather than walk through traditional galleries and wings, only to turn around and experience the same art while returning to the entrance hall, visitors were encouraged to ride elevators to the top of a spiral-shaped tower, the Great Rotunda, and descend via a gently sloping ramp along the spiral's perimeter. Adorning the tower's walls were works by Wassily Kandinsky, Piet Mondrian, and Joan Miró.

This specific vision for the building is no longer upheld, however. Some six years after the building's completion in 1959, the strictly abstract collection was augmented with figurative works by Impressionists Cézanne, Degas, and Renoir, and with paintings by Van Gogh and Picasso. The building was extended, and today the Great Rotunda is used only for temporary exhibitions, while the permanent collection is housed in the adjoining Tower. The Small Rotunda is used to display the "greatest hits" of the Impressionist and Post-Impressionist collection. The museum's temporary shows tend to relate to the Modern Movement, some very obviously, such as the conceptual abstraction of Daniel Buren, others more obliquely, such as art from the Aztec Empire, which influenced some early 20th-century avant-garde painters. **Adm**

Japan Gallery *wonderful woodblock prints* `10 F5`
1210 Lexington Avenue (at East 82nd Street) • 212 288 2241
>> www.japangalleryprints.com
Open 11am–6pm Tue–Fri, Sat by appointment

Branches bow under the weight of fresh snow while saints battle mythical beasts. Japan's tradition of woodblock printing fires the imagination, and this commercial gallery holds – and sells – some of the genre's most important examples of the past 200 years.

The Jewish Museum *all things Jewish* `10 E4`
1109 5th Avenue (at 92nd Street) • 212 423 3200
>> www.thejewishmuseum.org
Open 11am–5:45pm Sun–Wed, 11am–9pm Thu, 11am–5pm Fri

The Jewish Museum presents an unparalleled overview of Jewish art and culture. A stunning French Gothic house holds four floors of ceremonial art, photographs, paintings, textiles, sculptures, and video screenings. Each piece in the permanent collection – whether it be a self-portrait by Viennese artist Max Beckmann, a 3,000-year-old ceramic vase, or a vibrant 19th-century quilt from a Jerusalem workshop – encourages the viewer to explore how the object informs, or is informed by, Jewish identity.

Popular temporary exhibitions take place on the ground floor, such as *Kafka's Prague* and *Entertaining America: Jews, Media, and Broadcasting*, as well as retrospectives of individual Jewish artists, such as Marc Chagall and Chaim Soutine. A kosher café in the basement is on hand for refreshments.

Cooper-Hewitt National Design Museum *design classics* `10 E4`
2 East 91st Street • 212 849 8400
>> www.ndm.si.edu Open 10am–5pm Tue–Sat, 10am–9pm Fri, 10am–6pm Sat, noon–6pm Sun

Housed in the imposing Andrew Carnegie mansion, the Cooper-Hewitt is a shrine to design in all its forms. Exhibits range from a sketch of candelabra by Michelangelo to highly coveted Eames chairs. **Adm**

The Cloisters *portal to the Middle Ages*
Fort Tryon Park • 212 923 3700 • M4 bus or A train to 190th St.
>> www.metmuseum.org
Open 9:30am–5:15pm Tue–Sun (to 4:45pm Nov–Feb)

One of New York's most cherished assets seems, paradoxically, about as native to the Manhattan landscape as a Boston Red Sox fan at the Yankee Stadium. The Metropolitan Museum of Art's Cloisters is a neo-medieval composite of stained glass, painstakingly landscaped gardens, cavernous halls, and solemn chapels grafted onto the craggy northern fringes of Manhattan island.

It was the philanthropic might of John D. Rockefeller Jr. that facilitated the building's construction in 1938. The project was undertaken to provide a harmonious context for displaying the Met's superb collection of medieval European art and architecture. It provides a splendid setting for such masterpieces as Robert Campin's *Annunciation* triptych of 1425. It also integrates relics of medieval buildings, such as a 900-year-old apse from a Spanish church, seamlessly woven into a limestone wall. Elsewhere, a unicorn hunt is vibrantly portrayed through a series of 16th-century Dutch tapestries, and scores of ecclesiastical objects from the length and breadth of Europe are scattered throughout the complex. So complete is the illusion of medieval Europe that the Cloisters creates, the visitor experiences a sensation of distance, both temporal and geographical. Glimpsing New Jersey's rugged cliffs across the Hudson through a 12th-century portico is positively disorientating.

Turning to more earthly needs, during warm months visitors can stave off hunger at the on-site café in Bonnefort Cloister. But savvy diners take lunch at the nearby New Leaf Café *(see p51)* for moderately priced bistro fare, such as juicy sirloin burgers. **Adm**

El Museo del Barrio *Latin art* `10 E2`
1230 5th Avenue at 104th Street • 212 831 7272
>> **www.elmuseo.org** Open 11am–5pm Wed–Sun (to 8pm Thu)

Founded in 1969 by artists and activists from Spanish Harlem, El Museo del Barrio was a response to the lack of exhibition space for specifically Puerto Rican art. Since then, the museum has broadened its scope to the whole of the Caribbean and Latin America.

The permanent collection spans two millennia of art production, from Pre-Columbian artifacts to prints, paintings, installations, and film and video works by the latest generation of Latin American artists. Among more than 8,000 objects are wooden *santos* (colorful, often comical, depictions of Catholic saints that incorporate Afro-Caribbean motifs); fascinating documents of the early years of immigration in New York; and films of life in Spanish Harlem from the 1970s to the present day. The adjoining Teatro Heckscher is an enchanting venue for live Caribbean music, film screenings, and book readings. **Adm**

Studio Museum in Harlem `11 D3`
144 West 125th Street • 212 864 4500
>> **www.studiomuseuminharlem.org**
Open noon–6pm Wed–Sun (from 10am Sat)

The SMH is a contemporary art gallery and resource specializing in African-American culture. As well as holding a large permanent collection, the gallery puts on temporary exhibitions, such as its recent showcase for young Harlem photographers.

Prospect Park West *beautiful setting* `13 C5`
Between Union and 15th streets
>> **www.prospectpark.org**

This genteel stretch of 19th-century brownstone, brick, and limestone residences borders Prospect Park. Beginning at Grand Army Plaza's majestic Memorial Arch, a southward stroll takes you past the imposing bronze statue of the Marquis de LaFayette at 9th Street, the park's Concert Shell, and beautiful playgrounds.

>> *Prospect Park was landscaped by Olmsted & Vaux, the designers who also laid out Central Park*

Brooklyn Museum
of Art *world-class repository*

200 Eastern Parkway • 718 638 5000
>> www.brooklynmuseum.org
Open 10–5 Wed–Fri, 11–6 Sat & Sun (to 11pm first Sat of month)

The Beaux Arts BMA dates from 1893 and has as diverse and staggering a collection as its larger cross-river contemporary, the Metropolitan Museum of Art. This is no idle boast – spread over the five floors of the BMA is a collection that embraces Egyptian sarcophagi and mummy cases; statues, masks, and jewelry from Central Africa; Hiroshige's woodblock prints of *One Hundred Famous Views of Edo*; and a vast selection of paintings and sculpture from Europe and America, including works by Rodin, Degas, Pissaro, Matisse, Louise Bourgeois, and Mark Rothko. There is also a strong photography collection, with significant prints by Edward Weston and Paul Strand. On the Fifth floor, *American Identities* explores the American dream through exhibits that range from Native American totems to Georgia O'Keefe's 1948 meditation *Brooklyn Bridge*.

The BMA's First Saturday events (first Saturday of every month) make for one of the city's best nights out: free admission after 5pm, free concerts and dance performances, and a bar (cash only). **Adm**

Williamsburg Galleries

Priced out of Manhattan's lofts and studios during the late 1980s, frustrated but intrepid artists boarded the L Train and disembarked in Williamsburg, until then a predominantly Polish and Hasidic Jewish working-class neighborhood. There they found vacant industrial warehouses, which were easily converted into studios. Since then, Williamsburg artists have influenced tastes and styles worldwide, from fashion to painting to music. Supporting the neighborhood's visual arts scene from a spectacular c.1867 building is the **Williamsburg Art & Historical Center** (135 Broadway at Bedford Avenue), which mounts eclectic shows and performances by local artists. **Pierogi 2000** (177 North 9th Street) artists exhibit around the world, but visitors will always see at least one local artist featured at any time. Since 1992, not-for-profit **Momenta Art** (72 Berry Street) has given two artists per exhibition cycle a forum for what is often their first non-group show. The touring **Eyewash** gallery is quintessential Williamsburg: artists exhibit in multiple spaces around the neighborhood. Check **www.freewilliamsburg.com** for the latest exhibition information. For contact details of all the galleries mentioned here, *see p225*.

Brooklyn Historical Society 13 B4
local culture, historical setting
128 Pierrepont Street • 718 222 4111
>> www.brooklynhistory.org
Open 10am–5pm Wed–Sat (to 8pm Fri), noon–5pm Sun

Thousands of Brooklyn-related objects, from slave deeds to Brooklyn Dodgers baseball memorabilia, are housed in a stunning 1880s mansion. The BHS also arranges walking tours and outdoor concerts. **Adm**

Williamsburg Savings Bank Building 13 C4
opulent interior
1 Hanson Place, corner of Flatbush & Atlantic avenues

At night, Brooklyn's tallest building is distinguished by the neon red clock face of its 512-ft (156-m) tower. But the greatest highlight of this building (currently a branch of the HSBC bank) is its Neo-Romanesque interior: imposing iron chandeliers, mosaic-covered ceilings, intricately tiled floors, and graceful arches.

P.S.1 *cutting-edge contemporary art*
22–5 Jackson Ave. • 718 784 2084 • Ⓜ E or V to 23 St./Ely Ave.
>> www.ps1.org Open noon–6pm Thu–Mon

Modern art aficionados with adventurous tastes and an urge to break from the SoHo and Chelsea scenes need only venture as far as Long Island City to experience one of the world's foremost contemporary art institutions. Housed inside a late-19th-century high school building, P.S.1 consistently presents groundbreaking multimedia, painting, photography, and sculpture exhibitions that challenge conventions and blaze new aesthetic trails.

Featured artists have included the 1980s art star Keith Haring, actor/director/painter Dennis Hopper, and the late Spanish sculptor Juan Muñoz. A 1997 redesign by Frederick Fisher introduced a courtyard. Every summer, artists are selected to create thematic installations in this space for P.S.1's Saturday afternoon party series, Warm Up. The event draws a savvy crowd to hear top local DJs. **Adm**

>> *P.S.1's alliance with MoMA means that a ticket purchased at either establishment entitles entry to both* 109

performance

Broadway shows may be the big sellers, but the city's creative heart beats in a host of other artistic venues devoted to music, theater, dance, cinema, poetry, comedy, and literature. The official Music Under New York program promotes talents year-round on the subway and at street level, while the summer months bring superb outdoor entertainments, such as plays and opera in the parks.

CLASSICAL VENUES	DANCE & PERFORMANCE	CUTTING-EDGE

Barge Music
Fulton Ferry Landing, Brooklyn
With the Manhattan skyline in front of you and water lapping beneath, this is a magical setting for chamber music. *(See p130)*

>> *www.entertainment-link.com is a handy site which gives the percentage of seats already sold for a given performance.*

Carnegie Hall
881 7th Avenue
The three concert halls of this hallowed venue have hosted the world's best classical performers for more than a century. *(See p125)*

Brooklyn Academy of Music
30 Lafayette Avenue, Brooklyn
World-class dance and theater productions often preview here, especially during Brooklyn's international Next Wave festival. *(See p129)*

The Kitchen
512 West 19th Street
Experimental performances and more straightforward literary readings are combined at this Chelsea hub of creativity. *(See p120)*

New Jersey Performing Arts Center
One Center Street, Newark
International artists and the NJ Symphony Orchestra perform at this state-of-the-art complex. *(See p131)*

The Joyce Theater
175 8th Avenue
Dance is the main attraction at this former movie house. Mid-sized U.S. and international companies are showcased year-round. *(See p120)*

Bowery Poetry Club
308 Bowery
Rarely delivering anything mainstream, the Bowery plays host to literary performers who challenge the audience's minds. *(See p118)*

Alice Tully Hall, Lincoln Center
Broadway & Amsterdam, 62nd–66th Sts
This hall is known for spectacular performances and an energetic program of choir, quintet, and full orchestra concerts. *(See p126)*

The Public Theater
425 Lafayette Street
Five on-site theaters and the Shakespeare in the Park festival entrance drama fans. *(See p119)*

P.S.122
150 1st Avenue
East Village's innovative, not-for-profit arts center has two theaters offering some of the city's most daring productions. *(See p120)*

GIG VENUES

Tonic
107 Norfolk Street
The thing that sets this cool space apart from other gig venues is the highly diverse and experimental music it programs. *(See p117)*

Mercury Lounge
217 East Houston Street
There's a good bar scene in the front room here, while at the back, behind a deep red curtain, is a secretive room for live music. *(See p116)*

Cornelia Street Café
29 Cornelia Street
This intimate space hosts a wealth of musical styles, including jazz, a cappella singing, and the lilting rhythms of samba. *(See p115)*

Knitting Factory
74 Leonard Street
It's less cutting edge these days, but Knitting Factory still has a great music line-up. The air guitar competition always sells out. *(See p114)*

>> *The website www.nytheatre.com gives comprehensive listings.*

JAZZ & BLUES

Village Vanguard
178 7th Avenue
A jazz institution not to be missed for its good acoustics and line-up of great musicians. *(See p116)*

Lenox Lounge
288 Lenox Avenue
This famous Harlem venue has a local vibe. It attracts regulars from the neighborhood and jazz junkies from much farther afield. *(See p129)*

55 Bar
55 Christopher Street
Get close up and personal with jazz and blues maestros as you sip a drink and gaze at the photos of historic greats. *(See p116)*

Smoke
2751 Broadway
The Monday night jam session in this intimate room lures an audience of accomplished musicians and jazz devotees. *(See p127)*

COMEDY

The Comic Strip
1568 2nd Avenue
A stalwart of the stand-up tradition, this is a place to see both budding and established comedians. *(See p125)*

>> *For a basic listing of every kind of popular music, from bluegrass to hip-hop, go to www.citidex.com. It also gives info about comedy venues.*

Upright Citizen's Brigade
307 West 26th Street
An informal space that buzzes with off-the-cuff jokes and well-executed skits. *(See p121)*

Knitting Factory *experimental mecca* `1 D1`
74 Leonard Street • 212 219 3132
>> www.knittingfactory.com Open 5pm–4am nightly

Arriving here is like entering a funfair attraction; you're not sure which door to go through first. There are three main performance spaces – Main Space, Tap Bar, and Old Office – as well as a free bar area, where late-night jazz jams are often hosted. The media company that runs this venue, and also the Knitting Factory Record label, styles itself "a genre-bending presenter of established avant-garde." The types of music you're most likely to hear are experimental rock, klezmer, and jazz, though recent performances have also included an Eastern European women's choir. The Old Office is the most intimate space of the three and sometimes hosts poetry evenings and alternative screenings, as well as regular music slots. This has also been one of the venues used for the June JVC Jazz Festival. Tickets for all events can be ordered from the Knitting Factory website.

Film Forum *independent & vintage films* `3 C4`
209 West Houston Street • 212 727 8110
>> www.filmforum.com Box office 12:30pm–midnight daily

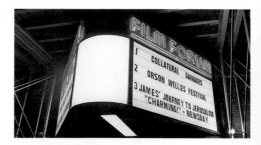

Cineastes can delight in this three-theater venue, where each screen has Dolby Digital Sound. The selection of films shown is widely varied, from old classics such as an Orson Welles season, to the latest underground hit. Director talks, fresh food concessions, and film-related merchandise are also offered.

S.O.B.'s *Latin beats* `3 C4`
204 Varick Street • 212 243 4940
>> www.sobs.com Open 6:30pm–4am Mon–Sat

Shake your body and celebrate the Sounds of Brazil (S.O.B.) – the very best in Latin, French Caribbean, salsa, hip-hop, reggae, and African beats. Live music is performed every night, with musicians coming from around the globe. For a free dance lesson, get here on a Monday or Friday night between 6pm and 8pm.

Blue Note *gold-standard jazz* `3 C3`
131 West 3rd Street • 212 475 8592
» **www.bluenotejazz.com**
Open from 6pm nightly; to 4am Fri & Sat

Now a franchised chain, with venues in Japan, Korea, and Europe, Blue Note first took root in Greenwich Village. The premise is simple: sophisticated surroundings for seriously good music (not just jazz), with the option of dinner service, and a classy interior to match the top-notch performers who come to play. Dizzy Gillespie, Ray Charles, and Sarah Vaughan have ripped the roof off the place in the past, and the club has also witnessed the talents of Oscar Peterson, George Benson, and Tony Bennett.

If it all sounds a little too highfalutin' for the gutsy world of live improvised music, join New York's poorer musicians, who turn up for the late-night Friday and Saturday jam sessions – it's a mere $5 cover. Blue Note is also known for the reasonable Sunday Jazz brunch and its Saturday afternoon master classes.

The Comedy Cellar *gritty stand-up* `3 C3`
117 MacDougal Street • 212 254 3480
» **www.comedycellar.com** Evening shows nightly

This basement space has had comics, famous and infamous, performing nightly for over 20 years. The cramped seating, brick wall backdrop and spotlit stage set the tone. The cover charge is normally $10–15, depending on the night, but you can get free passes via the website. Rude heckling isn't tolerated.

Cornelia Street Cafe *eclectic acts* `3 C3`
29 Cornelia Street • 212 989 9319
» **www.corneliastreetcafe.com** Evening shows nightly

Performed on a tiny stage in a narrow room beneath a restaurant, acts here have ranged from Inuit poetry to Suzanne Vega. In any given week you might encounter poetry and prose readings, one-act plays, comedy, singing, and live Latin, jazz, or samba music. Art on the walls changes regularly and is often for sale.

Performance

Duplex *kitsch & cabaret* `3 B3`
61 Christopher Street • 212 255 5438
Open 4pm–4am nightly

Anything goes in this dual-level space, which features a piano bar, complete with disco ball, on the first level, and an intimate-sized cabaret room, with pool table, upstairs. The monthly schedule is always packed, and usually includes comedy, cabaret, comedians, and open mic for singers of varying abilities.

55 Bar *NYC-style jazz/funk/blues* `3 B3`
55 Christopher Street • 212 929 9883
>> www.55bar.com Open 1pm–4am nightly

Walk down a few steps and soak up an atmosphere that's been brewing in this West Village stalwart since 1919. The music packs a punch in a space small enough for the vibes to resonate against the walls, which are hung with black-and-white photos of Miles Davis and John Coltrane.

Village Vanguard *amazing acoustics* `3 B2`
178 7th Avenue • 212 255 4037
>> www.villagevanguard.com Open from 8pm nightly

One of the world's most famous jazz venues, the Village Vanguard has hosted singers and musicians of phenomenal talent since 1935. It continues to take music very seriously, and socializing during sets is discouraged. Genres include mainstream jazz (for popular standards), bebop, fusion, Latin, and funk.

Mercury Lounge *musical excellence* `4 F4`
217 East Houston Street • 212 260 4700
>> www.mercuryloungenyc.com Open 6pm–4am nightly

The Mercury Lounge hosts a mix of new and established musical talent. You enter a long, narrow room dominated by a wooden, candle-lit bar. A heavy, deep-red curtain separates this from the performance space (with superb sound system), where Lou Reed, Jeff Buckley, and Tony Bennett have played.

Bowery Ballroom *music in style*
4 F5

6 Delancey Street • 212 533 2111 • Box office 866 468 7619
» www.boweryballroom.com

This Beaux Arts ballroom, dating from 1929, makes a wonderful setting in which to hear a band and have a drink. Although the venue has been fully updated to accommodate state-of-the-art acoustics and facilities, many of the building's architectural details have been retained. The mezzanine bar is wisely positioned in front of a gorgeous set of arched windows, providing a view of the city lights. The stage can be seen from the wooden ballroom area or the mezzanine. If you'd like a break from the music, you can drink more peacefully in the lower-level cocktail lounge. David Byrne, Beth Orton, Patti Smith, the John Spencer Blues Explosion, and DJ Shadow are among those who have played here. Tickets for shows often sell out, so buy early either by phone or at the box office, located at the Mercury Lounge *(see opposite)*, between noon and 7pm from Monday to Saturday.

Tonic *adventurous music*
4 G4

107 Norfolk Street • 212 358 7501
» www.tonic107.com Open from 7:30pm nightly

From jazz funk to the sounds of "industrial waste percussion" to the whirs of an electronic theremin to the bleeps of a palm pilot – the range of music and instruments at Tonic often surprises and inspires. The main space is hip, with its no-frills decor and basic seating; downstairs is Subtonic, where DJs spin eclectic beats.

Arlene's Grocery *multi-band options*
4 F4

95 Stanton Street • 212 358 1633
» www.arlene-grocery.com Open from 8pm nightly

It was, indeed, once a grocery store – hence the colorful frontage and welcoming atmosphere – and it gets a little crazy when more than four bands are billed in one evening. The music is invariably grunge, indie, pop, and metal. Come on Monday for a raucous and rocking Punk Rock Karaoke Night.

Bowery Poetry Club *literary café* `4 E4`
308 Bowery • 212 614 0505
» www.bowerypoetry.com Open 11am–midnight daily

First-time visitors with any anti-intellectual angst will soon feel at ease in this welcoming, unpretentious venue. Even imaginative readings for children are included on the bill.

The main glass doors open to a café with uneven wooden floorboards and mismatched tables, in which you can order organic goodies, espresso, juices, and alcoholic drinks. The back of the room widens out considerably to a high-ceilinged performance area with its own tables and chairs, which can pack in 200 word-lovers; there's also a smaller room for intimate readings. An alluring, slightly bohemian atmosphere is accentuated by local artists exhibiting their works on one wall, and flyers and notes about events and goods for sale pinned up on another. Readings include works by new writers and those of established poets and authors. Sunday brunch is a good time to come.

CBGB *echoes of rock history* `4 E4`
315 Bowery • 212 982 4052
» www.cbgb.com Open 6:30pm–3am nightly

Come here to pay respects to the world of punk and progressive rock. The Ramones, Blondie, The Police, and Talking Heads are among those who owe something to this venue. The bar's a bit cleaner, the music's changed to metal and new punk, but the basic gritty stage and loud amps are the same.

Landmark's Sunshine *film theater* `4 F4`
143 East Houston Street • 212 330 8182
» www.landmarktheatres.com

Formerly home to a Yiddish Vaudeville Theater, this beautifully renovated film house has five screens, all with Dolby Digital Sound and comfortable seats. Mostly foreign and independent films are shown. A good concession stand serves espresso and freshly baked snacks. For info about late-night screenings, *see p19*.

The Public Theater *integrity on stage* `4 E3`
425 Lafayette Street • 212 539 8650;
212 539 8750 for Shakespeare in the Park tickets (free)
>> www.publictheater.org
Box office 1–7:30pm (to 6pm Sun & Mon)

With five theaters, a private rehearsal space, and the recent addition of neighboring performance space/bar Joe's Pub, The Public Theater is a long-established venue for groundbreaking drama. It is where the musical *Hair* had its world premiere in 1967. The main building – formerly the Astor Library – has a grand entrance hall with the theaters leading off, and a small wine and coffee bar in the far corner. Joe's Pub focuses on experimental theater and solo performances of drama and music.

The company is also responsible for the summer Shakespeare in the Park season, performed from June to August at Central Park's Delacorte Theater. You can buy tickets from The Public Theater box office or at the park on the day of performance.

Nuyorican Poets Cafe *beats & poetry* `4 G3`
236 East 3rd Street • 212 505 8183
>> www.nuyorican.org Events nightly, except Mon

This once "underground" café has become a cutting-edge venue for people of all ethnicities to read, slam, rhyme, perform, or play an instrument. The dimly lit, cozy café is a place for contemplative, poetic thought by day and original spoken-word performances by night. *(See also p17.)*

C-Note *musical dive bar* `4 G2`
157 Avenue C • 212 677 8142
>> www.thecnote.com Open 7pm–4am (from 4pm weekends)

Live music – from jazz and blues to funk, rock, and country – is played nightly. C-Note also hosts superb jam sessions – jazz on Saturdays (4–7pm), blues on Sundays (10pm–3am) – and an open mic for singers and songwriters on Sundays (5–9pm). Have a go on the 1980s table version of the video game *Galaxian*.

>> *For information about outdoor summer film screenings in Bryant Park,* see p17

Performance

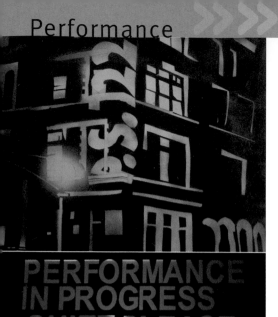

P.S.122 *innovative performances* 4 F2

150 1st Avenue • 212 477 5829 • Box office 212 477 5288
>> www.ps122.org
Open daily; box office 2–6pm Tue–Sun

This performance space in East Village was once a public school, a shadow of which is seen in the original stairwell, complete with wooden banisters and wrought-iron safety gates. In 1979 a small group of innovative performers began transforming the rooms into spaces for performance workshops, movement classes, and community meetings. The old school gym was converted into a theater in 1986, used by small avant-garde groups and cutting-edge productions. Now a major hub of creative energy, the not-for-profit arts center boasts two theaters and galleries, with a constantly changing program of theatrical, video, musical, and film presentations. Experimental in all that it does, and contributing much vibrancy to New York's arts community, P.S.122 has been nicely described as the "Petri dish of downtown culture."

The Kitchen *multimedia creations* 3 A1

512 West 19th Street • 212 255 5793
>> www.thekitchen.org Box office 2–6pm Tue–Sat

For many years, The Kitchen has brought together artists from varied disciplines, taking pride in its innovation. The two black-box theaters serve as backdrops for literary readings, multimedia installations, dance, and music. Family-friendly presentations often feature on Saturday afternoons.

The Joyce Theater *delightful dance* 3 B1

175 8th Avenue • 212 242 0800
>> www.joyce.org Box office noon–around 6pm daily

Presenting small- to medium-sized national and international companies, The Joyce Theater is a center of dance, from contemporary to traditional. The auditorium seats 452 in a functional interior that once housed a movie theater. Joyce's satellite space in SoHo (155 Mercer St.) hosts further performances.

Browse reviews online at >> www.enewyork.dk.com

Upright Citizen's Brigade *improv* `5 C5`
307 West 26th Street • 212 366 9176
>> www.ucbtheater.com Performances nightly (cash only)

Step into a world of zany and clever comic sketches and improvisation at the UCB Theater. Home-grown Brigade shows and visiting comic troupes are both on the schedule. Ticket prices are very reasonable, and you have the possibility of seeing future stars of the U.S. favorite TV show *Saturday Night Live*.

Kavehaz *gallery & music café* `6 E5`
37 West 26th Street • 212 343 0612
>> www.kavehaz.com Open 5pm–midnight or later nightly

The music and artwork on the walls dictate the ambience of the month at this popular Chelsea spot. Sample one of the featured wines or indulge in a hot drink gulped from a bowl as you listen to the music. Monday is reserved for an open mic singers' showcase; Wednesday is for the Ray Vega Latin Jazz band.

Gotham Comedy Club *funny shows* `6 E5`
34 West 22nd Street • 212 367 9000
>> www.gothamcomedyclub.com Shows nightly

This comfortable, casual comedy club is given an added air of sophistication by its solid oak bar and shimmering chandelier. The line-up mixes budding comics and surprise guests from the world of TV – comedians who may have appeared on *Conan O'Brien*, *The Tonight Show*, or on the Comedy Central network.

Hammerstein Ballroom *music venue* `5 C3`
311 West 34th Street • 212 279 7740
>> www.mcstudios.com Check website for upcoming events

Ambience and acoustics rate high at this Art Deco space with a capacity of 2,500. Historic fixtures and a beautiful ceiling mural have been kept, while there's enough rigging to support impressive light and sound equipment for shows by bands such as indie-rockers the Pixies or modern jazzers Medeski, Martin & Wood.

>> *For information on outdoor summer concerts series*, see p10

Performance

Rodeo Bar *country music crossover* `6 F5`
375 3rd Avenue • 212 683 6500
» www.rodeobar.com Open noon–4am daily; live music 10pm

Leave NYC and voyage into a world of bluegrass, rockabilly, flavors of country music, an amicable atmosphere, drinks served from a converted horse-trailer, and no cover charge for the entertainment! Refreshment comes in the form of Tex-Mex snacks, free peanuts, and powerful margaritas. Yeeee-haw!

The Soul Cafe *soul food* `5 B2`
444 West 42nd Street • 212 244 7685
» www.soulcaferestaurant.com Open all day from 11:30am

Attracting a mixed clientele of regulars and theater district visitors, this is a fun place to party with the almost nightly live entertainment. Have a drink in the bar and let the music take you. Also consider the Sunday gospel brunch (11:30am–3pm), for an uplifting mix of soul food and powerful song.

Roundabout/AA *magical theater space* `5 C2`
227 West 42nd Street • 212 719 1300
» www.roundabouttheatre.org

This repertory theater company has moved several times and is now based at the beautifully renovated American Airlines Theatre (formerly called the Selwyn), which was built in 1918. Slick productions often feature well-known guest actors; some shows are also performed at Studio 54 (254 West 54th St.).

B.B. King Blues Club *gospel & blues* `5 C2`
237 West 42nd Street • 212 997 4144
» www.bbkingblues.com Box office 10am–midnight daily

Legends such as James Brown and, of course, B.B. King himself have played in the club's Showcase Room. It has a tourist vibe, but the aim to entertain prevails, and wins over New Yorkers too. Food is served all day and there's nightly music at Lucille's, the more intimate space, named after B.B. King's favorite guitar.

To book tickets online, go to » www.enewyork.dk.com

Swing 46 *jazz & swing dance* `5 C1`
349 West 46th Street • 212 262 9554
>> www.swing46.com Open from 5pm nightly

Try your two-step or lindy between courses at this
dinner and dance club, or have drinks up by the bar –
away from the frenzy on the floor, but close enough
to hear the music. There's no dress code, but a bit of
sartorial elegance is encouraged. Bring your tap shoes
for the Tap Jam on Sundays between 5 and 8pm!

Don't Tell Mama *piano & cabaret* `5 C1`
343 West 46th Street • 212 757 0788
>> www.donttellmama.com Open from 6pm nightly (cash only)

Life is indeed a cabaret, and all believers need to visit
this venue at least once, either to listen or to perform.
Grab your Liza Minnelli songbook and come on over to
the piano bar or one of three intimate theaters, where
you can also eat. *The* place to hear the standards, see
diva wannabes, and enjoy hilarious musical comedy.

Rainbow Room *vintage sophistication* `6 E1`
30 Rockefeller Plaza, 65th Floor • 212 632 5100
>> www.cipriani.com
Open from 7pm Fri & Sat; Sunday brunch 11am–3pm

A glorious Art Deco institution with awesome views
from the 65th floor to help you forget the $150 per
person tab for dinner and dancing. Big band
orchestras play for the evening as you sway above the
shimmering lights of the city. Black tie is preferred.

City Center *music, drama & dance* `7 D5`
131 West 55th Street • 212 581 1212
>> www.citycenter.org

The colorful tiles and pillars of the beautiful Moorish
facade welcome you to the City Center. Inside, the
main stage is used for concerts and performances by
the Alvin Ailey, American Ballet, Paul Taylor, and
Martha Graham dance companies. The Manhattan
Theater Club performs in the center's smaller spaces.

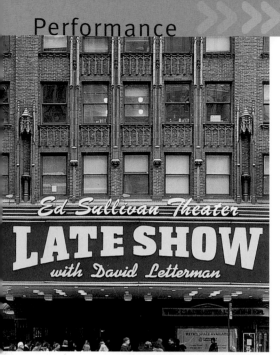

NBC Studios/
Ed Sullivan Theater *three seconds of fame?*

If you'd like to have your head filmed in the studio audience for NBC's news and entertainment *Today Show*, which goes out live on weekday mornings, hang around 49th Street between Fifth and Sixth avenues, between 8:30 and 10am, and join the masses who have the "Hi Mom, Bergen County Loves You" signs. You can also try your luck for last-minute studio audience tickets to see *Saturday Night Live* or *Light Night* with Conan O'Brien by lining up outside NBC's main lobby on the 49th Street entrance at 30 Rockefeller Plaza. Both lines often form before 7am (tickets are given out after 9am); unfortunately there are no guarantees that you'll get in.

It's easier to obtain tickets to see *The Late Show* with wise-cracking David Letterman, which is staged at the Ed Sullivan Theater at 1697 Broadway (Map 7 D5). For standby tickets, call 212 247 6497 at 11am on the day of the show (Monday to Thursday).

Florence Gould Hall *for Francophiles* 8 F4
55 East 59th Street • 212 355 6160
 www.fiaf.org Box office 11am–7pm Tue–Fri, 11am–3pm Sat

Associated with the French Institute and the location of a series of interesting lectures and weekly French films, this space is also open for productions ranging from light opera and ballet to various concerts. Acoustics are great in the main 400-person auditorium, while next door's Tinker Auditorium is more intimate.

Tickets for Broadway Theaters

The two main agencies selling theater tickets are **Telecharge** (212 239 6200, www.telecharge.com) and **TicketMaster** (212 307 4100, www.ticketmaster.com). These are convenient ways to purchase tickets, but you may be charged up to $9 extra for handling fees. If you want to try your luck at a discount agency on the day of performance, **TKTS** offers great deals on theater tickets – often 25–50% off the full price – but you will have to line up and you can't use a credit card. The main outlet is on the little island called Duffy Square at 47th and Broadway (Mon–Sat 3–8pm, Sun 11am–7:30pm; for matinees Wed & Sat 9am–2pm). The other outlet is at the South Street Seaport on the corner of John Street and Front Street (Mon–Sat 11am–6pm, Sun 11am–3:30pm).

The Comic Strip *stand-up showcase* `8 G1`
1568 2nd Avenue • 212 861 9386
» www.comicstriplive.com Shows nightly

Jerry Seinfeld started his career with a regular act here. There's a casual atmosphere, cabaret-style seating, and traditional stand-up. Thursday is "new talent night," while Mondays often feature comics from far and wide auditioning for regular spots. Reserve tickets by phone, and check out discounts on the website.

92nd Street Y *emporium of activity* `10 F4`
1395 Lexington Avenue • 212 415 5500
» www.92y.org

Established in the 19th century as a men's Hebrew association, the 92nd Street Y has since become a more diverse cultural institution. With a wide-ranging bill of artists, entrepreneurs, and politicians, the Y's two halls have hosted performances and talks by Yo-Yo Ma, Bill Gates, and Kofi Annan.

Carnegie Hall *supreme concert hall* `7 D5`
881 7th Avenue at 57th Street • 212 247 7800
» www.carnegiehall.org

Tchaikovsky conducted the Carnegie Hall's inaugural concert over a century ago and thus the standard was set. The main hall, the Isaac Stern Auditorium, seats just under 3,000; the Zankel Hall focuses on jazz and contemporary music; the smaller Weill Hall has good acoustics for recitals and chamber music.

Merkin Concert Hall *on-air sound* `7 B3`
129 West 67th Street • 212 501 3330
» www.elainekaufmancenter.org/merkin.htm

The resonance in this mid-sized auditorium is wonderful and it is often used for live radio recordings. Assorted performances cover classical, jazz, funk, and many other genres. Both the balcony and the orchestra seating provide good views, and the art gallery makes a nice diversion during intermissions.

Lincoln Center for the Performing Arts

7 B3

rich pickings for culture vultures

Straddling Broadway and Amsterdam between
62nd Street and 66th Street
Box office 212 546 2656 • Tours 212 875 5350
» www.lincolncenter.org

One of the world leaders in performing arts since the 1960s, Lincoln Center has 12 resident organizations, including a Chamber Music Society, a Film Society, Jazz at Lincoln Center, The New York City Ballet, Metropolitan Opera, New York City Opera, and the New York Philharmonic.

Formerly the slum area of Lincoln Square, the 15-acre site was first envisaged as an arts complex in the 1950s, the scheme being eventually realized with the support of John D. Rockefeller and President Eisenhower, among others. The **Philharmonic Hall** opened in 1962, and was followed a few years later by the **New York State Theater**, the **Vivian Beaumont Theater**, the **Metropolitan Opera House**, and the **Alice Tully Hall**. Altogether there are nearly 20 performance spaces and a host of other facilities, including a library and studios for budding musicians and actors. Tours of the complex run regularly and last an hour, focusing on history, stories, and architecture.

The central outdoor fountain, designed by American Modernist architect Philip Johnson, is a popular meeting point before a show. It is also close to the spot where the Christmas tree, bedecked in musical instrument ornaments, stands during the holiday period. **Damrosch Park** hosts a free outdoor concert series, usually in August. The **Mostly Mozart Festival** is a perennial favorite, while **Midsummer Night Swing** features a wide range of dance music.

Renovations are expected to take place over the next few years to give some of the buildings a facelift and to enhance acoustics. The Vivian Beaumont Theater, beyond the reflecting pool and Henry Moore sculpture, has already been refurbished and hosts wonderful theatrical productions.

Makor *culture with hip twist* 7 C3
35 West 67th Street • 212 601 1000
>> www.makor.org

Frequented by a 20- to 30-something crowd, Makor – associated with the 92nd Street Y *(see p125)* – offers film, discussions, theater, and music, including jazz, funk, and a cappella. Allow time to relax in the lobby lounge before a show, or have a drink in the café. There's a healthy singles scene here too.

Stand-Up NY *heard the one about…?* 7 B2
236 West 78th Street • 212 595 0850
>> www.standupny.com

Stand-Up is the only comedy club on the Upper West Side, so it's a popular venue for locals. Get to know your table neighbors up close and personal as you sit in on a string of comics delivering their routines. The standard ranges from decent to hilarious, and past circuit performers include Robin Williams.

Symphony Space *reggae & throat-singing* 9 B3
2537 Broadway • 212 864 5400
>> www.symphonyspace.org Box office noon–7pm Tue–Sun

This newly renovated complex offers a vast array of theater, film, dance, and music. The main Peter Jay Sharp Theatre – which seats nearly 700 on a gentle slope with plenty of legroom – is often used by guest musicians of the World Music Institute. The Leonard Nimoy Thalia building now includes a café.

Smoke *hot jazz, no tobacco* 9 B2
2751 Broadway • 212 864 6662
>> www.smokejazz.com Open 5pm–4am most nights

Red velvet curtains and low-hanging chandeliers set the scene in this cozy jazz bar/lounge. If you can't accessorize with an instrument, then at least bring an attentive pair of ears, because the live music is taken seriously here. There's seating for 70, with overflow accommodated at the bar.

Performance

Apollo Theater *where stars are born* 11 D3
253 West 125th Street • 212 531 5300
>> www.apollotheater.com
Box office 10am–6pm Mon, Tue, Thu, Fri; 10am–8:30pm Wed;
noon–6pm Sat

The Apollo – Harlem's top attraction – has made such
an important contribution to music history and the
cultural life of New York that it was designated a
National Landmark in 1983. Originally a burlesque
theater, in the 1930s the venue became a showcase
for African American musicians, singers, dancers,
and comedians, who would perform at the theater's
Amateur Night. The careers of many internationally
famous musicians and singers were launched here –
Ella Fitzgerald and Michael Jackson were among
those who were first recognized at the Apollo.

Today, the venue welcomes any talent good enough
to withstand the potential boos from the crowd on
Wednesday's Amateur Night. Latino music has also
been showcased since 2001, and *Showtime at the
Apollo* is produced as a syndicated television program.

As well as coming here to see a performance, it is
also worth taking a close look around the theater. The
lobby Walk of Fame highlights some of the eminent
past performers, such as James Brown, Aretha
Franklin, and Duke Ellington. The guided backstage
tour offers fascinating oral anecdotes and musical
history. You'll also get to touch the renowned Tree of
Hope – in reality, a wooden stump mounted on an
Ionic column. Legendary in the show business world,
it is touched by performers before they start their act
to bring them good luck.

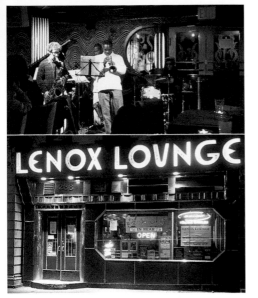

Lenox Lounge *booze & Billie Holliday*

11 D3

288 Lenox Avenue (between 124th & 125th streets)
212 427 0253
➤➤ www.lenoxlounge.com Open noon–4am daily

Lenox is a leading music club with a solid repertoire of live jazz, DJs, and an open jam session on Monday nights. The front bar is Art Deco in character, and the lounge has been restored to its original plush design, including built-in banquettes and zebra stripes in the back room. Southern-style food is served all day.

A sense of history permeates the proceedings – jazz heroes such as Miles Davis, Billie Holiday, and John Coltrane have played in this space. And Malcolm X is said to have spent many an hour at the Lenox before being galvanized by the political fight. Nowadays, the live music ranges from mainstream jazz through to more esoteric genres. Use the front room for mingling – the clientele includes regulars, locals, and jazz aficionados – and then head to the back for listening and dining pleasure.

Brooklyn Academy of Music *performing arts center*

13 C4

30 Lafayette Avenue • 718 636 4100
➤➤ www.bam.org Box office noon–6pm Mon–Sat

Far more than just a music academy, the BAM is a hive of cultural activity, offering live music, opera, dance, film, and theater. The academy's first production was in 1861, and the legendary Ellen Terry was one of the first actors to perform here.

The main building straddles most of the block and has a grand lobby. The Rose Cinema has four screens and very comfortable seating. The Howard Gillman Opera House has a capacity of a little over 2,000, while the smaller Harvey Lichtenstein Theater holds 874. From Thursday to Saturday, you can also catch live performances in the BAM café, which is a great place for a quick drink or light meal before or after a show. The famed Next Wave Festival takes place over three months in the Fall and features modern and experimental works from around the globe.

➤➤ *For a listing of performance venues by type, see pp226–7*

Performance

Warsaw *pierogi & pro sound* 13 C1

261 Driggs Avenue • 718 387 0505
>> www.warsawconcerts.com

A curious collaborative doubling: hip music venue and main ballroom of the Polish National Home. Some nights feature indie and rock groups; others involve Polish festivals and Polka dance evenings. The bistro offers *kielbasa* (sausage) and *pierogi* (small pies), and the bar serves strong Polish beer.

Barge Music *classical music on the water* 13 A3

Fulton Ferry Landing • 718 624 4061
>> www.bargemusic.org
Performances at 7:30pm Thu, Fri & Sat; 4pm Sun

This chamber music concert space is absolutely worth the trip for the quality of the performers, the unique setting, and the superb views of the Manhattan skyline and Brooklyn Bridge.

As suggested by the venue's name, performances do, indeed, take place on the water, in a converted barge that features wood paneling and an open fireplace. Seating arrangements cater to a maximum of just 125, which encourages an intimacy and immediacy for the audience and the musicians.

The barge does move gently during performances but there's little danger of sea-sickness.

Unusually for chamber music, there is no regard for the seasons, and the concert hall is used year-round. Highly polished performances of Mozart, Bach, Schubert, Debussy, and Prokofiev might all feature in a typical month, and guest musicians add zest to the program. A fortnight in December each year is given over to Bach's Brandenburg Concertos.

Before a concert, allow time to wander around the revamped ferry landing and enjoy some ice cream at the Brooklyn Ice Cream Factory. Round off the evening by taking a yellow New York water taxi (718 742969, www.nywatertaxi.com) back to Manhattan.

New Jersey Performing Arts Center (NJPAC) *notable in Newark*

One Center Street, Newark • 888 GO-NJPAC (466-5722)
>> www.njpac.org • Train from Penn Station (New York) to Penn Station (Newark), then LOOP shuttle or short walk to NJPAC
Box office noon–6pm Mon–Sat; 10am–3 pm Sun

Newark has never looked so appealing. This stunning, multi-million-dollar arts complex was built in 1997, breathing new life into a downtrodden city and giving Manhattan residents and tourists alike reason enough to cross the water to New Jersey.

The architecture of the main part of the complex – defined by glass and brick, and cubed shapes – was the brainchild of Barton Myers and honors the idea of casual urban living. The two performance spaces, Prudential Hall (2,730 seats) and Victoria Theater (514 seats) are wonderfully appointed and functional, with first-rate sight lines and excellent acoustics for all seats. The Alvin Ailey American Dance Theater and the New Jersey Symphony Orchestra are regular performers. The complex has also hosted touring productions of musicals (*Les Misérables*, *The Mikado*) and such diverse performers as Yo-Yo Ma, the Vienna Boys Choir, Lauryn Hill, and teen band 'N Synch.

Getting to the NJPAC is not too difficult, but does involve either walking five blocks from Newark's Penn Station, or taking the purple-signed LOOP shuttle bus for one dollar. The complex has two restaurants: the Theater Square Grill, which has a lounge bar, and the Calcada restaurant, which offers alfresco dining.

Sports Venues

New York has several capacious sports venues. The **Yankee Stadium** was built for the famous baseball team in 1923, and is fun to visit via the Yankee Clipper ferry. **Shea Stadium** is home to the New York Mets baseball team and lies beneath a flight path to LaGuardia airport. The Beatles famously played here in 1965 and 1966. Part of the Meadowlands complex, **Giants Stadium** is the home of three soccer teams: the New York Giants, New York Jets (both always sold out), and Metrostars. **Madison Square Garden** is home to ice hockey team New York Rangers and basketball teams Knicks and Liberty. The Garden also hosts big-name concerts, monster truck rallies, wrestling, boxing, and top dog and cat shows. For contact details, *see p227*.

>> *For information about getting tickets to watch the Knicks at Madison Square Garden, see p17*

bars & clubs

From super-cool cocktail lounges to dark old ale houses to neighborhood joints with jukeboxes and pool tables, New York has bars to suit everyone. For those in search of an energetic night out, downtown and Chelsea have the most lively DJ bars and clubs, though Brooklyn is catching up fast. More laid-back drinkers may prefer to slip into an easy chair in the swanky cocktail bars of midtown and the Upper East Side.

DJ BARS	GAY BARS & CLUBS	STAR BARS
Beauty Bar 231 East 14th Street Expect plenty of 70s and 80s punk and glam rock at this lively East Village bar, decked out like an old-fashioned beauty salon. *(See p144)*	**Cubbyhole** 281 West 12th Street Cheeky decor, mammoth Martinis, and a relaxed, friendly vibe are enjoyed by a predominantly lesbian clientele here. *(See p148)*	**2A** 25 Avenue A Downtown rockers The Strokes are among the street-credible names associated with this Alphabet City dive bar. *(See p141)*
Sullivan Room 218 Sullivan Street The warm tones and cushy alcoves induce a loungy atmosphere, the mood matched by soulful house played by resident DJs. *(See p146)*		**Hiro** 366 West 17th Street Japanese-themed Hiro is a top spot for the city's youthful models, musicians, and actors to congregate. *(See p150)*
TriBeCa Grand's Studio Room 2 Avenue of the Americas The Studio attracts a knowledgeable crowd, appreciative of the club's top DJ talent, such as Junior Sanchez and LCD Soundsystem. *(See p183)*	**Roxy** 515 West 18th Street Evoking the last days of disco, the cavernous Roxy hosts the city's longest running, most popular gay club night on Saturdays. *(See p149)*	**Serena** Chelsea Hotel, 222 West 23rd Street This subterranean lounge caters to artists and film makers hoping to become a part of the Chelsea Hotel's eventful history. *(See p149)*
Uncle Ming's 225 Avenue B Fashion-conscious Lower East Siders flock to Ming's to hear retro electro beats and bask in the dim light of ancient chandeliers. *(See p146)*	**Stonewall** 53 Christopher Street With regular drag shows, this icon of 60s gay activism is as much about pleasure as politics. *(See p147)*	**Bungalow 8** 515 West 27th Street A tribute to Tinseltown, with palms, mock sunsets, and a strict door policy to help homesick Hollywood babies feel at ease. *(See p150)*
»» *In New York there are strict laws governing where you can dance. Dancing is permitted in clubs, but not in the city's DJ bars unless they are hosting special events.*		
	Trash 256 Grand Street, Brooklyn Punk-glam vinyl upholstery, beautiful gay boys and girls, and the dirtiest rock 'n' roll weekend parties east of Alphabet City. *(See p156)*	

HISTORIC BARS

Bemelmans Bar
Carlyle Hotel, 35 East 76th Street
This uptown lounge has a whimsical mural by *Madeline* creator, Ludwig Bemelmans. *(See p153)*

McSorley's Old Ale House
15 East 7th Street
The furnishings, robust ales, and good cheer remain largely unchanged since the days when Abraham Lincoln drank at this inn. *(See p142)*

White Horse Tavern
567 Hudson Street
This bar attained fame when, as legend has it, poet Dylan Thomas met his demise after a whiskey-drinking session here. *(See p147)*

Chumley's
86 Bedford Street
A favorite of writers thirsting for liquid inspiration ever since the 1920s Prohibition era. *(See p146)*

ALFRESCO DRINKING

Glass
287 10th Avenue
Beyond the sleek, Cubist bar here lies a patio surrounded by bamboo trees – the destination of choice for local sophisticates. *(See p150)*

Gowanus Yacht Club
323 Smith Street, Brooklyn
Typifying summer in Brooklyn, this convivial, all-outdoor bar lures a young clientele with cheap beer and nightly barbecues. *(See p155)*

Barramundi
147 Ludlow Street
A Lower East Side rarity, Barramundi has a flower-filled garden, complete with fairytale lighting. *(See p140)*

Ava Lounge
Majestic Hotel, 210 West 55th Street
On warm nights Ava's best feature is its patio filled with stylish cocktail-quaffers. Times Square lies within view. *(See p152)*

B-Bar & Grill
40 East 4th Street
At the crossroads of East Village and West Village, B-Bar invites both camps into its large, illuminated back patio. *(See p143)*

DANCE CLUBS

Cielo
18 Little West 12th Street
Seasoned DJs combine with a full-on crowd of clubbers in this small venue for nights of enjoyable mayhem on a sunken dance floor. *(See p148)*

Volume
Wythe Ave. & North 13th St., Brooklyn
Underground hip-hop DJs, electro producers, and other creative music makers get Brooklynites moving at this warehouse. *(See p156)*

>> *The website http://nyc.flavorpill.net gives a roundup of forthcoming club nights and DJs playing in the city's bars.*

Avalon
47 West 20th Street
A church converted into a cavernous dancing and lounging space for Ibiza-scale crowds of clubbers and top international DJs. *(See p149)*

Galapagos
70 North 6th Street, Brooklyn
Brooklyn's home for performance art, films, and irresistible DJ parties. Musical styles include glam rock, techno, and new wave. *(See p157)*

Pussycat Lounge *trash & banter*

1 D4

96 Greenwich Street • 212 349 4800
>> www.pussycatlounge.com Open Mon–Sat from around 9pm

A quiet block near Ground Zero adopts a delectably sleazy air when the Pussycat Lounge opens up for the night. Skip the first floor's depressing, 60s-style go-go strip club, and head upstairs for trashy burlesque shows, live bands, and ribald weekend dance parties. Try to wear something a little daring. **Adm**

Winnie's *Chinatown's livelist karaoke bar*

2 E1

104 Bayard Street • 212 732 2384
Open noon–4am daily

Someone is singing, and probably butchering, your favorite song right now at Winnie's. Know before you go: 1. You'll pay $1 per song; 2. Swinging the microphone is not allowed; 3. You should anticipate sharing any well-known chorus (such as in Neil Diamond's *Sweet Caroline*) with the boisterous young crowd.

Antarctica *chilled beer hall*

3 C5

287 Hudson Street • 212 352 1666
>> www.antarcticabar.com
Open from 4:30pm Mon–Fri, from 7pm Sat

The owners of Antarctica claim that their bar has been in continuous business since the year in which Guinness was invented: 1759. You don't have to believe this, but there is certainly a feeling of age about the weathered wood floor planks, shining brass taps, and the picture of 19th-century, mustachioed drinkers on the wall. The overall effect is not of Earth's last frontier either, though Antarctica's location in the far reaches of SoHo lends it a certain remoteness that's appealing.

The bar has received many plaudits for its down-to-earth appeal in an upscale neighborhood. It has also won the "Best Bar to Shoot Pool" title from *NY Mag*. Booth seating and pitchers of beer ensure a merry crowd. Check the website to see if your first name qualifies you for free drinks on the night.

THOM's Bar *classy hotel bar*

60 Thompson Street • 212 219 2000

>> www.60thompson.com Open from 5pm nightly

3 C5

The boutique hotel bar craze that swept Manhattan in the 1990s shows no signs of fatigue at this bar set in the lobby of the sleek 60 Thompson Hotel.

A sense of occasion starts to build from the moment you approach the chic SoHo address. The glass entrance is grandly set back from the curb and manned by cordial, black-clad doormen. You'll be directed up to THOM's Bar, which instantly gives the impression of classic sophistication with its leather parlor chairs, massive marble fireplace, and lofty ceilings. Modern touches can be seen in the lacquer-black bar, gracefully arching chrome lamps, and strongly geometric purple sofas and banquettes.

A typical weekend night attracts an international, casually fashionable crowd partial to specialty cocktails. The signature THOM is a blend of the very pure Skyy citrus vodka, fresh lime, and mint. Sidecars, lychee Martinis, Tom Collins, and others are deftly mixed by bartenders who look as if they've stepped off the pages of hip lifestyle magazine *Wallpaper**.

On particularly crowded nights, patrons have no compunction about taking their drinks to the adjacent lobby, where the acid jazz music plays at lower decibels than in the bar, and where seating does not come at such a premium.

ñ *atmospheric Spanish bar* 3 D5
33 Crosby Street • 212 219 8856
Open from 5pm nightly (to 4am Fri & Sat; cash only)

The labyrinthine lanes of Madrid's old quarter lie a considerable distance from SoHo, but past midnight – especially on Wednesdays – this somewhat desolate stretch of Crosby Street adopts a distinctly *madrileño* mood. As you open the door to ñ (pronounced "enyay"), the insistent, passionate rhythms of flamenco immediately grab you.

An intimate and authentic Spanish tapas bar, ñ is just wide enough to accommodate a few musicians and dancers for its Wednesday flamenco showcase. It compensates for its diminutive size, however, with a genial, Iberian atmosphere. An international mix of artists and professionals gathers at the long, gleaming copper bar to choose from a selection of 20 sherries and affordable Spanish wines by the glass. Among the popular tapas plates are savory toasted almonds, addictive, briny olives, and luscious *tetilla con membrillo*: mild, creamy cheese served with a sweet quince paste.

At weekends patrons pack four-deep at the bar, which can result in brusque drink service, but weeknights – Wednesdays excepted – are comparatively quiet and easygoing. A homely bar, ñ concedes few points to its style-driven downtown environs. Except, that is, for the one-way glass on the bathroom doors. Fear not, however: you can be assured that the only visibility afforded is experienced from inside the stall looking out.

Temple Bar *for lounging lovers* 4 E4
332 Lafayette Street • 212 925 4242
Open from 5pm Mon–Sat, from 7pm Sun

Exuding luxury and romance from every dimmed Deco wall lamp, Temple Bar is a favorite destination among amorous NoHo couples. Discreet servers bring deftly mixed Martinis to the table, while the sultry crooning of one female jazz legend or another drifting from the speakers raises the seduction ante.

Pravda *Russian speakeasy* `4 E4`
281 Lafayette Street • 212 226 4944
» www.pravdany.com Open from 5pm Mon–Sat, from 6 Sun

Keen eyes are indispensable for locating this subterranean SoHo destination, indicated by a lone red lamp atop an iron banister. At the entrance, crimson velvet curtains part to reveal a sprawling lounge painted terra cotta and furnished with burgundy parlor chairs, candlelit cocktail tables, and leaded glass wall lamps. Combined with the Cyrillic characters and Roman numerals stenciled on low ceiling arches, the scene evokes the gritty romance of a Moscow train station, circa 1929. Statuesque, black-clad servers weave between throngs of chic patrons, balancing cocktail trays laden with generous vodka shots, single-malt Scotches and house specialties such as the Nolita: chilled mango-infused vodka, apricot liqueur, and lime juice. In true vodka-room style, Pravda also offers an appealing menu of European finger foods, from garlicky mussels and fries to smoked-fish plates and caviar.

Upstairs, a diminutive lounge, with no more than one couch and a tiny bar, is a prime spot for amorous couples – providing, that is, they can blissfully ignore the constant parade of drinkers traipsing up to use Pravda's bathrooms.

Lansky Lounge *discreet cocktail bar* `4 G4`
104 Norfolk Street • 212 677 9489
» www.lanskylounge.com Open from 6pm nightly

A spacious, modern bar, named after one of the neighborhood's most notorious sons, Jewish gangster Meyer Lansky. The uptown, attractive crowd enters through the "speakeasy" entrance, distinguished by the neon letter "L." Excellent classic cocktails, plus DJs spinning hip-hop on Wednesdays and weekends.

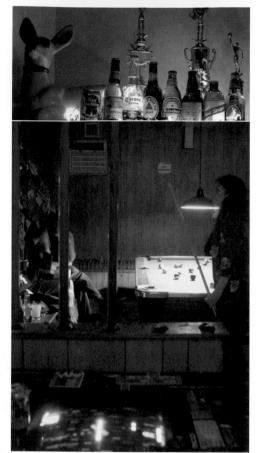

Welcome to the Johnson's *the real dive bar*

123 Rivington Street • 212 420 9911
Open 3:30pm–4am Mon–Fri, noon–4am
Sat & Sun (cash only)

While some New York bars may classify themselves as "dives," a close inspection often reveals that the shabby decor has been painstakingly cultivated, the jukebox song catalogue caters only to esoteric tastes, the place is full of elitist poseurs, and the beer is $7 a glass. Whereas the genuine requirements of an American dive bar are cheap beer, anthemic rock music, decrepit furniture, and graffitied bathrooms – nothing else will do.

Fortunately, there is a Lower East Side bar that delivers the requisite attributes with just the right touch of self-assured, devil-may-care attitude: Welcome to the Johnson's – or, as it's known to the regulars, The Johnson's.

Though it opens mid-afternoon, the fun really begins from around 5pm, as the neighborhood's young musicians, professionals, and students make themselves comfortable on thrift-shop sofas. The favorite beer, Pabst Blue Ribbon, is absurdly cheap. Diversions involve playing pool on a warped billiard table, waging intergalactic warfare on the vintage video game machine, and feeding dollar bills into the hard-rocking juke.

A word of caution: The Johnson's gets very crowded after 10pm. Also, the bathroom stalls are not for the squeamish. Consider yourself informed.

Barramundi *backpackers' hangout*

147 Ludlow Street • 212 529 6900
Open 7:30pm–4am Sun–Thu, 6pm–4am Fri & Sat

Young travelers feel at home at this funky, Australian-owned Lower East Side bar. An international crowd sips reasonably priced beverages on the back room's couches while gesturing at the otherworldly wall sculptures. During summer, Barramundi's garden (which closes at 10pm) is a beautiful setting.

Slipper Room *lively entertainment* `4 F4`

167 Orchard Street • 212 253 7246
>> www.slipperroom.com Open from 8pm nightly

Five dollars is usually all that's required to experience anything from burlesque and classic vaudeville theater to cash-prize trivia nights at this inviting Lower East Side lounge. The crowd changes according to the event schedule, but patrons infallibly arrive equipped with sharp wits and playful attitudes.

Parkside Lounge *easygoing joint* `4 G4`

317 East Houston Street • 212 673 6270
>> www.parksidelounge.com Open from mid-afternoon daily

Cheap beers, generous cocktails, and zero attitude draw neighborhood residents young and old to the Parkside. In the afternoon, the affable crowd's banter mixes with the jukebox's classic country. Nighttime arrivals head straight to the back room, where bluegrass bands and burlesque troupes perform.

Chez es Saada *North African vibe* `4 F4`

42 East 1st Street • 212 475 2220
>> www.chezessaada.com Open from 6pm nightly

Follow the trail of fresh rose petals from the undistinguished street-level lounge down into a sumptuous Moroccan-style grotto. Here, fashionable lovebirds steal kisses across candlelit alcove tables, singles flirt at the bar over signature plum Martinis, and North African rhythms evoke a world far away.

2A *rocking bar & upstairs lounge* `4 F3`

25 Avenue A • 212 505 2466
Open from 4pm daily

For better or worse, 2A has become an easy place to spot a hip celebrity. New Wave and punk music from the 70s set the tone at the street-level bar. The couch-filled upstairs lounge is cozier, with a more flirtatious atmosphere. Though most of the clientele drinks beer, 2A's red wine selection should not be overlooked.

KGB *vodka & old Russia* `4 E3`

85 East 4th Street • 212 505 3360
>> www.kgbbar.com Open from 6pm nightly

Detached from the frenetic barhopping of nearby
2nd Avenue is this Bolshevik-red, dimly lit den of
Soviet nostalgia. Staff keep glasses full of vodka or
Central European imported pilsners, while bookish
patrons turn up for occasional readings by guest
novelists. Vintage Leninist posters adorn the walls.

Swift Hibernian Lounge *Celtic vibe* `4 E3`

34 East 4th Street • 212 260 3600
Open noon–4am daily

A mural depicting Irish satirist Jonathan Swift raising
a pint of Guinness welcomes Irish expats, NYU
students, and everyone else besides to this spacious
public house. Come for Swift's extensive draft beer
selection, hearty pub food, sharp-witted bartenders,
weekly live Irish music, and infectious cheer.

McSorley's *historic ale house* `4 E3`

15 East 7th Street • 212 473 9148
Open from 11am Mon–Sat, from 1pm Sun

Reputedly New York's oldest bar, McSorley's hasn't
changed much since Civil War president Abraham
Lincoln hoisted his tankard here. You'll still find
sawdust littering the wooden floor, drinkers from
around the globe crowding the rustic booths, and
robust dark and pale ales on draft. *(See also p17.)*

Angel's Share *cocktails with a Tokyo flavor* `4 E2`

8 Stuyvesant Street • 212 777 5415
Open from 7pm nightly

Standing is not allowed, nor are groups exceeding
four people, but with these criteria met, Angel's Share
is a wonderful place for cocktails. In fact, you might
not find better classic mixes anywhere downtown.
There's an extensive sake selection and delicate
Japanese bar snacks too. Service is exemplary.

Nevada Smith's *soccer-oriented bar* `4 E2`

74 3rd Avenue • 212 982 2591
>> www.nevadasmiths.net Open nightly

Diehard soccer fans, behold your Manhattan headquarters. Upstairs, jersey-wearing Europeans and a
dusting of Americans sip pints while watching their
favorite teams on TV. Downstairs, the scene is different, with dim lighting, polished wooden furnishings,
and, on Thursdays, stand-up comedy.

B-Bar & Grill *East-West Village crossover* `4 E3`
40 East 4th Street • 212 475 2220
Open noon–4am daily

Barring an electrical blackout, one cannot miss the B-Bar: a neon red sign protrudes from the facade, while the patio's towering trees sparkle under a multicolored blanket of festive lights. Aside from its physical situation between New York's East and West villages, this former petrol station possesses other attributes that distinguish it as the nocturnal crossroads of the East/West divide. The fabulous outdoor patio – with its nicely spaced tables and bar – draws equal numbers of conservative West Villagers and their counterculture-embracing neighbors to the east. The dichotomy continues inside the handsome dining room and at the bar. Retro vinyl booths, wood-beamed ceilings, and mammoth framed photographs suggest a hip, East Side sensibility; yet it is executed with polish befitting a refined West 4th Street bistro.

Neighborhood allegiances aside, everybody shares in their love for B-Bar's cocktails. Take note, however: the pretty pastel hues of apple, lychee, and water-melon Martinis belie their explosive potency. Regarding the "Grill" portion of the name, B-Bar offers a varied, if somewhat uneven, American diner menu. But the crowd-pleasing, always-busy, prix-fixe brunch on the weekend brings the nighttime vibe into broad daylight: chatty crowds, outside seating when the weather's fine, and an unlimited supply of Mimosas and Bloody Marys.

Bar Veloce *Italian-style wine bar* `4 E2`
175 2nd Avenue • 212 260 3200
>> www.barveloce.com Open from 5pm nightly

This comfortable, sleek little wine bar would not look out of place on the elegant streets of Florence. A smart menu of Italian snacks, from toasted panini to Nutella and fruit plates, gives peckish drinkers something to nibble while choosing a wine. Glasses are priced under $10, bottles up to $80.

Beauty Bar *intimate theme bar* `4 E2`
231 East 14th Street • 212 539 1389
>> www.beautybar.com Open 5pm–4am nightly (from 7 Sat, Sun)

True to its name, the place is swathed in retro beauty-salon kitsch. East Village rockers and NYU graduate students sip potent cocktails bearing names like "Aqua Net" at the bar, while 70s glam rock and punk blare from the speakers. Check out happy hour for deals on drinks. Manicures are on offer too.

Lotus `3 A2`
409 West 14th Street • 212 243 4420
>> www.lotusnewyork.com Open 10pm–4am Tue–Sun

It's been several years since this sleek, sexy club opened its black lacquer doors in a neighborhood best known for wholesale meat butchers, rumbling garbage trucks, and transvestite prostitutes. In so doing, Lotus helped blaze the trail that converted the Meatpacking District into a hotbed of nightlife.

Imitated throughout the city, Lotus's design is still the best, with three distinct areas for lounging upstairs, pan-Asian dining on the ground floor, and dancing below. The place exudes a subtle Eastern warmth, with a mix of blonde and cherry woods, rusty-red walls, and half-moon banquettes. The cocktail menu features signature blackberry Caipirinhas. Regulars have their preferred nights: Friday's house party GBH pulls in a serious dance crowd, while Saturday's blend of 80s pop and contemporary hip-hop draws a more mainstream, uptown element. **Adm**

Korova Milk Bar *homage to a cult film* 4 F2
200 Avenue A • 212 254 8838
>> www.korovamilkbar.com Open from 7pm nightly

From the rounded, swooping white script above the doorway to the geometric zebra stripes lining the entrance hall, visitors to Korova know a distinctive visual experience awaits them. The entire place is a homage to Stanley Kubrick's 1971 film about brutality and youth, *A Clockwork Orange*; indeed, the bar takes its name from the film (it was the haunt of Malcolm Macdowell's band of miscreants). Once inside, film buffs will immediately recognize many references, such as the stark white, wigged and lipsticked mannequins protruding from the walls. The cinematic homage continues with wall-mounted video monitors and curvaceous, matching black and white recliners swathed in vinyl and velvet, perched on a platform opposite the exceptionally long bar. Korova is a final destination on the East Village/Alphabet City barhopping circuit, so before midnight the spacious floor has room to spare.

After midnight, 70s punk and glam blares, while a throwback bunch of mods, punks, and stragglers recounts the night's wanderings over cheap beer, Jack Daniel's shots, and wicked vodka gimlets. For those who possess the stomach for it at such an hour, Korova's series of signature cocktails, Molokos (of course), should not be missed. The Moloko is an ice cream-based concoction, mixed with any number of liqueurs and flavorings, served in a Martini glass and kept cool in an ice-filled miniature fishbowl.

Rue B *Gallic-style retreat* 4 G2
188 Avenue B • 212 358 1700
Open from noon Mon–Fri, from 10am Fri & Sat

Rue B's seductive air renders any intention of East Village barhopping pointless. The Parisian-style bar is decked out with comfy banquettes, offers respectable French wine, bistro menus, and – its *coup de grâce* – hosts live jazz with no cover charge. With all that on offer, there's no need to go anywhere else.

>> *DJ bars usually charge an entrance fee after around 10 or 11pm*

Uncle Ming's *cozy, crazy lounge* `4 G2`
225 Avenue B, 2nd Floor • 212 959 8506
≫ www.unclemings.com Open from 6pm nightly

Discreetly plying its trade above a liquor store, this
unmarked lounge has the atmosphere of a party that's
strictly for the in-crowd. Deep purple and pink lighting,
old chandeliers, gorgeous bartenders serving strong
cocktails, and DJs spinning electro beats inspire a
flirtatious atmosphere among the cool clientele.

Sullivan Room *relaxed clubbing* `3 C3`
218 Sullivan Street • 212 252 2151
≫ www.sullivanroom.com Open from 10pm Thu–Sun

This modest, subterranean West Village jewel is one
of those rare spaces in which you can feel comfortable whether you've come to dance to soulful house,
lounge around with friends, or converse at the bar.
A refreshing lack of attitude comes with the territory;
you might even toast the DJ after his set. **Adm**

Vol de Nuit *Belgian beer & cheer* `3 C3`
148 West 4th Street • 212 982 3388
Open from 7:30pm nightly

Behind an inconspicuous door on West 4th, Vol de
Nuit counts eight Belgian brews on draft – each
served in its appropriate style of glass – and dozens
of others in bottles. Snacks are wonderful: Belgian
fries served in paper cones, and mussels paired with
irresistible sauces. There's an outdoor courtyard too.

Chumley's *former speakeasy* `3 B3`
86 Bedford Street • 212 675 4449
Open from mid-afternoon Mon–Fri, from 11am Sat & Sun

"Eighty-sixed," the American bartender's code for
denying service to a particularly inebriated patron,
evolved from the address of this institution in the
1920s Prohibition era. Booth seating and yellowing
portraits of famed writers who once sipped their pints
here round out the warm, convivial pub atmosphere.

Stonewall *famous & still fabulous* `3 B3`
53 Christopher Street • 212 463 0950
Open from 3pm daily

When this bar's predominantly gay male clientele resisted a police raid in 1969, the ensuing riot touched off NYC's gay activist movement. Stonewall demands reverence, but it's also a fun place. Campy 60s pop music and multicolored lighting dominate the main bar, and drag queens strut their stuff nightly.

Blind Tiger Ale House *serious beers* `3 B3`
518 Hudson Street • 212 675 3848
»www.blindtiger.citysearch.com
Open from lunchtime daily

West Village beer connoisseurs hoist their pints at the convivial Blind Tiger. No fewer than 24 microbrews chill on draft. It's one of New York's most friendly, casual places for mid-week beer drinking. Go on Wednesday evening for free cheese pairings.

White Horse Tavern *writers' haunt* `3 B3`
567 Hudson Street • 212 243 9260
Open from 11am daily

Few New York buildings, let alone bars, shelter as many literary ghosts as the White Horse Tavern. Before the West Village became a gentrified expanse of French bistros and NYU dormitories, this circa-1880 bar was a favorite spot for the neighborhood's bohemian writers to brood over 20-cent ales. But the address attained infamy in 1953, when – as legend has it – the Welsh poet and dramatist Dylan Thomas dropped dead outside, the victim of undiagnosed diabetes and untold whiskeys.

Fittingly, posters from Thomas's theatrical productions line the dark wood walls. Grandfather clocks, white porcelain horses, a pressed tin ceiling – even the bartenders' amiable rapport with afternoon regulars – evoke a bygone era. But things turn decidedly 21st-century after work and at weekends, when crowds fill the bar and adjoining dining rooms.

Bars & Clubs

Cubbyhole *one for the girls* `3 B2`
281 West 12th Street • 212 243 9041
Open from mid-afternoon daily

If the suspended goldfish figurines, Chinese lanterns, and whimsical bar stools at this lesbian bar don't charm you, perhaps this will: half-price drinks until 7pm, all-you-can-drink specials on Saturday nights, and notoriously mammoth Martinis. Cubbyhole ladies are very friendly, and the mood is always casual.

Rhône *cavernous wine bar* `3 A2`
63 Gansevoort Street • 212 367 8440
» www.rhonenyc.com Open from 5:30pm Mon–Sat

Tucked among the Meatpacking District's industrial-chic nightclubs, Rhône is an enormous wine bar with a copper bar and futuristic, lime-green recliners. Gallery owners, fashion models, and downtown professionals sip any of 30 vintages available by the glass, and nibble from French-Indochinese tasting plates.

Cielo *award-winning dance club* `3 A2`
18 Little West 12th Street • 212 645 5700
» www.cieloclub.com Open 10pm–4am Wed–Sat

Soulful house with interjected Latin grooves leave patrons little choice but to abandon their soft suede banquettes and storm the sunken dance floor. Co-owned by DJ Nicolas Matar (well known on the Ibiza scene), Cielo attracts knowledgeable clubbers and top-drawer DJs from around the world. **Adm**

Daytime Bars

When a thirst for something stronger than bottled water strikes you during midtown sightseeing, these bars make welcome stops. The daytime crowd at **Rudy's Bar & Grill** in Hell's Kitchen is as friendly as any you'll find, and Miles Davis on the jukebox makes a welcome change from the classic rock barrage of neighboring bars. Murray Hill's campy **Cabin Club at Pinetree Lodge** has a huge back patio where potent fruit slushes are dispensed to a fun, flirty crowd. Afternoon sophistication abounds at the rooftop **Mica Bar**, within blocks of the United Nations. A parlor atmosphere pervades the **Hudson Hotel's Library Bar**, where chessboards, architecture books, and a purple-felt billiard table are all at guests' disposal. For full addresses, *see p228*.

Roxy *perennially popular nightclub*   `3 A1`
515 West 18th Street • 212 645 5156
▶▶**www.roxynyc.com** Open Wed, Fri & Sat nights

Friday-night house, salsa, and hip-hop extravaganzas tend to see this most massive of Chelsea clubs overrun by a young clientele. By contrast, Wednesday Roller Skating nights offer a fun, often hilarious, and sometimes bruising reminder of disco's last days. Saturday brings NYC's biggest gay party. **Adm**

Avalon *Chelsea club with attitude*   `3 C1`
47 West 20th Street • 212 807 7780
▶▶**www.nyavalon.com** Check website for club nights

Avalon occupies hallowed ground on two counts: it's housed in a Gothic church and is the former address of Limelight, a legendary 1980s club that engendered near-religious devotion among its regulars. These days, a mixed gay and straight crowd comes to lounge and dance to the sounds of the world's top DJs. **Adm**

Eugene *upscale schmoozing post*   `6 E5`
27 West 24th Street • 212 462 0999
▶▶**www.eugenenyc.com** Open from 5pm Thu–Sat

Realized in Art Deco retro, Eugene is a spacious supper club designed with big spending in mind. Well-dressed Flatiron professionals nibble tuna tartare in the cream-hued dining room, then settle themselves onto burgundy banquettes and ottomans in the adjacent lounge. There's dancing on weekends.

Serena *soft pink lounge*   `5 C5`
Chelsea Hotel, 222 West 23rd Street • 212 255 4646
Open from 6pm Mon–Fri, from 8pm Sat & Sun

It's had a makeover to meet fire-safety standards, but the home of pop culture personalities hasn't lost its touch. The Chelsea's subterranean Serena lounge delights with its new velvet couches and pink walls up front, and Moroccan motifs in the adjacent rooms. Celebrity sightings are frequent.

▶▶ *For advice on tipping in bars,* see p233

apanese theme **3 A1**
7 0212
Open from 10pm nightly

e Hotel is Chelsea's
f the moment. Fashion
sake, while, behind a
luminescent rice paper wall, more energized guests
move to 80s pop, rock remixes, and electro in Hiro's
sizeable ballroom. Not famous? Try a weeknight.

Glass *receptacle for the beautiful people* **5 B5**
287 10th Avenue • 212 904 1580
Open Tue–Fri 6pm–4am, Sat 8pm–4am

An ultra-cool design and Brazilian electro rhythms
draw Chelsea's gallery set to Glass like magnets. In
summer, the bamboo-filled patio is the site for one of
Manhattan's most exclusive people-watching scenes.
Models, artists, and curators mingle over *caipiruva*
cocktails, made from cachaça rum and crushed grapes.

Bungalow 8 *West Coast seduction* **5 B4**
515 West 27th Street • 212 629 3333
Open from 10pm nightly

Nightlife impresario Amy Sacco delivers a cozy, albeit exclusive,
Hollywood Hills-inspired lounge to Chelsea's young style mavens.
Strike your most unaffected L.A. pose – $30 glass of champagne
in hand – amid swimming pool murals, quirky designer furniture,
and potted palms. A digital "sunset wall" stands in for that most
essential of Californian ingredients – the sun setting on the ocean.

Spirit *holistic nightlife* **5 B4**
530 West 27th Street • 212 268 9477
≫ www.spiritnewyork.com Open from 10pm Fri & Sat

Eastern and Native American religions have inspired
this "wellness club." Spirit has three zones: Mind, a
holistic spa with massage rooms; Body, an immense
dance space, where superstar DJs such as David
Morales and Roger Sanchez play; and Soul, an
organic restaurant, overlooking the dance floor. **Adm**

Copacabana *salsa, meréngue & samba* `5 B3`
560 West 34th Street • 212 239 2672
>> www.copacabanany.com Open 10pm–5am Tue, Fri–Sun

With its plush beige banquettes and Art Deco palm-
frond motifs, the capacious Copa evokes the glamour
of a 1940s supper club in Havana. Massive dance
floors and a stage that can accommodate NYC's
largest ensembles make for unforgettable evenings.
Dress strictly to impress. **Adm**

The Ginger Man *distinguished ale house* `6 E3`
11 East 36th Street • 212 532 3740
>> www.gingermanpub.com Open from lunchtime daily

This handsome bar includes all the accoutrements of
a classic pub: lustrous woods, booth seating, and
hearty food. Despite the preponderance of vintage
Guinness signage, it is Belgian ales and single-malt
Scotches that fill the glasses of most of the gathered
regulars and visitors to this watering hole.

Campbell Apartment *pricey cocktails* `6 F2`
15 Vanderbilt Avenue, Southwest Balcony,
Grand Central Terminal • 212 953 0409
Open 3pm–1am Mon–Sat, 3–10pm Sun

For all its restored Beaux Arts splendor, Grand Central
Station can still be a hassle. But the sting of crowds
and late trains can be swiftly soothed by the divine
cocktails at Campbell Apartment. Formerly the office
of 1920s railroad tycoon John W. Campbell, it looks
every bit the inner sanctum of a prosperous American
industrialist, with dark wood paneling, monstrous
stone fireplace, and intricate, leaded glass windows.

Suited midtown professionals unwind on comfy
parlor furniture or on high bar stools, tapping feet to
swing and calypso rhythms. The deceptively potent
libations include Prohibition Punch – a mix of passion
fruit juice, cognac, Grand Marnier, and champagne.
A small balcony provides more privacy for latter-day
John W.s to discuss mergers and acquisitions. Note:
no sneakers, jeans, or baseball caps are allowed.

Métrazur *Grand Central splendor* `6 F2`
East Balcony, Grand Central Terminal • 212 687 4600
»» www.charliepalmer.com/metrazur
Open 11:30am–3pm Mon–Fri, 5–10:30pm Mon–Sat

Métrazur packs enough panache to lure rail travelers and non-commuters alike to Grand Central's East Balcony. Smart professionals relish Charlie Palmer's beautifully crafted cocktails, such as the Riviera: Dubonnet, Grand Marnier, blood orange and lime juice.

Single Room Occupancy *discreet bar* `7 C5`
360 West 53rd Street • 212 765 6299
Open from 7:30pm Mon–Sat

This Theater District cubbyhole might be midtown's best-kept secret. Ring the outdoor buzzer, and a member of staff will show you into a dark bar, where chic patrons sip Malbecs and full-bodied Brooklyn Monster Ale served in elegant glassware. House music pounds from the stereo.

Ava Lounge *modernist vision at the Majestic* `7 D5`
Top of Majestic Hotel, 210 West 55th Street • 212 956 7020
»» www.avaloungenyc.com Open from 5pm daily

The 1950s Golden Age of cocktail culture is evoked here through gorgeous linear furnishings, geometric patterns on the bar, designer Martinis, and jazzy house music. The outdoor patio comes into its own in summer – the perfect place to be mesmerized by the blinking commercialism of nearby Times Square.

Flûte *Theater District champagne lounge* `7 D5`
205 West 54th Street • 212 265 5169
»» www.flutebar.com Open 5pm–4am Mon–Sat

Velvet couches, Belle Époque poster art, discreet alcoves, and cuddling couples create a cozy, romantic mood. Choose your bubbly from 100 bottles (18 are available by the flute). Tasting plates feature smoked salmon, tuna tartare, and foie gras. Live jazz and DJs play Thursday through Saturday.

Russian Vodka Room *for connoisseurs* `7 C5`
265 West 52nd Street • 212 307 5835
>> www.rvrclub.com Open from 4pm daily

Gloss, glamour, and rampant pretension are the usual hallmarks of Manhattan lounges with extensive vodka selections. Fortunately, the Russian Vodka Room dodges this unsavory trend. The block's boisterous theater crowds rarely even notice RVR's black awning amid the twinkling lights, which means that proceedings inside the windowless lounge are intimate and relaxed. East Europeans, young and old, sit at the crescent-shaped wood bar or alcove tables, talking animatedly over music from a resident pianist.

No fewer than 50 varieties of the potent spirit fill the shelves. The curious, large glass jars you may notice above the coat rack hold luscious, home-made vodka infusions – try a bracing shot of horseradish, tangy cranberry, or mellow pear. An extensive menu of appetizing Russian delicacies, from borscht to caviar, is also available.

Baraonda *Italo-Latin festivity* `8 G2`
1439 2nd Avenue • 212 288 8555
>> www.baraondany.com Open from 6pm Mon–Sat

Baraonda single-handedly proves that staid Upper East Siders can, in fact, party. Around midnight, the restaurant transforms into a Latin American dance house, with samba, techno, and *rock en español* compelling revelers to gulp down sangría and dance on the tables. (Skip the middling, overpriced food.)

Bemelmans Bar *cabaret & cocktails* `8 E1`
Carlyle Hotel, 35 East 76th Street • 212 744 1600
>> www.thecarlyle.com Open 11am–2am daily

Ludwig Bemelmans, creator of the *Madeline* children's book series, painted the exquisite zoological mural enveloping this superb uptown piano lounge. Top cabaret acts, subdued lighting, polished woods, and peerless classic cocktails set the tone for incomparably romantic evenings. Attire can be casual.

Jimmy's Uptown *jazz & more in Harlem* `11 D3`

2207 Adam Clayton Powell, Jr. Boulevard • 212 491 4000
Open from early evening daily; also for gospel brunch Sun

Jimmy Rodriguez gives classic Southern soul food a gourmet twist (think filet mignon with horseradish grits). After dinner, the slick dining room transforms into one of Harlem's hottest clubs, with live jazz, R&B, and reggae. Local hip-hop impresarios Sean Combs and Russell Simmons are among Jimmy's fans.

Lunatarium *rave venue in Brooklyn* `13 A3`

Lunatarium @ DUMBOLUNA, 10 Jay Street • 718 813 8404
>> www.lunatarium.com Open from around 10pm Sat

Little more than a warehouse in Brooklyn's riverfront DUMBO neighborhood, Lunatarium evokes the heady days of NYC's nascent rave culture. Three rooms please the crowd with booming sound and kaleidoscopic lighting. Amazing views of Lower Manhattan make the trek even more worthwhile. **Adm**

Frank's Lounge *DJ bar* `13 B4`

660 Fulton Street • 718 625 9339
>> www.frankscocktaillounge.com Open from 5pm nightly

New York's best classic 1960s soul and R&B jukebox sets the weeknight mood for warm nights of bonhomie among the clientele and the bar staff. Weekends are when DJs play hip-hop and soulful house, and the modest dance floor is jam-packed with Brooklyn's urban style elite.

Zombie Hut *surprisingly refined lounge* `13 B4`

261 Smith Street • 718 855 2736
Open from 5pm nightly

The cartoonish name suggests tiki bar clichés such as plastic palms and grass skirts, but this intimate cocktail lounge on Brooklyn's restaurant row is a dreamier, plusher evocation of Polynesia. Young couples share potent Mai Tais by the stone fireplace, while jazzy electronic music plays.

Gowanus Yacht Club *local gem* `13 B4`
323 Smith Street • 718 246 1321
Open May–Oct: from mid-afternoon daily

Summer in Carroll Gardens means strolls in the park and beers at the Yacht Club. Nautical only in name, this tiny outdoor bar feels as convivial as a suburban backyard. Patio furniture, sizzling burgers and festive lights keep a hip crowd lingering long after their cheap domestic beers have been drained.

Great Lakes *graduates' gathering* `13 C4`
284 5th Avenue • 718 499 3710
Open from 6pm nightly

This spacious Park Slope favorite, with its worn couches, young, amiable crowd, and cracking indie-rock jukebox, suggests a college dormitory lounge for grown-ups. Defend your thesis anew over a Brooklyn Lager while making friends at the bar or out on the sidewalk with the banished smokers.

Bars with Views

For all the millions of dollars sunk into New York's myriad theme bars and luxe lounges, a bar with appealing views will have endless allure. **Sky Bar**, atop the Herald Square outpost of the La Quinta Inn chain, offers ample proof. The 14th-floor terrace compensates for the diminutive size of its split outdoor/indoor patio and undistinguished drinks by providing spectacular views of the Empire State Building, which literally towers above you. It's a popular gathering spot for the neighborhood's young after-work crowd.

The **Boat Basin Café** presents as rarified a setting for drinking beer and quaffing burgers as any in New York: a quirky, spacious complex, with limestone archways in its outdoor courtyard that are reminiscent of a Moorish grotto. Watch sailboats ply the Hudson from your shaded, riverfront patio table along with sociable Upper West Side couples and families. The preferred retreat among young, cosmopolitan travelers keen on seeing and being seen is the new Hotel Gansevoort's aptly named **Plunge Bar**, adjacent to the hotel's rooftop pool. Sleek patio furniture and an unfalteringly beautiful clientele are formidable distractions from the 360-degree views. Equally polished, though not as style obsessed, is the **High Bar** at the revamped Gramercy Hotel. Legendary hotelier Ian Schrager fills the bar's outdoor roof garden with comfy furnishings befitting a living room, which are in turn filled by celebrities from music and film.

As a counterpoint to all this refinement, nothing matches the gritty charm of hoisting your plastic beer cup at the weathered bar of **Ruby's** at Coney Island, where salty breezes and the boardwalk's colorful, wonderful spirit can be enjoyed free of charge. For full addresses, *see pp227–8*.

» *Another café-bar with a superb view over Central Park is The Met's Roof Garden Café (see p172)*

Bars & Clubs

Buttermilk Bar *Brooklynite classic* `13 C5`
557 5th Avenue • 718 788 6297
Open from 6pm nightly

Operated by the same people as Great Lakes *(see p155)*, Buttermilk is remote by Park Slope standards, but worth seeking out for its hip young atmosphere. There's an excellent indie-rock jukebox, ample booth seating, and Brooklyn Brewery beers on tap. A locals' local, Buttermilk's a place to chat with Brooklynites.

Larry Lawrence *easy-going lounge* `13 C2`
295 Grand Street • 718 218 7866
Open from 6pm nightly

This bi-level Williamsburg space flaunts all the polished-wood sophistication of a Manhattan lounge, without the pretension. Downstairs, neighborhood professionals and artists sip reasonably priced Martinis and wines by the glass. Upstairs, smokers enjoy the skyward views from a garden-like atrium.

Volume *brash newcomer to the club scene* `13 B1`
Wythe Ave. & N. 13th St., Williamsburg • 718 388 3588
≫www.volume.tv Check website for events

Volume's stark, cavernous warehouse design provides an ideal setting for massive weekend house music parties. Club kids and Williamsburg artists mix things up at avant-garde electronica showcases, installation artist/DJ collaborations – even dodgeball tournaments. The cover charge varies accordingly.

Trash *gay & lesbian bar* `13 C2`
256 Grand Street • 718 599 1000
Open 5pm–4am nightly

Trash (formerly Luxx, then Toybox) has quickly established itself as the bar of choice for Williamsburg boys and girls who like to rock. Glittery vinyl booths fill with young, flirtatious singles every night, but it's at its most jam-packed on Fridays and Saturdays, when the tiny backroom is used for dancing.

Spuyten Duyvil *Belgian beers/wicked fun* `13 C2`
359 Metropolitan Avenue • 718 963-4140
Open from 5pm nightly

A hundred different bottled beers and six rotating cask ales await beer connoisseurs at this cozy Williamsburg bar. The bright red facade hints at merriment. Inside, you'll find locals sampling rare Belgian brews, snacking on hot *soppressata* (spicy salami) sandwiches, and sharing group toasts.

Galapagos *playhouse for the arty*   `13 B2`

70 North 6th Street • 718 782 5188
›› www.galapagosartspace.com Open from 6pm nightly

Almost every New York neighborhood boasts a space where the values, styles, and habits of its residents fuse into something emblematic. For Williamsburg – Brooklyn's much-hyped bastion of artistic activity – it is Galapagos. Anchoring North 6th Street's minimally appointed bistros, cutting-edge boutiques, and two or three remaining vacant warehouses, the venue gives voice to local musicians, wall space to film-makers and painters, and a great excuse for visitors from farther afield to visit Williamsburg.

A soft magenta spotlight points out the door, beyond which sits a huge reflecting pool and, above

it, a projection screen suspended in the air. Behind this theatrical entrance, the performance and bar area fills up with the neighborhood's hip young members of Brooklyn's arts and music scene. Lushly illuminated with ingenious spotlighting, the intimate stage hosts everything from avant-garde rock bands to risqué burlesque troupes – usually enthusiastically supported by friends in the audience.

Ocularis, a weekly film series, features domestic and international cinema. A film's director or one of its actors is often invited along for a post-screening discussion. Weekends bring DJs spinning electro, rock 'n' roll, soul, breakbeats, and more.

Some nights carry a cover charge, so check the website for information about scheduled events.

›› *For a listing of bars & clubs by category,* see pp227–9

streetlife

Away from the well-known tourist destinations are neighborhoods where New Yorkers shop, eat, and just hang out. To experience the variety and energy of authentic NY life, you need to visit places frequented by recent immigrants as well as born-and-bred New Yorkers. This chapter is the insider's view of where things happen for the locals – snapshots of street culture in a bubbling, bustling metropolis.

Streetlife

1 D4

Lunchtime on Wall Street *Finance District frenzy*

For a quintessential New York phenomenon, head to Wall Street between noon and 2pm on a weekday, and join the fast-paced business crowd for lunch. There are numerous delis and sandwich shops, including **Cosi**, **Pret a Manger**, the **Green Market**, and the **Amish Fine Food Market**. Be warned, though: ordering a sandwich in this high-powered financial district is not for the timid. Decide in advance what you want and be prepared to bark your order to an impatient server, who will yell "next" if you show any hesitation.

Once you've got through this experience, sit on the steps of **Federal Hall**, opposite the **Stock Exchange**. This is a good place for gazing along the concrete canyons. Alternatively, find a space in **Bowling Green Park** (south end of Broadway) or by the river in **Battery Park**. For a little calm after the lunchtime storm, **Trinity Church** (Map 1 D4) offers daily tours at 2pm, and Thursday afternoon music concerts at 1pm.

Canal Street *chopsticks & bargains*

2 E1

A visit to New York isn't complete without a walk along the main thoroughfare of Chinatown. Canal Street is always crowded with cars and people: a jumble of languages making themselves heard within the din.

Street vendors peddle NYC T-shirts, counterfeit Rolex watches, and all manner of cheap knick-knacks. Ignore these and focus instead on the fresh produce, red bean buns, and Chinese paraphernalia in the stores on Canal St. and the quieter side streets of Bayard, Pell, and Mott. The **Chinatown Ice Cream Factory** on Bayard (No. 65) is an essential stop in summer; **HSF** (No. 46) is fantastic for dim sum. **Great NY Noodle Town** on Bowery (No. 281) is another good food stop.

For an insight into the local culture and history, visit the **Museum of Chinese in the Americas**, at the intersection of Mulberry and Bayard. The **Mahayana Buddhist Temple** on Canal St. (No. 133) is another Sino-American establishment that's worth a look; with a bright yellow facade it's impossible to miss.

West 4th Street Courts
on 6th Avenue *sport on the streets* `3 C3`

A simple area of asphalt by West 4th Street has become so popular for basketball that it has been officially recognized by the NYC Parks Department. Casual "pick-up" games occur year-round, and a summer tournament draws semi-pro players from around the world. Get in on the action: grab a hotdog from a street vendor, and cheer the players.

Meatpacking District *gentrified area* `3 A2`

This historic district in the westernmost pocket of West Village, just below 14th Street, is undergoing rapid change. In its 19th-century heyday, the area housed over 200 slaughterhouses and meatpacking plants. A handful of these remain, but most of the meat business has moved up to the Bronx or out of the city altogether. The former meat storage facilities – many of them listed as landmarks – are being reborn as cafés, restaurants, galleries, bars, and chic stores, and the Meatpacking District is now the hangout of models and celebrities. A shiny limousine is more often spotted than a side of beef these days. Remnants of the past can be seen, however, in architectural details. The curious metal awnings over the roads, for example, would have protected the meat as it was being moved off the trucks.

Cobbled **Gansevoort Street** was once a notorious spot for transvestite and she-male prostitutes. Diner/bistro **Florent** *(see p38)* opened on this street in 1985, pioneering the area's path to gentrification. Other established venues include **Cielo** *(see p148)*, a club where dancing is taken seriously, and French bistro **Pastis** *(see p221)*. High-end fashion boutiques **Stella McCartney** *(see p73)*, **Alexander McQueen** *(see p223)*, and **Jeffrey** *(see p74)* are steps away at 14th Street, while designer furniture is available at **Karkula Gallery** and **Vitra** *(see p224 for both)*. The former Gansevoort Docks now form part of the **Hudson River Park**. A waterside path is used by pedestrians, runners, cyclists, and roller-bladers, and leads past some scenic piers.

Tompkins Square Park Dog Run *canine romps* `4 G2`

If Fluffy isn't wearing the latest Burberry sweater, that's okay, so long as he's behaving and not sporting a spiked, pronged, or pinched collar. Toys aren't allowed either because "toys cause fights." These are some of the many rules, carefully displayed at the entrance to the dog run at Tompkins Square Park. This singular spot is the culmination of the American obsession with regulations and the New Yorker's need to give his or her dog room to promenade and socialize.

Once the preserve of drug users and prostitutes, the park is decidedly bourgeois now – the orderly dog run and its prim owners are a testament to that. Once you have gazed at the dog-walking spectacle over the fence (no people without dogs allowed in, and vice versa), stroll along 9th Street and avenues A and B. In contrast to the dog run, these roads have a funkier vibe. Notable cafés include **Itzocan** (438 E. 9th St.), and **Rue B** and **DT–UT** on Avenue B (Nos. 188 & 41, respectively).

Chelsea Flea Market & Union Square Markets *deals for steals* `3 D1`

Outdoor Market open 8am–5pm Sat & Sun • Union Square Greenmarket open 8am–6pm Mon, Wed, Fri & Sat • Holiday Market open from day after Thanksgiving until Christmas Eve

Chelsea's weekend flea and antiques markets are prime for finding anything from belt buckles and old buttons to botanical drawings, maps, vintage clothing, axes, and lace. The **Outdoor Market** on the northwest corner of 24th Street and 6th Avenue is a mélange of curios and furniture. **Antiques Garage** and **Antiques Annex** are geared more towards antique treasures, but also harbor a fair share of junk. Both are worth a browse; there's a $1 admission to get into the Annex. A few blocks further south, **Union Square Greenmarket** showcases farmers' stalls offering fruit, vegetables, fish, meat, and baked goods. During winter, the **Holiday Market** takes over – a mine of handmade jewelry, T-shirts, candles, massage oil, paintings, and hats.

Subway Passages: Grand Central to Times Square 6 F2 *underground music*

Grand Central Station and Times Square are connected by an underground Shuttle train, and the subway passages at either end of the short route are abuzz with New York energy, as bustling workers swarm through the passageways on their way to and from work. In these tunnels you'll also find excellent musicians, their performances good enough to make even the most determined commuter slow down to catch a few bars. While you may come across the occasional "rogue" performer – who'll set up and play wherever there's space – most are part of the MTA's Music Under New York program. The scheme promotes a variety of music, including jazz, Cajun, African, classical, Asian, and bluegrass. A stringent audition process held each year ensures that a high standard is maintained. Look for the authorized performers, who display an orange and black "Music Under New York" banner.

125th Street *gateway to Harlem* 11 D3

One of the main roads in Harlem, 125th Street came to prominence during the Harlem Renaissance of the 1920s, when it became synonymous with dancing and jazz clubs. Since then the street has been the main commercial center for Harlem's predominantly black community and, over time, has provided the backdrop to civil rights activism and a creative flourishing of music, painting, literature, and drama.

Having gone through a prolonged period of economic depression and attendant crime problems, 125th street is back to being a vibrant thoroughfare again, with a mix of gentrified boutiques, mainstream chains, and street vendors. Some would argue that the soul of Harlem has moved to smaller side streets, but 125th remains the hub. For tours of Harlem, check out **Harlem Spirituals**, **Radical Walking Tours**, or **Big Apple Jazz Tours** *(see p231)*. See if you can catch a gospel service at the Lenox Lounge *(see p129)* or some Southern-style cooking at **Amy Ruth's** *(see p220)*.

>> *For information about Harlem's famous Apollo Theater,* see p128

Brooklyn Heights Promenade
13 A4

sublime views of Manhattan

This is one of the best vantage points for a panorama of Manhattan. It's also a great place to enjoy a stroll – alone, hand in hand with a lover, or lead in hand with your dog. Grab an espresso at **Connecticut Muffin** on Montague (the main commercial street) and head towards the water to get onto the walkway.

A favorite spot for both locals and visitors, the promenade offers a mix of calm (despite the fact that it overlooks the Brooklyn to Queens expressway), and excitement – a thrill instilled by the awesome view of Manhattan that confronts you every time you look across the water.

The strip isn't very long, but you can combine the stroll with a perusal of Brooklyn Heights and its beautifully maintained brownstones. Back on Montague Street, there are several decent places to eat, such as **Theresa's** restaurant (No. 80), which offers tasty and authentic Polish fare alongside grilled cheese and hamburgers. Retail stores include **Heights Books** (No. 109), which specializes in second-hand publications.

Alternatively, you can take a different route from the promenade and walk along Columbia Heights to the Fulton Ferry landing, where you can buy an ice cream at the **Brooklyn Ice Cream Factory** before catching a water taxi over to Manhattan. To extend your walk further, cross via the Brooklyn Bridge.

Red Hook Food Stalls
spice & soccer 13 B5

Corner of Bay and Clinton streets
Sat & Sun (end of April to first weekend in Oct)

Weekends in Red Hook's playing fields are dedicated to soccer, socializing, soaking up rays, and working one's way through as much delicious, home-cooked Latin American food as possible. Mexico, Honduras, Guatemala, and Colombia are all well represented. Try out your Spanish, and be willing to experiment.

Bedford Avenue *Williamsburg's heart* `13 C2`

Williamsburg is a compact area in north Brooklyn, packed with the accessories of bourgeois bohemia – funky cafés, hip bars, renovated lofts, fashion boutiques, and a few more trendy cafés. And Bedford Avenue is at its pulsating heart. This is an area that has changed dramatically in the last ten years, and some bemoan the arrival of Brooklyn's hip young things, who have pitched camp, placed their laptops on the counters of every café and bar in sight, and by their very presence have raised the rents. However, others are grateful for the attention the neighborhood is receiving and are happy to see some of the disused factories converted into apartments, stores, and clubs.

It is true that some of the grit may have been replaced by something funkier, lighter, and more affluent, but it is possible to find an earthy feel to the neighborhood once you look beyond the iPods and messenger bags (which you can pick up for a snip at **Brooklyn Industries**, No. 162). This is an eclectic locale, incorporating a Hasidic community in South Williamsburg, a profusion of artists, and a Polish contingent that has spilled over from Greenpoint. The Polish influence can be seen and tasted in places such as **Cukiernia** (a Polish bakery at No. 223) and **S & B Polish Restaurant** (No. 194).

The Bedford Avenue strip is most lively between North 6th and 10th streets. For a cool coffee stop, try **Verb Café** (No. 218), and watch the locals sitting at rickety wooden tables, indulging in java, listening to off-beat music, and playing checkers. The Verb is connected to a mini-mall that houses a variety of establishments, including an Internet café, the famed **Bedford Cheese Shop**, a vintage clothing store, and the bookstore **Spoonbill and Sugartown** *(see p88)*. Try **Bliss Café** (No. 191) for veggie delights, or a slice of delicious pizza at **Anna Maria's** (No. 179). Noteworthy stops are **Metaphors** (No. 195) for women's clothing and **Spacial** *(see p89)* for interior design. Check out the **Brooklyn Lager Brewery** (79 N. 11th St.), and take a free tour on Saturday (last tour 4pm) or indulge in Friday Night's Happy Hour (6–10pm).

For the art scene in Williamsburg, see p108

Brighton Beach

Boardwalk *sea, sand, and snacks*

Ⓜ B, Q to Brighton Beach; F, D, Q to Coney Island/Stillwell Ave.

The Russian enclave of Brighton Beach at the southern tip of Brooklyn, also known as "Little Odessa," has much to offer for a day trip from Manhattan. The Brighton Beach Boardwalk is alive with Slavic languages, chess games, the smell of the ocean, and a whiff of borscht wafting from one of the boardwalk cafés. For the area's best food and prices, however, go off the boardwalk and eat "inland" at **Café Glechik** (3159 Coney Island Avenue) or **Café Arbat** (306 Brighton Beach Avenue). Try the *vareniki* (similar to *pierogi* or ravioli) and drink a wholesome fruit compote. If you want to pick up snacks to take back to the waterfront, **M & I International Food Market**
(249 Brighton Beach Avenue) has an impressive selection of Eastern European delicacies.

The boardwalk provides a vantage point for a lovely beach and water view. If you walk all the way along it, you'll reach Coney Island, where you can't miss the **New York Aquarium** (www.nyaquarium.com) and **Astroland** (www.astroland.com). This amusement park has the famed and rickety-looking Cyclone rollercoaster, which now has National Landmark status.

For the full Brighton Beach/Coney Island experience, have a **Nathan's Hotdog** from the original outpost on the corner of Surf and Stillwell. This is where the July 4th Hotdog Eating Championships take place. If you visit in mid- to late June, check www.coneyisland.com to find out when New York's aquatic version of Mardi Gras, the Mermaid Parade, struts down Surf Avenue.

Roosevelt Avenue *vibrancy and spice*

Ⓜ **Roosevelt Avenue subway station is served by the 7, E, F, V, G and R trains**

Roosevelt Avenue is one of the main thoroughfares through the Queens neighborhood of Jackson Heights, and is a veritable smorgasbord of cultures and food, including Colombian, Chinese, Indian, Pakistani, Korean, and Mexican. As soon as you leave the subway station, your olfactory sense starts working overtime to decipher the wafts of exotic ingredients that are being mixed in various kitchens. The area may lack aesthetic appeal, but it compensates in variety and vitality.

Along the adjacent 74th Street, you'll find stores full of phonecards, toys, food, and confections. For a meal try **Jackson Diner** (No. 37), or visit **Patel Brothers Market** (No. 27) to see myriad fresh and dried Asian spices and vegetables. Also on 74th Street, you'll find dazzlingly intricate jewelry as well as colorful saris and beautiful silk cloth in **Sahil Sari Palace** (Nos. 37–55).

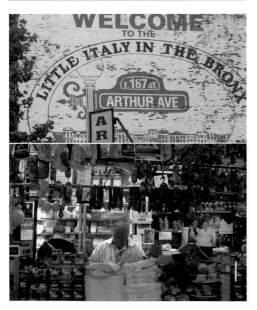

Arthur Avenue *a mini Little Italy*

Ⓜ **4 or D subway train to Fordham Rd then No.12 bus east; 2 or 5 subway train to Pelham Parkway then No.12 bus west**
≫ **www.arthuravenuebronx.com**

Another testament to the New York patchwork of ethnic communities, Arthur Avenue, in the north Bronx, is suffused with southern Italian traditions. The strip offering the best in Italian produce is between 187th Street and Crescent Avenue. Here you can find some of the freshest and tastiest Italian food on this side of the Atlantic. The **Egidio Pastry Shop** (622 E. 187th St.) sells scrumptious chocolate cakes and excellent *cannoli* (deep-fried tubes of pastry with a sweetened ricotta filling), along with superb espresso. You can buy the best home-made pasta and ravioli (rolled out and cut right in front of you) from **Borgatti's** (632 E. 187th St.). Shops and stalls tease the senses with an array of salamis, parmigianos, pastas, mozzarella, and seafood. Italian is spoken widely on the street and there's a relaxed, family-oriented vibe. *Mangia!*

≫ *Combine a visit to Arthur Avenue with a trip to the Botanical Gardens or Wave Hill (see p175)*

havens

In New York, there's no need to leave the city limits in order to find a piece of nirvana. Along with parks and gardens, there are yoga centers, spas, churches, and tea rooms to retreat to. Vantage points at the tops of the city's towers provide inspirational views. And out at its farthest reaches – whether at Wave Hill in the Bronx or in the marshlands of Jamaica Bay – you may well discover an unexpected "wild" side to New York.

The River Project *waterside pleasures* `1 B1`
Pier 26, off West St. • 212 233 3030
>> www.riverproject.org Open 11am–5pm daily

Just a few steps from Tribeca, this "estuarium" and research center is a perfect place to come for a deep breath or to confess to the marine gods for having just eaten sushi at neighboring Nobu *(see p38)*. Watch the boats and learn a bit about the local marine life from informative displays and the friendly volunteer staff.

Bliss SoHo *top-notch spa* `3 D4`
568 Broadway, 2nd Floor • 212 219 8970
>> www.blissworld.com
Open 9:30am–8:30pm Mon–Fri; 9:30am–6:30pm Sat

Forget about the outside world for a couple of hours, slip on a soft robe and slippers, and indulge in home-made brownies, apples, and fresh juices while you wait for your chosen treatment. Bliss has two locations in New York, but the SoHo spot – the Bliss flagship – is the one to seek out. Both men and women are pampered here, in a space reminiscent of a ship's interior. Treatments cater for the whole body, from head to toes, but the Bliss forte is facials.
The trademarked Triple Oxygen Treatment and Fully Loaded facials are extremely popular with beauty-conscious New Yorkers. Alternatively, book a basic facial and add on treatments from an amazing à-la-carte menu, which offers masks, lip plumping, and capillary zapping. The changing rooms have saunas, steam rooms, and showers for further relaxation.

Angel Feet *divine foot relief* `3 B3`
77 Perry Street • 212 924 3576
Open 10am–9pm Mon, Tue, Thu & Fri, 10am–8pm Sat & Sun

As the name of this jewel-box sized basement room suggests, a reflexology session here is truly heavenly. The treatment rids feet of soreness and is given while you sit in one of two plush chairs that take up most of the intimate space. Relaxing music, candles, and a fragrant water mist for the feet add to the experience.

Jivamukti Yoga
Center *for body and spirit*
`4 E3`

404 Lafayette Street, 3rd floor • 212 353 0214
>> www.jivamuktiyoga.com Open 8am–9pm Mon–Thu,
8am–6:30pm Fri, 9am–6:30 pm Sat & Sun

Calm your senses and align your posture with one of
a vast selection of hatha yoga classes, offered
throughout the day. Jivamukti, with two Manhattan
locations, has made yoga accessible to New York's
masses. You can simply drop in for a class or join an
open meditation session, but it's generally worth
calling ahead to check that space is available.

Throughout the building, the aroma of fragrant oils,
mellow music, mood lighting, and a soothing
waterfall help the process of relaxation. Massage
treatments, workshops, lectures, and yoga
demonstrations are held regularly. Take note: the
etiquette at the center dictates that shoes are to
be taken off before you enter the clean, loft-like
studio areas and changing rooms.

Wild Lily Tea Room *zen relaxation*
`5 B5`

511a West 22nd Street • 212 691 2258
>> www.wildlilytearoom.com Open 11am–10pm Tue–Sun

Take time out from shopping, gallery hopping, and
sightseeing at a place that takes tea very seriously.
There's no need to be stressed out by the range of
teas available; if you'd like to venture away from a
regular teabag, staff will guide you through a wide
selection of loose black tea blends, and jasmine,
ginseng, green, barley, and berry teas.

With a maximum capacity of 32 people, Wild Lily
isn't big, but the high ceilings and tiny goldfish pond
in the front create a fresh, airy, and Zen-like ambience.
As you sip your tea, enjoy the simplicity of the Japanese
decor, and the neat bento boxes, trays, and tea sets.
The food is fresh, inventive, and tasty, encompassing
traditional British fare, such as scones with clotted
cream, as well as more intriguing concoctions, such
as pea and yogurt soup, and green-tea cake. If you
feel like something stronger, sake is also available.

>> *For a selection of other fine tea rooms,* see p31

The Spa at the Mandarin Oriental *luxurious respite*
7 C4

80 Columbus Circle at 60th St., 35th Floor • 212 805 8880
>> www.mandarinoriental.com Open 9–9 Mon–Fri, 9–7 Sat & Sun

It's not cheap, but this spa is worth the expense! Splurge on wonderful body treatments, including exotically named massages such as Life Dance and Balinese Body. Herbal infusions are prepared daily by a chef (and are free), and almonds and dried fruits are offered in the Tea Lounge, which has stunning views of the Hudson River and the West Side of Manhattan. The decor is inspired by crisp Asian simplicity, elegance, and style: tiny candles line the carefully appointed hallway, and orchid buds decorate surface tops. Be sure to take advantage of the many amenities available as part of a visit to the spa, such as the Vitality Pool, the amethyst-crystal steam room (where eucalyptus oil is available to soften the skin), and the "rainforest experience" shower. Round it all off with some quality time in the Relaxing Room.

Top of the Tower @ Beekman Tower Hotel *26th-floor calm*
6 G1

3 Mitchell Place, at 49th St. & 1st Ave. • 212 980 4796
Open 4pm–1am Sun–Thu, 4pm–2am Fri & Sat

A jewel of a space with wonderful views and a full cocktail menu. The calm atmosphere, unhurried service, and superb vantage point take you far away from the street-level clamor. Get a table by the window, from where the roof slopes vertiginously downward.

The Iris and B. Gerald Cantor Roof Garden *art & leisure*
8 E1

The Metropolitan Museum of Art, 1000 5th Avenue, at 82nd St.
>> www.metmuseum.org Open May–late Fall: 10am–4:30 Tue–Thu & Sun, 10am–8:30pm Fri & Sat

Gorgeous views, sculpture in the foreground, and wine or cappuccino to lift your spirits. The joys of an elevated outdoor space are combined with art from the Met's collection and the whole of Central Park as a backdrop.

Conservatory Gardens at Central Park *floral sanctuary*

`10 E2`

Entrance on 5th Avenue and 105th Street • 212 360 2766
>> www.centralparknyc.org Open 8am–dusk daily

Wildflowers, pruned rare roses, trimmed hedges, trees, and a thousand other floral delights are carefully arranged within these 6 acres, the most studiously tended area in Central Park. It's no wonder that New York brides scramble for permits for wedding ceremonies within these garden walls, or that school teachers are keen to bring classes for story-time sessions.

The central fountain is glorious in spring, when the wisteria that surrounds it bursts with purple, violet, pink, and white blossoms. Two more fountains are set closer to Fifth Avenue, one encircled by concentric rings of flowers. The fragrance, peace, and quiet of this garden is perfect for sitting on a bench, writing postcards, and taking time to reflect. There are free tours (rain or shine) on Saturdays from April to October; meet at Vanderbilt Gate on Fifth and 105th Street at 11am.

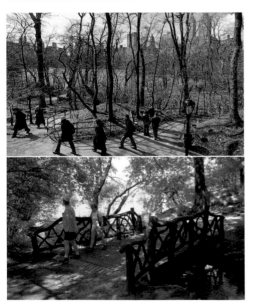

The Ramble at Central Park *green mazes*

`7 D2`

Enter via 5th Ave. or Central Park West between 72nd and 80th
>> www.centralparknyc.org

The Ramble is the perfect place to get lost in a web of winding paths which cross 36 acres of wonderfully dense wooded areas, encompassing ponds, small bridges, and rocky outcrops. The wilderness factor in this pocket of Central Park is so great that the National Audubon Society has ranked the Ramble as one of the top 15 bird-watching sites in the whole of the U.S., putting it among National Parks such as Yosemite and geographical regions like the Everglades. If you visit early in the morning, you'll see die-hard birders at their regular spots, sporting binoculars and sipping cups of coffee or hot chocolate. The rest of the day brings a more diverse crowd, most of them with a more leisurely interest in a lunchtime stroll or a rendezvous. Note that the Central Park website refers to The Ramble within the Great Lawn section of the park.

>> *The Ramble is a great place for a wander after visiting the Met* (see p103)

The Rotunda at The Pierre *traditional tea*

8 E4

The Pierre Hotel, 2 East 61st Street • 212 838 8000
Afternoon tea served 3–5:30pm daily

This is New York's best spot for afternoon tea. The atmosphere is gracious and welcoming, with a high, domed ceiling above, and linen and fresh flowers at your table. Choose a three- or five-course tea, depending on your appetite for sandwiches and cakes.

The Cathedral Church of St. John the Divine *glorious peace*

9 B1

1047 Amsterdam Avenue at 112th Street • 212 316 7540
>> www.stjohndivine.org Open 7–6 Mon–Sat, 7–7 Sun

Begun in 1892 but still unfinished, St. John's will be one of the largest cathedrals in the world when completed. However, its size and huge vaulted ceilings do not intimidate; rather, the church envelops you, and encourages a sense of well-being. Smaller chapels are reserved for prayer during the day, and services are held in the nave on Sunday at 11am and 6pm, with the Cathedral Choir in full voice. The organ, however, was damaged in a fire in 2001, and is awaiting repair once sufficient funds are raised.

Stained glass, intricately carved altars, and fine stonework is found throughout the cathedral, alongside modern interpretations of religious icons. These include a three-paneled, white and gold-leaf altarpiece by the late graphic designer and artist Keith Haring. As you walk down the central aisle, look up at the stunning Great Rose Window, an extraordinary creation made from over 10,000 pieces of stained glass in patterns dominated by hues of vibrant royal blue and calming indigo.

Next to the cathedral is a **Children's Sculpture Garden**, which exhibits a selection of bronze animal sculptures created by school children aged between 5 and 18. After your visit, head to the **Hungarian Pastry Shop** across the street on Amsterdam Avenue. There you can collect your thoughts, have a snack, and mingle with the erudite Columbia University set.

Wave Hill *escape to an estate*

675 West 252nd Street • 718 549 3200 • Ⓜ Riverdale
>> **www.wavehill.org** Open Spring & Summer: 9am–5:30pm
Tue–Sun (to 9pm Wed); Fall & Winter: 9am–4:30pm Tue–Sun

It's hard to believe that you're still within NYC limits
(the Bronx no less) when you visit the well-situated
and beautifully laid out garden and cultural center of
Wave Hill. Part of Wave Hill's mission is to connect
people with nature; to this end it presents impressive
horticultural and art exhibits, and offers an array of
environmental workshops, and musical and literary
performances. Regular events include story telling,
poetry readings, and chamber music and jazz
concerts. T'ai chi is taught in the grounds too.

The café at Wave Hill House is a great spot, partly
for the sustenance it offers, but mostly for the exceptional views. For another great view, walk along one
of the paths through the white-columned pergola
covered in flowering plants, and look downriver to the
suspension cables of the George Washington Bridge.

Prospect Park *the lungs of Brooklyn* `13 D5`

Wollman Rink: 718 282 7789; Prospect Park Zoo: 718 399
7339; Kensington Stables: 718 972 4588
>> www.prospectpark.org

Designed by the dynamic duo of landscape design
Olmstead and Vaux (the planners of Central Park),
Prospect Park is a lesser-known but equally enjoyable
green playground for New Yorkers – Brooklynites in
particular. It's a place to cycle, run, stroll, picnic, bird-
watch, and skate, and every season has something to
offer. Winter is the time for ice-skating at the
Wollman Rink; summer brings colorful local festivals
and concerts at the Bandshell. Prospect Park Zoo is a
year-round family favorite, and other perennial
attractions include horse-back riding on a track by
Kensington Stables, and birding at the beautiful
Audubon Center (www.prospectparkaudubon.org).
Locals often use the park drive, also known as the
loop, for bike riding, roller-blading, and running.
Check the website for a list of seasonal events.

Brooklyn Botanic Garden *paradise* `13 D4`
1000 Washington Avenue • 718 623 7200
>> **www.bbg.org** Open 8am–6pm Tue–Fri, 10am–6pm Sat & Sun; closes at 4:30pm Oct–Mar

Your olfactory and visual senses will be sharpened in the wonderfully maintained BBG. A visit here may be rewarded by bluebells in late spring or the scent of roses in summer, while May's Cherry Blossom Festival will transport you to the orchards of Asia *(see p10)*.

Jamaica Bay Wildlife Refuge *an antidote to city life* `2 C4`
Crossbay Boulevard, Broad Channel • 718 318 4340
Ⓜ **A train to Broad Channel** Open sunrise to sunset daily

This wild habitat in the huge bay south of JFK airport is where New Yorkers go to escape the intensity of the city and delight instead in tranquillity, bird-watching, and walking. The train takes an hour from Manhattan, allowing you to adjust to a different pace and prepare for another world. The journey is interesting as well: before the train reaches Broad Channel stop, it travels along a stretch of track surrounded by marsh and water on either side, which heightens a sense of remoteness.

Walking to the refuge from the stop is straight-forward. Go along Noel Road until you reach Crossbay Boulevard and turn right; the refuge entrance will be on your left after 10–15 minutes. On the way, you'll pass waterfront houses on stilts and wooden platforms.

The visitor center has a small but informative interpretive area explaining the history and features of the refuge, including the abundant wildflowers. Jamaica Bay is a regular rest stop for migrating birds, and teems with airborne life as thousands of shore, land, and water birds flock to its wetlands; over 320 species have been spotted. Benches along the main path allow you to sit, observe, and listen to bird songs. Particularly captivating, though, is the contrast of freshwater ponds, marshes, and wildlife set against the distant skyline of Manhattan.

For more peaceful corners of New York, browse >> **www.enewyork.dk.com**

Noguchi Sculpture
Museum *intimacy, solitude, design*
32–7 Vernon Boulevard, Long Island City (entrance on
33rd Road) • 718 204 7088 • Ⓜ N & W trains to Broadway
≫ www.noguchi.org Open year round; closed Mon & Tue

Several million dollars-worth of renovation work has
ensured that this museum (which reopened in 2004
after a two-and-a-half-year closure) will continue to
inspire. It has an intimacy that's not often found in art
spaces; the renovations have not contributed to a
"blockbuster experience" in the manner of the downtown museum revamps, but rather have attempted to
refine the concrete and wood space.

This Museum is a tribute to the Japanese-American
sculptor, landscaper, and set designer Isamu Noguchi,
who established a studio in this Queens neighborhood in 1961. Noguchi created beautiful pieces made
of materials such as wood, marble, basalt, and metal,
and his sculptures are in a multitude of shapes and
textures. The museum is designed to eliminate

distractions while you contemplate the work, allowing
the art of Noguchi to be the sole focus of attention.
The space – its aesthetic a refined, pared-back
Modernism – contains several galleries; some are
exposed to the elements, others are fully enclosed.
There is also a garden, with a majestic, fully grown
Katsura tree and a wonderfully subtle fountain
sculpture. At its center is what appears to be a
bottomless pool.

The park is a place to reflect, to relax, and to
appreciate art without having to fight a crowd or have
museum attendants hovering over your shoulder.
There's an on-site café for light snacks, and a store
that stocks a wide range of design books and
Noguchi's trademark rice-paper lamps.

While in the area, it's also worth dropping by the
Socrates Sculpture Park, a little further north on
Vernon Boulevard. On the bank of the East River, the
park exhibits temporary installations of sculpture by
international contemporary artists.

hotels

The independent hotel scene is stronger in New York than in any other major city. More than half the hotels are not affiliated to a national or international chain, which means that they are particularly good at providing individuality, character, and style. Rooms don't come cheap, but there are deals to be had with a little planning. Check hotel and reservation agency websites to get the best deals.

ROMANTIC HIDEAWAYS	GASTRONOMIC	LIVE LIKE A LOCAL

Soho House New York
29–35 9th Avenue
Enjoy the rooftop pool, soak in a generously sized tub, or romp around your private "playroom" – perfect for romantic trysts. *(See p184)*

>> *www.in-newyorkmag.com lists hotel restaurants in the city.*

Bevy's SoHo Loft
70 Mercer Street
With Bevy and fellow guests for company, a stay here is like sharing a spacious apartment right in the middle of SoHo. *(See p182)*

St. Regis
2 East 55th Street
Plush and luxurious, St. Regis is a place to pamper and be pampered. Excellent bathrooms and great service. *(See p186)*

Harlem Flophouse
242 West 123rd Street
The fun, jazzy vibe of the Flophouse will instantly make you feel part of New York. Interior details evoke early 20th-century Harlem. *(See p190)*

Bed & Breakfast on the Park
113 Prospect Park West, Brooklyn
This small hotel is just steps away from lovely Prospect Park. Its top-floor room has prime views and a four-poster bed. *(See p191)*

Hotel Wales
1295 Madison Avenue
The place to stay for a delicious and hearty breakfast, including fresh scones and fluffy omelets, at Sarabeth's Kitchen. *(See p191)*

1871 House
East 62nd Street
Many suites or studios here come with a kitchenette and fireplace, so you can pretend you've got your own pied-à-terre. *(See p188)*

The Mark
25 East 77th Street
With an extensive wine list and fine French-American cuisine, The Mark's restaurant offers a refined dining experience. *(See p189)*

Union Street B&B
405 Union Street, Brooklyn
A warm ambience and well-stocked bookshelves (and even a welcome for pet dogs) make this B&B feel like a family home. *(See p191)*

Mercer Hotel
147 Mercer Street
If you can tear yourself away from the hotel's elegant rooms and deep tubs, the Mercer Kitchen is a fashionable haunt for fine dining. *(See p182)*

>> *www.affordablenewyorkcity.com lists B&Bs and fully furnished apartments. These offer good value for stays of over a week and even better value if you are in town for a month or more.*

BEST OF THE BARGAINS	STYLE STATEMENTS	GREAT LOCATION

Washington Square Hotel
103 Waverly Place
Super budget prices for clean, if flowery, rooms in a desirable Village location. Breakfast is also included in the price. *(See p183)*

>> *The hippest areas are the easy-going downtown neighbourhoods, such as SoHo and the Village, but the largest concentration of hotels is midtown, close to the theaters and department stores.*

Chelsea Inn
46 West 17th Street
The Chelsea Inn has low rates and kitchenettes in the rooms. It is set in a great location two blocks from Union Square. *(See p185)*

>> *Hotel prices will usually be quoted without tax. Be sure to check the figure once City and State taxes are added.*

Four Seasons
57 East 57th Street
Ideal for shopping sorties on Madison Avenue – afterwards you can drop your bags and put up your feet in the luxurious spa. *(See p188)*

Chelsea Lodge
318 West 20th Street
A spotless lodge, with wooden floors, TVs, and shower stalls in every room. Toilets are shared, hence the bargain rates. *(See p185)*

Hudson
356 West 58th Street
The spectacular courtyard, roof terrace and other lounging spaces here were created by Philippe Starck and the hotelier Ian Schrager. *(See p187)*

The Stanhope
995 5th Avenue
Right opposite the Metropolitan Museum of Art, The Stanhope is also very handy for the space and greenery of Central Park. *(See p190)*

60 Thompson
60 Thompson Street
Comfort and style are the themes throughout. How many hotels have chairs specially designed and named for them? *(See p182)*

Abingdon Guest House
13 8th Avenue
Feel the pulse of the West Village right outside the door of these stately townhouses. Each room is individually decorated. *(See p183)*

Morgans
237 Madison Avenue
The original "lifestyle hotel," with design touches that create a magical, understated aesthetic throughout. *(See p187)*

W New York, Union Square
201 Park Avenue South
Just off Union Square, you'll be within easy walking distance of such funky neighborhoods as West Village, Chelsea, and Gramercy. *(See p185)*

Bevy's SoHo Loft *three great rooms* `3 D5`

70 Mercer Street • 212 431 8214
>> www.sohobevy.com

Bevy – known to many as the "SoHo Mom" – is a real character, who relishes lively conversation with her guests. Her loft is a funky, renovated industrial space, filled with paintings and colorful fabrics. There are just three rooms, but each is characterful and spacious, with very high ceilings. Great location. **Moderate**

SoHo Grand Hotel *pet-friendly place* `3 D5`

310 West Broadway • 800 965 3000
>> www.sohogrand.com

Pets are made very welcome here – indeed, if you haven't brought your own furry friend, you'll be offered a fish as a room companion. A selection of CDs is also provided, and you can buy the fish and discs if you like them. As for the 360 rooms: some are small, but all the beds are big and comfy. **Cheap/Moderate**

Mercer Hotel *minimalist finesse* `3 D4`

147 Mercer Street • 212 966 6060
>> www.mercerhotel.com

In a solid 1890 building near the Village, the Mercer focuses on style and service. The 75 rooms are light and minimally furnished, and the bathrooms come with large soaking tubs and Swedish Face Stockholm cosmetics. The Mercer Kitchen restaurant is worth a visit, and a fine spot for celebrity spotting. **Expensive**

60 Thompson *SoHo taste* `3 C5`

60 Thompson Street • 877 431 0400
>> www.60thompson.com

60 Thompson has 100 rooms and suites, all with music and DVD systems. The setting is modern, with a sleek interior design, plush bedding, and marble bathrooms. Check out the high-backed 60 Thompson chairs, designed exclusively for the hotel by Thomas O'Brien of Aero Studios. **Expensive**

Tribeca Grand Hotel *hip & stylish* `3 C5`

2 Avenue of the Americas • 212 519 6600
>> www.tribecagrand.com

Built in 2000, this hotel attracts a cool clientele. All rooms
lead off from the Church Lounge, the hub of its atrium-style
layout. The guest rooms match simple, modern design with top
technology in the form of great sound systems and high-speed
Internet access. The hotel offers the same deal on fish and CDs
as its older sister, the Soho Grand *(see opposite)*. **Expensive**

Washington Square Hotel *location, location* `3 D3`

103 Waverly Place • 800 222 0418
>> www.wshotel.com

This budget option is in a prime Village location, close
to many attractions by foot or subway. The rooms are
a little floral and frilly, but the lobby has a smart, Art
Deco style. Complimentary continental breakfast
makes this even better value for downtown. **Cheap**

Abingdon Guest House *Village comfort* `3 B2`

13 8th Avenue • 212 243 5384
>> www.abingdonguesthouse.com

Two landmark townhouses in West Village have been
converted into a guest house with nine rooms. Each
room has its own style, as suggested by the names –
"Martinique," "Ambassador," and so on. Prices vary
according to size and decor. Light breakfasts and
lunches are served at its Brewbar café. **Moderate**

Old Establishments

With an enviable location at the foot of Central
Park, the **Plaza Hotel** maintains its reputation for
providing the ultimate in service and comfort. The
Carlyle on Madison Avenue has been appreciated
since the 1930s for its understated elegance,
superb service, and striking Art Deco design. The
hotel's Café Carlyle is popular with a well-heeled
Upper East Side crowd. No stranger to scandal and
creativity, the **Hotel Chelsea** has a thousand stories
to tell. Each room and apartment is different, and
much of the building is occupied by long-stay residents. A great slice of bohemia, the Chelsea has
welcomed many writers and musicians, from Mark
Twain and Tennessee Williams to Bob Dylan and
Sid Vicious. For individual hotel details, *see p229.*

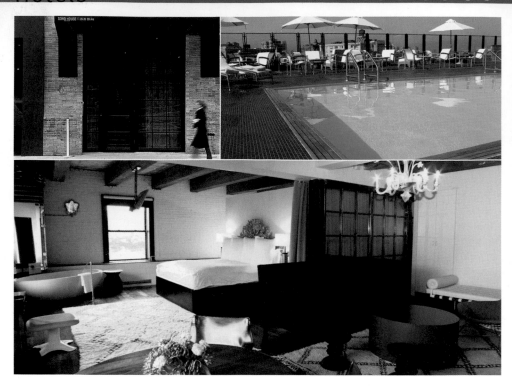

Soho House

3 A2

New York *chic hotel in the Meatpacking District*

29–35 9th Avenue • 212 627 9800

»» www.sohohouse.com

Blink and you'll miss the entrance to Soho House – a level of discretion you'd expect of a hotel that doubles as a private members' club. Staying at the hotel gives you access to the club facilities, which include a fitness room, a private screening room, a restaurant and bar, a drawing room and library, a games room with pool table and pinball, and an elegantly comfortable club room. The Cowshed Spa offers a variety of healthy treatments and a soothing environment. The "Cowshed" products are produced by hand in the UK, home of the original, London Soho House. The prime facility, however, is the rooftop pool. Although not a place for serious laps, the pool is great for a quick dip, and the deck around it has chaise longues, umbrellas, tables, chairs, and a full bar with light snacks. The roof area is open year round, with a heated marquee in winter.

The comfortable guest rooms are classified according to size, and are labeled (in ascending order) playpen, playroom, playhouse, and playground. Mini-bars are stocked with all sorts of temptations, including Ben & Jerry's ice cream in the freezer, and chilled Martini glasses. The decor is an eclectic mix, with touches of luxury such as freestanding, rolltop bathtubs. The rooms remain functional, however, with state-of-the-art gadgets such as surround-sound entertainment systems and wireless Internet access throughout the whole building. **Expensive**

Maritime Hotel *nautical swank* `3 A1`
363 West 16th Street • 212 242 4300
>> www.themaritimehotel.com

The rooms here have a maritime theme, complete with porthole windows and an appealing blue-and-white color scheme for the bedding. Rates are reasonable, and the location is great for Chelsea and the Meatpacking District. There's 24-hour room service, a roof terrace, and a sushi bar. **Moderate**

Chelsea Lodge *fresh, clean & friendly* `3 B1`
318 West 20th Street • 800 373 1116
>> www.chelsealodge.com

Toilets are shared at this low-priced lodge, but each of the 22 refurbished rooms has wooden floors and high ceilings, and is well appointed, with a shower stall, sink, TV, and double bed. You also have the option to pay extra for a suite with more amenities. The place is bright and on a quiet side street. **Cheap**

Chelsea Inn *affordable charm* `3 C1`
46 West 17th Street • 800 640 6469
>> www.chelseainn.com

Ask for a quiet room at the back of this renovated 19th-century townhouse in a great downtown location. The budget-priced rooms all have kitchenettes and TVs, and the shared bathrooms are decorated with charming, colorful painted murals. Continental breakfast is included in the price. **Cheap**

W New York, Union Square *stylish* `3 D1`
201 Park Avenue South • 212 253 9119
>> www.whotels.com

The signature style of the "W" hotel chain involves subdued lighting and touches of purple in the otherwise minimalist white decor. Rooms are sleek, with comfy feather beds, and the service is impeccable. The dramatic lobby has a soaring stair-case and areas of sand, grass, and marble. **Moderate**

>> *The price categories used are based on a hotel's rack rate, but discount deals are frequently available*

Bryant Park Hotel *high-tech & colorful* `6 E2`
40 West 40th Street • 877 640 9300
>> www.bryantparkhotel.com

The plush red of the lobby desks and rug is the first thing you notice. Throughout the hotel, the simple lines of Scandinavian-inspired furniture are juxtaposed nicely with Tibetan rugs and cashmere throws. Rooms have super sound systems as well as Internet access, and the bathtubs are generously sized. **Moderate**

Royalton *theatrical style* `6 E2`
44 West 44th Street • 800 606 6090
>> www.ianschragerhotels.com

In the heart of the Theater District, this Ian Schrager hotel *(see also Morgans, opposite)* has a stunning lobby that's almost like a runway. Sit on the chairs at the side and socialize, or slip into the Round Bar for cocktails and people-watching. For the best views, try to get a deal on a deluxe room or suite. **Moderate**

St. Regis *Beaux Arts beauty* `8 E5`
2 East 55th Street • 800 759 7550
>> www.stregis.com

Built in 1904 by John Jacob Astor IV, this luxurious hotel is meant to be a home away from home. The rooms even have doorbells. Original details are mixed with modern amenities, including flat-screen TVs in the bathrooms and high-speed Internet access. The hallways are wonderfully airy and bright. **Expensive**

The Peninsula *discriminating modernity* `8 E5`
700 5th Avenue at 55th Street • 800 262 9467
>> www.peninsula.com

The 1905 landmark building and deluxe, spacious rooms are as much a draw here as the ultra-modern facilities, which include Internet connections and "silent fax machines" in all the boldly colored rooms. Remote controls in the bathrooms can be used to operate speaker phones, TVs, or radios. **Expensive**

Morgans *understated sophistication*   6 E3
237 Madison Avenue • 800 606 6090
>> www.ianschragerhotels.com

The concept of the "boutique hotel" originated at Morgans. Defined not by size (as with the grand hotels of the past) but by a unique sense of style and coolness, the hotel was an instant hit with fashion-conscious travelers. Morgans, designed in the late 1980s, recreates the ambience of an apartment house. The lobby is functional, with a small side office for the helpful and knowledgeable concierge. Decorative themes include the black-and-white checkerboard motif, reminiscent of old New York cabs, seen subtly in the elevator, in the pattern of the hallway carpets, and in the sleek stainless steel and glass bathrooms (which are also adorned with fresh flowers).

Renowned designer Andrée Putman planned the interiors, mixing materials such as raw silk, corduroy, maplewood, and formica. All rooms have grey, white, and beige color schemes, and feature banquettes and original Robert Mapplethorpe photographs – which have had to be bolted to the wall. Communal spaces include the "living room," with free computer access, and a welcoming area conducive to playing scrabble, reading, or writing.

The famed restaurant Asia de Cuba is where break-fast is served (included in the price), and Morgans Bar has a lively night scene and superb cocktails. Owner Ian Schrager has replicated his hotel philosophy with other New York establishments, including the Hudson *(below)* and the Royalton *(opposite)*. **Expensive**

Hudson *cosmopolitan, affordable & urbane*   7 C4
356 West 58th Street • 800 606 6090
>> www.ianschragerhotels.com

Over 800 rooms are priced at various scales so that the surfer dude can mix with the film producer in the swanky Hudson Bar. Note that the rooms tend to be very small – the concept at this Ian Schrager hotel is that you'll spend most of your time in the beautiful and funky communal spaces. **Moderate**

Hotels

Four Seasons *contemporary panache* 8 E5
57 East 57th Street • 212 758 5700
>> www.fourseasons.com

There's nothing understated about the Four Seasons – just look at the immense lobby with its cathedral-like ceiling, marble floors, and floral arrangements as large as refrigerators. As a modern facility, the hotel was built with the savvy customer in mind. Even the most modest rooms have generous dimensions – 500 sq ft (47 sq m) rivals the floorspace of many New York studio apartments. Rooms on the top floors offer great city views, including the sweep of Central Park. The windows open to let in a bit of fresh air, and curtains can be opened from the bed with a switch. All bathrooms have Bulgari products, a glass-enclosed shower, and a deep tub that fills in 60 seconds. Other gadgets include a flat screen TV in the bathroom, and a top-quality CD player/radio. The on-site spa and fitness center offers a "floating sensory escape," perfect for defeating jetlag. **Expensive**

1871 House *country-style feel* 8 F4
East 62nd Street • 212 756 8823
>> www.1871house.com

This beautifully renovated brownstone building is close to Central Park and an upscale shopping zone, but the quiet, leafy street makes you forget you're in the heart of the city. There's no common area for guests, but the spacious, high-ceilinged rooms, suites, and studios are ideal for lounging, and most have working fireplaces – quite a treat for a New York property. The keepers even provide duraflame logs to burn.

So long as you don't require 24-hour room service, these cozy, relaxing accommodations are a good option. The whole place is furnished with antiques and the decor is warm and homey. If you are traveling in a group of four or more, reserve the Great Room and Cottage combination; both have access to a lovely garden, the "cottage space." Some rooms have kitchenettes, but the hotel is close to many eateries. A four-night minimum is usually expected. **Moderate**

The Lowell *intimate retreat* 8 F4
28 East 63rd Street • 212 838 1400
>> www.lowellhotel.com

With 23 rooms and 47 suites, The Lowell focuses more on comfort than numbers. High-profile guests stay here to escape the paparazzi. The suites offer options such as wood-burning fireplaces, terraces, and kitchenettes. Orchids in every room are another high-quality detail, and there's an airy fitness room too. **Expensive**

Melrose *highly accommodating hotel* 8 F4
140 East 63rd Street • 212 838 5700
>> www.melrosehotelnewyork.com

Formerly the Barbizon Hotel, the Melrose has been renovated to accommodate every need of luxury-loving travelers, whether it's plush bedding, Internet access, modern gadgetry, or a well-equipped gym. It's also well situated, only three blocks from Central Park and up the street from Bloomingdales. **Moderate**

The Pierre *New York landmark* 8 E4
5th Avenue at 61st Street • 212 838 8000
>> www.fourseasons.com

A top hotel since 1930, The Pierre is a bastion of old-fashioned gentility, and is the perfect place to return to after a shopping spree at neighboring Bergdorf's. Attentive staff perform to a backdrop of chandeliers and Art Deco details. The **Rotunda** *(see p174)* is on hand for afternoon tea; Café Pierre offers full meals. **Expensive**

The Mark *Upper East Side elegance* 8 F1
25 East 77th Street • 212 744 4300
>> www.themarkhotel.com

An air of sophistication permeates the lobby and generously sized rooms of this hotel, part of the Mandarin group. Inspiration for The Mark's exquisite Neo-Classical interior is said to have come from the work of 19th-century English architect Sir John Soane. Service is thorough and professional. **Expensive**

Hotels

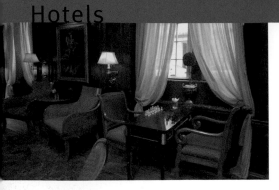

The Stanhope *refined luxury* 8 E1

995 5th Avenue at 81st Street • 212 774 1234
>> www.stanhopepark.hyatt.com

The staff here pride themselves on personal touches, such as knowing many of the guests' names and catering to individual needs. All the rooms are furnished with antiques and the bathrooms have Molton Brown products. Head down to the cozy ground-floor library for tea, coffee, and games of chess. **Expensive**

Harlem Flophouse *jazz-related fun* 11 D4

242 West 123rd Street • 212 662 0678
>> www.harlemflophouse.com

A small brass plaque is the only thing that sets the Flophouse apart from the other residences on this quiet, tree-lined brownstone block. The first thing you'll notice upon entering is the sound of jazz, drifting softly from the mantelpiece radio in the charming front room. It has been a B&B since 2000, and the owner has worked on various parts of the house to restore original details, including patterned tin ceilings, wooden moldings, and a downstairs dining room for parties.

A touch of faded glory and fresh renovation add to the appeal and charm of the four guest rooms. Each has a sink, but bathrooms are shared – a claw-foot tub in one is nicely set right under a sky light. All beds are firm, with good mattresses, and the rooms are named after notable people with either jazz or Harlem connections – often both. There are no TVs, but alarm clocks are provided. There's a smoking room in the basement and guests have access to the garden, for summer barbecues, relaxation, and reflection. Hearty and delicious breakfasts of eggs, grits, sausage, and yogurt are available at an extra charge.

The Flop House is conveniently located for subway trains and buses (the M60 can bring you right here from LaGuardia airport), and is close to the Apollo Theater *(see p128)*, Lenox Lounge *(see p129)*, and the Harlem Studio Museum *(see p107)*. The Flophouse also hosts occasional art exhibitions in the common area on the main floor. **Cheap**

Hotel Wales *classic & fresh* `10 E4`
1295 Madison Avenue • 866 925 3746
>> www.waleshotel.com

This Upper East Side boutique hotel has an intimate feel. Aveda products and fresh flowers feature in the comfortable rooms, and free coffee is available day and night. The roof deck is a great place from which to watch the buzzing city, and adjacent Sarabeth's Kitchen whips up fantastic omelets and soups. **Moderate**

Union St B&B *bohemian charm* `13 B4`
405 Union Street, Brooklyn
718 852 8406

Floral wallpaper, wooden floors, and music boxes in each of the six rooms create a charming, warm, and homey atmosphere. The continental-style breakfast includes good strong coffee. Owner Angelique is a history buff, and provides a well-stocked bookshelf of local historical books for perusal. **Cheap/Moderate**

Bed & Breakfast on the Park *Victorian time machine* `13 C5`
113 Prospect Park West • 718 499 6115
>> www.bbnyc.com

The fixtures here have been lovingly restored to maintain an ambience of Victorian gentility. Reserve the Lady Liberty Room for a four-poster bed, great city views, and exclusive access to the roof garden. Breakfast includes home-made pastries. **Moderate**

Accommodations Agencies

Hotel rates can be rather mysterious: the officially quoted "rack rate" may say one thing, but certain packages, the time of year, and discounts found on the web can give a completely different price. If you get the timing right, you can slice a lot of money off your room price. At weekends in off-peak seasons, for example, hotels often offer rooms at discounted rates. Accommodations agencies with websites to try include: **www.simply-newyork.com**, **www.a1-discount-hotels.com**, and **www.hotels.com**.

Also, if you're interested in longer stays – a duration of seven days or more – and are thinking about subletting an apartment, try **www.sublet inthecity.com**, **www.citysublets.com**, and **www.newyorkhabitat.com**.

>> *Thanksgiving and Christmas are busy periods – you'll need to make early reservations at these times*

New York Street Finder

Almost every listing in this guide includes a
(boxed) page and grid reference to the maps in
this section. The few entries that fall outside the
area covered by these maps give transport
details instead. Maps 1 to 12 cover the whole of
Manhattan, while Brooklyn is shown on Map 13.
An index of the street names follows on
pp207–209.

The Outer Boroughs

Key to Street Finder

▪	Sight/public building	⊗	Post office
Ⓜ	Subway station	Ⓟ	Parking
Ⓡ	Railroad station	═	Railroad line
⊖	Ferry terminal	▬	Pedestrian street
⊜	Bus terminal	▦	Expressway
⊕	Heliport		
⊜	Aerial tramway		
❶	Tourist information office		
⊕	Hospital with emergency room		
⊜	Police station		
⊕	Church		
⊙	Synagogue		

Scale of maps 1–12

0 metres   500

0 yards   500

Scale of map 13

0 kilometres   1

0 miles   1

Street Finder Index

Street Finder Index

Downtown

Restaurants

Chinatown

Golden Unicorn (p25) $
18 East Broadway (Map 2 F1)
Chinese

Peking Duck House (p25) $$
28 Mott Street (Map 2 E1)
Chinese

HSF (p160) $$
46 Bowery (Map 2 E1)
Chinese

Chinatown Ice Cream $
Factory (p160)
65 Bayard Street (Map 2 E1)
Ice Cream Parlor

Great NY Noodle Town (p160) $
Bowery at Bayard Street
(Map 2 E1)
Chinese

East Village

2nd Avenue Deli (p33) $$
156 2nd Avenue (Map 4 E2)
Deli

Angelica Kitchen (p32) $
300 East 12th St (Map 4 E2)
Vegetarian

Bao (p29) $
111 Avenue C (Map 4 G3)
Vietnamese

Crif Dogs (p36) $
113 St. Mark's Place (Map 4 F3)
American

Daily Chow (p30) $
2 East 2nd Street (Map 4 E3)
Asian

DT–UT (p162) $
41 Avenue B (Map 4 G2)
Café

The Elephant (p27) $$
58 East 1st Street (Map 4 F4)
French/Thai

Mermaid Inn (p31) $$
96 2nd Avenue (Map 4 E3)
Seafood

Mud Spot (p31) $
307 East 9th Street (Map 4 E2)
www.themudtruck.com
Café

Paul's Palace (p31) $
131 2nd Avenue (Map 4 E3)
American

Pommes Frites (p36) $
123 2nd Avenue (Map 4 E3)
Belgian

Pylos (p30) $$
128 East 7th Street (Map 4 F3)
Greek

Rue B (p162) $
188 Avenue B (Map 4 G2)
Café

Sobaya (p32) $/$$
229 East 9th Street (Map 4 E2)
Japanese

Le Souk (p29) $$
47 Avenue B (Map 4 G3)
North African

Le Tableau (p29) $$
511 East 5th Street (Map 4 F3)
French

Yaffa Cafe (p30) $
97 St. Mark's Place (Map 4 F3)
Middle Eastern

Little Italy

Cafe Gitane (p27) $
242 Mott Street (Map 4 E4)
North African

Cafe Habana (p27) $
229 Elizabeth St (Map 4 E4)
Cuban/Mexican

Housing Works $
Used Book Café (p15)
126 Crosby Street (Map 3 D5)
Café

Lower East Side

Alias (p28) $$
76 Clinton Street (Map 4 G4)
American

Bereket (p27) $
187 East Houston St
(Map 4 F4)
Turkish

Cube 63 (p28) $$
63 Clinton Street (Map 4 G4)
Japanese

Fried Dumpling (p36) $
99 Allen Street (Map 4 F4)
Chinese

'inoteca (p28) $$
98 Rivington Street (Map 4 F4)
Italian

WD-50 (p28) $$$
50 Clinton Street (Map 4 G4)
American

Lower Manhattan

Amish Fine Food Market (p160)
17 Battery Place (Map 1 D5)
Downtown/Lower Manhattan

Cosi Downtown (p160) $
55 Broad Street (Map 1 D4)
Deli/Sandwich Shop

Pret a Manger (p160) $
60 Broad Street (Map 1 D4)
Deli/Sandwich Shop

Meatpacking District

Bonsignour (p72)
35 Jane Street (Map 3 B2)
Bakery

Florent (pp38 & 161) $$
69 Gansevoort Street (Map 3 A2)
American/European

Pastis (p161)
9 Ninth Avenue (Map 3 A2)
French

Nolita

Mud Spot (p31) $
307 East 9th Street (Map 3 DE)
www.themudtruck.com
Coffee

SoHo

Balthazar (p25) $$
80 Spring Street (Map 3 D5)
French

Blue Ribbon Sushi (p33) $$
119 Sullivan Street (Map 3 C4)
Japanese

Dean & DeLuca (pp13, 65) $
560 Broadway (Map 3 D4)
Bakery/Deli

L'Ecole (p26) $/$$
462 Broadway (Map 3 D5)
French

Mercer Kitchen (p25) $/$$
99 Prince Street (Map 3 D4)
French/American

Tribeca

66 (p24) $$$
241 Church Street (Map 1 D1)
Chinese

Acappella (p24) $$$
1 Hudson Street (Map 1 C2)
Italian

Chanterelle (p38) $$$
2 Harrison Street (Map 1 C1)
www.chanterellenyc.com
French

Montrachet (p24) $$$
239 West Broadway
(Map 1 C1)
European

Nobu (p38) $$$
105 Hudson Street (Map 1 C1)
212 219 0500, www.myriad
restaurantgroup.com
Japanese

West Village

Babbo (p34) $$$
110 Waverly Place
(Map 3 C3)
Northern Italian

BB Sandwich Bar (p36) $
120 West 3rd Street (Map 3 C3)
Deli

Blue Ribbon $/$$$
Bakery (p33)
33 Downing Street (Map 3 C4)
European

Cones (p36) $
272 Bleecker Street (Map 3 C3)
Ice Cream Parlor

Deborah (p13) $
43 Carmine Street (Map 3 C4)
Brunch

Jane (p26) $$
100 West Houston Street
(Map 3 D4)
American

Joe (p31) $
141 Waverly Place
212 924 6750 (Map 3 C3)
Café

**John's of
Bleecker Street** (p35) $
278 Bleecker Street (Map 3 C3)
Pizzeria

Magnolia Bakery (p71) $
401 Bleeker Street (Map 3 B3)
Downtown/West Village

Mamoun's (p36) $
119 MacDougal St. (Map 3 C3)
Middle Eastern

Mary's Fish Camp (p37) $$
64 Charles Street (Map 3 B3)
Seafood

Mud Truck (p31)
14th Street and Broadway
(Map 3 D2)
www.themudtruck.com
Café

NY Dosas (p37) $
West 4th Street & Sullivan
Street (Map 3 C3)
Vegetarian

**Otto Enoteca
and Pizzeria** (p34) $$
1 5th Avenue (Map 3 D3)
Italian

La Palapa Rockola (p34) $$
359 6th Avenue (Map 3 C3)
Mexican

Sumile (p38) $$$
154 West 13th Street (Map 3 C2)
Japanese

Paris Commune (p13) $
411 Bleecker Street (Map 3 B3)
Brunch

Pepe Rosso's (p36) $
149 Sullivan Street (Map 3 C4)
Italian

Tartine (p38) $$
253 West 11th Street
(Map 3 B2)
French

Tea & Sympathy (p31)
108 Greenwich Ave. (Map 3 C2)
British

Tomoe Sushi (p33) $$
172 Thompson Street (Map 3 C4)
Japanese

Wallse (p37) $$$
344 West 11th Street
(Map 3A3)
Austrian

Shopping

East Village

Kiehl's (p77)
109 3rd Avenue (Map 4 E2)
Health & Beauty

St. Mark's Sounds (p78)
16 St. Mark's Place
(Map 4 E3)
Music

The Strand (p77)
828 Broadway (Map 4 D2)
Books

Little Italy

The Apartment (p66)
101 Crosby Street (Map 3 D4)
Interiors

Calypso (p67)
280 Mott Street (Map 4 E4)
Fashion

Hable Construction (p68)
230 Elizabeth St. (Map 4 E4)
Interiors

INA (p67)
21 Prince Street (Map 4 E4)
Fashion

Mayle (p68)
242 Elizabeth Street
(Map 4 E4)
Fashion

Rescue Nail Spa (p66)
21 Cleveland Place (Map 4 E5)
Health & Beauty

SCO (p67)
230 Mulberry Street
(Map 4 E4)
Health & Beauty

Lower East Side

ALife Rivington Club (p69)
158 Rivington Street (Map 4 F4)
Shoes & Accessories

Shop (p70)
105 Stanton Street (Map 4 F4)
Fashion

Teany (p70)
90 Rivington Street (Map 4 F4)
Food

TG-170 (p69)
170 Ludlow Street (Map 4 F4)
Fashion

Lower Manhattan

Century 21 (p60)
22 Cortland Street (Map 1 D3)
Fashion

Green Market (p160)
Farmer's market at Bowling
Green Park (Map 1 D4)
Food Market

**Amish Market
Downtown** (p160)
17 Battery Place (Map 1 D4)
Food Market

Meatpacking District

Alexander McQueen (p161)
417 West 14th Street (Map 3 A2)
Fashion

Bonsignour (p72)
35 Jane Street (Map 3 B2)
Food

Jeffrey (pp74 & 161)
449 West 14th St. (Map 3 A2)
Department Store

MXYPLYZYK (p73)
125 Greenwich Ave (Map 3 B2)
Interiors

Stella McCartney (p73)
429 West 14th St. (Map 3 A2)
Fashion

Vitra (p161)
29 9th Avenue (Map 3 A2)
Interiors

Nolita

Bond 07 By Selima (p68)
7 Bond Street (Map 3 D3)
Shoes & Accessories

LAFCO (p69)
285 Lafayette Street (Map 4 E3)
Health & Beauty

Rafe (p68)
1 Bleecker Street (Map 4 E4)
Shoes & Accessories

SoHo

Barney's Co-Op (p62)
116 Wooster Street (Map 3 D4)
Fashion

Clio (p63)
92 Thompson Street (Map 3 C4)
Interiors

Le Corset by Selima (p62)
80 Thompson Street
(Map 3 C5)
Lingerie

Costume National (p63)
108 Wooster Street (Map 3 D4)
Fashion

Dean & DeLuca (p65)
560 Broadway (Map 3 D4)
Food

Helmut Lang (p62)
80 Greene Street (Map 3 D5)
Fashion

**Hotel Venus by
Patricia Field** (p60)
382 W. Broadway (Map 3 D5)
Fashion

Kate Spade Travel (p60)
59 Thompson Street (Map 3 C5)
Shoes & Accessories

Kate's Paperie (p66)
561 Broadway (Map 3 D4)
Stationery

Keiko (p61)
62 Greene Street (Map 3 D5)
Fashion

Kirna Zabete (p63)
96 Greene Street (Map 3 D4)
Fashion

Miu Miu (p63)
100 Prince Street (Map 3 D4)
Fashion

Moss (p64)
146 Greene Street (Map 3 D4)
Interiors

Pearl River Mart (p61)
477 Broadway (Map 3 D5)
Department Store

Angel's Share (p142)
8 Stuyvesant Street
(Map 4 E2)
Cocktail Lounge

Bar Veloce (p144)
175 2nd Avenue (Map 4 E2)
Bar

Beauty Bar (p144)
231 East 14th Street (Map 4 E2)
DJ Bar

Chez es Saada (p141)
42 East 1st Street (Map 4 F4)
Bar

KGB (p142)
85 East 4th Street (Map 4 E3)
Bar

Korova Milk Bar (p145)
200 Avenue A (Map 4 F2)
Bar

Lansky Lounge (p139)
104 Norfolk Street (Map 4 G4)
Cocktail Lounge/DJ Bar

**McSorley's Old
Ale House** (p142)
15 East 7th Street (Map 4 E3)
Ale House

Nevada Smith's (p142)
74 3rd Avenue (Map 4 E2)
Bar

Parkside Lounge (p141)
317 East Houston Street
(Map 4 G4)
Bar

Rue B (p145)
188 Avenue B (Map 4 G2)
Bar

Swift Hibernian Lounge (p142)
34 East 4th Street
(Map 4 E3)
Ale House

Uncle Ming's (p146)
225 Avenue B, 2nd Floor
(Map 4 G2)
DJ Bar

Little Italy

ñ (p138)
33 Crosby Street
(Map 3 D5)
Bar

Lower East Side

Arlene's Grocery (p117)
95 Stanton Street (Map 4 F4)
Bar & Music Venue

Barramundi (p140)
147 Ludlow Street (Map 4 F4)
Bar

Slipper Room (p141)
167 Orchard Street (Map 4 F4)
Bar

**Welcome to the
Johnson's** (p140)
123 Rivington Street
(Map 4 F4)
Bar

Lower Manhattan

Pussycat Lounge (p136)
96 Greenwich Street
(Map 1 D4)
Bar

Meatpacking District

Cielo (pp148 & 161)
18 Little West 12th Street
(Map 3 A2)
Club

Cubbyhole (p148)
281 West 12th Street
(Map 3 B2)
Bar

Rhône (p148)
63 Gansevoort Street
(Map 3 A2)
Bar

Nolita

B-Bar & Grill (p143)
40 East 4th Street (Map 4 E3)
Bar

Pravda (p139)
281 Lafayette Street (Map 4 E4)
Cocktail Lounge

Temple Bar (p138)
332 Lafayette Street (Map 4 E4)
Cocktail Lounge

SoHo

Antarctica (p136)
287 Hudson Street (Map 3 C5)
Bar

THOM's Bar (p137)
60 Thompson Street (Map 3 C5)
Cocktail Lounge

West Village

Blind Tiger Ale House (p147)
518 Hudson Street (Map 3 B3)
Ale House

Chumley's (p146)
86 Bedford Street (Map 3 B3)
Bar

Lotus (p144)
409 West 14th Street
(Map 3 A2)
DJ Bar

Stonewall (p147)
53 Christopher Street
(Map 3 B3)
Bar

Sullivan Room (p146)
218 Sullivan Street (Map 3 C3)
DJ Bar

Vol de Nuit (p146)
148 West 4th Street (Map 3 C3)
Ale House

White Horse Tavern (p147)
567 Hudson Street
(Map 3 B3)
Ale House

Havens:
Parks & Gardens

Lower Manhattan

Battery Park (p160)
Battery Place & State Street
(Map 1 D4)
www.bpcparks.org

Havens:
Spas & Treatments

SoHo

Angel Feet (p170)
77 Perry Street (Map 3 B3)

Bliss SoHo (p170)
568 Broadway (Map 3 D4)

Jivamukti Yoga Center (p171)
404 Lafayette Street
(Map 4 E3)

Hotels

Meatpacking District

**Abingdon
Guest House** (p183) $$
13 8th Avenue (Map 3 B2)

**SoHo House
New York** (p184) $$$
29–35 9th Avenue (Map 3 A2)

SoHo

Bevy's SoHo Loft (p182) $$
70 Mercer Street (Map 3 D5)

60 Thompson (p182) $$$
60 Thompson Street (3 C5)

Mercer Hotel (p182) $$$
147 Mercer Street (Map 3 D4)

SoHo Grand Hotel (p182) $-$$
310 West Broadway (Map 3 D5)

Tribeca

**Tribeca Grand
Hotel** (p183) $$$
Two Avenue of the Americas
(Map 3 C5)

West Village

**Washington Square
Hotel** (p183) $
103 Waverly Place (Map 3 D3)

Midtown

Restaurants

Chelsea

Biltmore Room (p40) $$$
290 8th Avenue (Map 5 C5)
International

City Bakery (p39) $
3 West 18th Street (Map 3 C1)
Bakery

**Grand Sichuan
International** (p39) $
229 9th Avenue (Map 5 C5)
Chinese

Red Cat (p39) $$
227 10th Avenue (Map 5 B5)
International

Whitney Museum of American Art at Altria (p100)
120 Park Avenue at 42nd Street (Map 6 F2)
Museum

Theater District

Carnegie Hall (p125)
881 7th Avenue at 57th Street (Map 7 D5)
Concert Hall

International Center of Photography (p100)
1133 Ave. of the Americas (Map 5 D2)
Art Gallery

Museum of Modern Art (p101)
11 West 53rd Street (Map 8 E5)
Museum

Museum of Television and Radio (p103)
25 West 52nd Street (Map 8 E5)
Museum

Rose Museum at Carnegie Hall (p100)
154 West 57th Street, 2nd Floor (Map 7 D5)
Museum

Performance

Chelsea

Hammerstein Ballroom (p121)
311 West 34th Street (Map 5 C3)
Music Venue

The Joyce Theater (p120)
175 8th Avenue (Map 3 B1)
Dance

The Kitchen (p120)
512 West 19th Street (Map 3 A1)
Combined Arts Center

Upright Citizen's Brigade (p121)
307 West 26th Street (Map 5 C5)
Comedy

Flatiron

Gotham Comedy Club (p121)
34 West 22nd Street (Map 6 E5)
Comedy

Kavehaz (p121)
37 West 26th Street (Map 6 E5)
Music Venue

Gramercy

Rodeo Bar (p122)
375 3rd Avenue (Map 6 F5)
Music Venue

Hell's Kitchen

The Soul Cafe (p122)
444 West 42nd St. (Map 5 B2)
Music Venue

Theater District

B.B. King Blues Club & Grill (p122)
237 West 42nd St. (Map 5 C2)
Jazz & Blues Venue

City Center (p123)
131 West 55th Street (Map 7 D5)
Combined Arts Center

Don't Tell Mama (p123)
343 West 46th Street (Map 5 C1)
Cabaret

Ed Sullivan Theater (p124)
51 West 52nd Street (Map 7 D5)
TV Studio

NBC Studios (p124)
Between 5th & 7th avenues from 47th to 51st streets (Map 6 E1)
TV Studio

Rainbow Room (p123)
30 Rockefeller Plaza, 65th Floor (Map 6 E1)
Ball Room

Roundabout Theatre Company @ The American Airlines Theatre (p122)
227 West 42nd St. (Map 5 C2)
Theater

Swing 46 (p123)
349 West 46th Street (Map 5 C1)
Ball Room

Sports Arenas

Flatiron

Madison Square Garden (p131)
Map 6 E5
Sports Arena

Bars and Clubs

Chelsea

Avalon (p149)
47 West 20th Street (Map 3 C1)
DJ Bar

Bungalow 8 (p150)
515 West 27th Street (Map 5 B4)
Bar

Copacabana (p151)
560 West 34th Street (Map 5 B3)
Ball Room

Glass (p150)
287 10th Avenue (Map 5 B5)
Bar

Hiro (p150)
366 West 17th Street (Map 3 A1)
Bar

Plunge Bar (p155)
18 9th Avenue (Map 3 A1)
Bar

Roxy (p149)
515 West 18th Street (Map 3 A1)
Club

Serena (p149)
Chelsea Hotel, 222 West 23rd Street (Map 5 C5)
Bar

Spirit (p150)
530 West 27th Street (Map 5 B4)
Bar

Flatiron

Eugene (p149)
27 West 24th Street (Map 6 E5)
Club

Gramercy

High Bar (p155)
2 Lexington Avenue (Map 6 F5)
Bar

Hell's Kitchen

Rudy's Bar & Grill (p148)
627 9th Avenue (Map 5 C1)
Bar

Murray Hill

Campbell Apartment (p151)
15 Vanderbilt Ave., Southwest Balcony,

Grand Central Terminal (Map 6 F2)
Bar

The Ginger Man (p151)
11 East 36th Street (Map 6 E3)
Bar

Métrazur (p152)
East Balcony, Grand Central Station (Map 6 F2)
Cocktail Lounge

Theater District

Ava Lounge (p152)
210 West 55th Street (Map 7 D5)
Bar

Flûte (p152)
205 West 54th Street (Map 7 D5)
DJ Bar

Russian Vodka Room (p153)
265 West 52nd Street (Map 7 C5)
Bar

Single Room Occupancy (p152)
360 West 53rd Street (Map 7 C5)
Bar

Turtle Bay

Mica Bar (p148)
252 East 51st Street (Map 6 F1)
Bar

Top of the Tower @ Beekman Tower Hotel (p172)
3 Mitchell Place at 49th Street & First Avenue (Map 6 G1)
Bar

Havens: Spas & Treatments

Theater District

The Spa at the Mandarin Oriental (p172)
80 Columbus Circle at 60th Street, 35th Floor (Map 7 C4)

Hotels

Chelsea

Chelsea Inn (p185) $
46 West 17th Street (Map 3 C1)

Chelsea Lodge (p185) $
318 West 20th Street (Map 3 B1)

Index by Area

Hotels *continued*

Hotel Chelsea (p183) $$
222 West 23rd Street
(Map 5 C5)

Maritime Hotel (p185) $$
363 West 16th Street
(Map 3 A1)

Gramercy

**W New York,
Union Square** (p185) $–$$
201 Park Avenue South
(Map 3D1)

Murray Hill

Morgans (p187) $$$
237 Madison Avenue
(Map 6 E3)

Theater District

Bryant Park Hotel (p186) $$
40 West 40th Street
(Map 6 E2)

Four Seasons (p188) $$$
57 East 57th Street (Map 8 E5)

The Peninsula (p186) $$$
700 5th Avenue at 55th Street
(Map 8 E5)

The Plaza (p183) $$$
5th Avenue at Central Park
South (Map 8 E4)

Royalton (p186) $$
44 West 44th Street (Map 6 E2)

St. Regis (p186) $$$
2 East 55th Street (Map 8 E5)

Upper East Side

Restaurants

Annie's (p47) $
1381 3rd Avenue (Map 8 F1)
American

Atlantic Grill (p48) $$
1341 3rd Avenue (Map 8 F1)
Seafood

Candle 79 (p48) $$
154 East 79th Street (Map 8 F1)
Vegetarian/Vegan

Geisha (p46) $$$
33 East 61st Street (Map 8 E4)
Japanese

March (p47) $$$
405 East 58th Street (Map 8 G4)
Asian

Mezzaluna (p47) $$
1295 3rd Avenue (Map 8 F2)
Italian

Rotunda at the Pierre (p174)
The Pierre Hotel, 2 East 61st
Street (Map 8 E4)
Tea Room

Serendipity 3 (p47) $
225 East 60th Street (Map 8 F4)
American

Sushi of Gari (p49) $$$
402 East 78th Street (Map 8 G1)
Japanese

Via Quadronno (p31)
25 East 73rd Street (Map 8 F2)
www.viaquadronno.com
Italian

Shopping

ABH Designs (p84)
401 East 76th Street (Map 8 H1)
Interiors

Barney's New York (p82)
660 Madison Avenue
(Map 8 E4)
Department Store

Bra Smyth (p82)
905 Madison Avenue
(Map 8 E2)
Lingerie

Christian Louboutin (p83)
941 Madison Avenue
(Map 8 E2)
Shoes & Accessories

Clyde's (p83)
926 Madison Avenue
(Map 8 E2)
Heath & Beauty

Diane B (p83)
1414 3rd Avenue (Map 8 F2)
Fashion

Dylan's Candy Bar (p82)
1011 3rd Avenue
(Map 8 F4)
Food

Liliblue (p83)
955 Madison Avenue
(Map 8 E2)
Shoes & Accessories

La Perla (p82)
777 Madison Avenue
(Map 8 E3)
Lingerie

Searle (p84)
1124 Madison Avenue
(Map 10 E5)
Fashion

Art & Architecture

Asia Society (p103)
725 Park Avenue. at 70th
Street (Map 8 F2)
Gallery

**Cooper-Hewitt National Design
Museum** (p105)
2 East 91st Street
(Map 10 E4)
Museum

Frick Collection (p102)
1 East 70th Street
(Map 8 E2)
Museum

Guggenheim Museum (p104)
1071 5th Avenue at 89th Street
(Map 10 E4)
Museum

Japan Gallery (p105)
1210 Lexington Avenue
(Map 10 F5)
Art Gallery

The Jewish Museum (p105)
1109 5th Avenue at 92nd
Street (Map 10 E4)
Museum

**Metropolitan Museum
of Art** (p103)
1000 5th Avenue (Map 8 E1)
Museum

El Museo del Barrio (p107)
1230 5th Avenue at 104th
Street (Map 10 E2)
Museum

**Whitney Museum of
American Art** (p101)
945 Madison Avenue
(Map 8 E2)
Museum

Performance

92nd Street Y (p125)
1395 Lexington Avenue
(Map 10 F4)
Combined Arts Center

The Comic Strip (p125)
1568 2nd Avenue (Map 8 G1)
Comedy

Florence Gould Hall (p124)
55 East 59th Street (Map 8 F4)
Combined Arts Center

Bars

Baraonda (p153)
1439 2nd Avenue (Map 8 G2)
Bar

Bemelmans Bar (p153)
Carlyle Hotel, 35 East 76th
Street (Map 8 E1)
Bar

Havens: Parks & Gardens

**Conservatory Gardens at
Central Park** (p173)
5th Avenue at 110th Street
(Map 10 E2)

**The Iris and B. Gerald Cantor
Roof Garden** (p172)
Metropolitan Museum of Art,
1000 5th Avenue
(Map 8 E1)

**The Ramble at
Central Park** (p173)
5th Avenue between 72nd and
80th streets (Map 7 D2)

Hotels

1871 House (p188) $$
East 62nd Street (Map 8 F4)

The Carlyle (p183) $$
Madison Avenue at 76th Street
(Map 8 E1)

Hotel Wales (p191) $$
1295 Madison Avenue
(Map 10 E4)

The Lowell (p189) $$$
28 East 63rd Street (Map 8 F4)

The Mark (p189) $$$
25 East 77th Street (Map 8 F1)

The Melrose (p189) $$
140 East 63rd Street
(Map 8 F4)

The Pierre (p189) $$$
5th Avenue at 61st Street
(Map 8 E4)

The Stanhope (p190) $$$
995 5th Avenue at 81st Street
(Map 8 E1)

Upper West Side

Restaurants

Aix (p51) $$$
2398 Broadway (Map 9 B4)
French

El Malecón II (p50) $
764 Amsterdam Avenue (9 B3)
Caribbean

Ouest (p49) $$$
2315 Broadway (Map 9 B5)
American

Pasha (p50) $$
70 W. 71st Street (Map 7 C2)
Turkish

Picholine (p50) $$$
35 West 64th Street (Map 7 C3)
European

Tavern on the Green (p38)
Central Park West between
66th and 67th sts. (Map 7 C3)
212 873 3200
www.tavernonthegreen.com
American

Shopping

Blades Board & Skate (p84)
120 West 72nd Street
(Map 7 B2)
Sporting Goods

**Housing Works
Thrift Shop** (p85)
306 Columbus Avenue
(Map 7 C2)
Thrift Store

Intermix (p84)
210 Columbus Avenue
(Map 7 C3)
Fashion

Super Runners (p85)
360 Amsterdam Avenue
(Map 7 B1)
Sporting Goods

Zabar's (p85)
2245 Broadway
(Map 7 B1)
Food

Performance

**Lincoln Center for the
Performing Arts** (p126)
Straddling Broadway and
Amsterdam Avenue between
62nd and 66th streets
(Map 7 B3)
Performing Arts Center

Makor (p127)
35 West 67th Street
(Map 7 C3)
Combined Arts Center

Merkin Concert Hall (p125)
129 West 67th Street
(Map 7 B3)
Concert Hall

Smoke (p127)
2751 Broadway
(Map 9 B2)
Jazz Venue

Stand-Up NY (p127)
236 West 78th Street
(Map 7 B2)
Comedy

Symphony Space (p127)
2537 Broadway (Map 9 B3)
Combined Arts Center

Bars & Clubs

Boat Basin Café (p155)
West 79th St. at Henry Hudson
Parkway (Map 7 A1)
Bar

Library Bar (p148)
Hudson Hotel, 356 West 58th
Street (Map 7 B4)
Bar

Hotels

Hudson Hotel (p187) $$
356 West 58th Street (Map 7 C4)

Above Central Park

Restaurants

Columbus University

Symposium (p51) $$
544 West 113th St. (Map 11 B5)
Greek

Fort Tryon

New Leaf Café (p51) $$
Fort Tryon Park
American

Harlem

Amy Ruth's (p163) $
113 West 116th St. (Map 11 D5)
212 280 8771
American

Shopping

Harlem

Demolition Depot (p86)
216 East 125th St. (Map 12 G3)
Interiors

Xukuma (p86)
183 Lenox Avenue (11 D4)
Fashion/Interiors

Art & Architecture

Fort Tryon

The Cloisters (p106)
Fort Tryon Park
Museum

Harlem

**Studio Museum in
Harlem** (pp107 & 163)
144 West 125th Street
(Map 11 D3)
Museum

Performance

Harlem

Apollo Theater (p128)
253 West 125th Street
(Map 11 D3)
Music/Combined Arts Venue

Lenox Lounge (p129)
288 Lenox Avenue between
124th & 125th streets
(Map 11 D3)
Jazz Venue

Clubs

Harlem

Jimmy's Uptown (p154)
2207 Adam Clayton Powell, Jr.
Blvd. (Map 11 D3)
Club

Hotels

Harlem

**The Harlem
Flophouse** (p190) $
242 West 123rd Street
(Map 11 D4)

Brooklyn

Restaurants

Brooklyn Heights

**Brooklyn Ice Cream
Factory** (p164) $
Fulton Ferry Landing
(Map 13 A4)
Ice Cream Parlor

Connecticut Muffin (p164) $
115 Montague Street
(Map 13 A4)
Bakery

Noodle Pudding (p51) $$
38 Henry Street (Map 13 A3)
Italian

The River Café (p52) $$$
1 Water Street (Map 13 A3)
International

Theresa's (p164) $$
80 Montague St. (Map 13 A4)
Polish

Index by Area

Brooklyn

Restaurants *continued*

Carroll Gardens

The Grocery (p52) $$
288 Smith Street (Map 13 B4)
American

Joya (p52) $
215 Court Street (Map 13 B4)
Thai

Coney Island

Café Arbat (p166)
306 Brighton Beach Avenue
Eastern European

Café Glechik (p166)
3159 Coney Island Avenue
Eastern European

Nathan's Famous $
Hotdogs (p166)
Corner of Surf &
Stillwell avenues
American

Fort Green

Butta'Cup Lounge (p54) $$
271 Adelphi Street
(Map 13 C3)
American

i-Shebeen Madiba (p54) $$
195 DeKalb Avenue
(Map 13 C3)
South African

LouLou (p53) $$
222 DeKalb Avenue
(Map 13 C3)
French

Park Slope

Al Di La (p53) $$
248 5th Avenue
(Map 13 C4)
Italian

Convivium Osteria (p53) $$
68 5th Avenue
(Map 13 C4)
Italian

DiFara Pizzeria (p54) $
1424 Avenue J
Pizzeria

Park Slope Chip Shop (p53) $
383 5th Avenue (Map 13 C4)
British

Williamsburg

Anna Maria's (p165) $
179 Bedford Avenue
(Map 13 C2)
Pizzeria

Bamonte's (p55) $$
32 Withers Street
(Map 13 C1)
Italian

Bliss Café (p165)
191 Bedford Avenue
(Map 13 C2)
Vegetarian

Cukiernia (p165) $
223 Bedford Avenue
(Map 13 B2)
Bakery

Peter Luger $$$
Steak House (p55)
178 Broadway (Map 13 B2)
American

Planet Thailand (p55) $
133 North 7th Street
(Map 13 C2)
Thai/Japanese

Relish (p55) $$
225 Wythe Avenue (Map 13 D2)
American

S & B Polish Restaurant (p165)
194 Bedford Avenue
(Map 13 C2)
Restaurant

Verb Café (p165) $
218 Bedford Avenue
(Map 13 C2)
Café

Shopping

Boerum Hill

Breukelen (p87)
369 Atlantic Avenue
(Map 13 B4)
Interiors

Butter (p87)
389 Atlantic Avenue
(Map 13 B4)
Fashion

Brooklyn Heights

Heights Books (p164)
109 Montague Street
(Map 13 A4)
Books

Park Slope

Loom (p87)
115 7th Avenue (Map 13 C5)
Interiors

Nest (p88)
396A 7th Avenue
(Map 13 C5)
Interiors

Williamsburg

Beacon's Closet (p89)
88 North 11th St. (Map 13 B1)
Thrift Store

Bedford Cheese Shop (p165)
218 Bedford Avenue
(Map 13 C2)
Food

Brooklyn Industries (p165)
162 Bedford Avenue
(Map 13 C2)
Shoes & Accessories

Brooklyn Lager Brewery (p165)
79 North 11th Street
(Map 13 C2)
Food

Earwax Records (p165)
218 Bedford Avenue
(Map 13 C2)
Music

Isa (p89)
88 North 6th Street
(Map 13 B2)
Fashion

Metaphors (p165)
195 Bedford Avenue
(Map 13 C2)
Fashion

Mini Minimarket (p88)
218 Bedford Avenue
(Map 13 B2)
Fashion

Moon River Chattel (p91)
62 Grand Street (Map 13 B2)
Interiors

Spacial (pp89 & 165)
199 Bedford Avenue
(Map 13 B2)
Interiors/Fashion

Spoonbill &
Sugartown (pp88 &165)
218 Bedford Avenue
(Map 13 C2)
Books

Two Jakes (p91)
320 Wythe Avenue (Map 13 B2)
Interiors

Art & Architecture

Boerum Hill

Brooklyn Historical
Society (p109)
128 Pierrepont Street
(Map 13 B4)
Museum

Brooklyn Museum
of Art (p108)
200 Eastern Parkway
(Map 13 D4)
Museum

Williamsburg Savings Bank
Building (p109)
1 Hanson Place, corner of
Flatbush and Atlantic avenues
(Map 13 C4)
Modern Architecture

Park Slope

Prospect Park West (p107)
between Union and 15th
streets (Map 13 C5)
Historic Buildings

Williamsburg

Momenta Art (p108)
72 Berry Street (Map 13 B1)
Art Gallery

Pierogi 2000 (p108)
177 North 9th Street
(Map 13 B1)
www.pierogi2000.com
Art Gallery

Williamsburg Art & Historical
Center (p108)
135 Broadway at Bedford
Avenue (Map 13 B2)
Art Gallery

Connect up with other parts of town on ≫ www.enewyork.dk.com

Performance

Brooklyn Heights

Barge Music (p130)
Fulton Ferry Landing
(Map 13 A3)
Concert Hall

Fort Green

Brooklyn Academy of Music (BAM) (p129)
30 Lafayette Avenue
(Map 13 C4)
Performing Arts Center

Greenpoint

Warsaw (p130)
261 Driggs Avenue (Map 13 C1)
Music Venue

Bars & Clubs

Boerum Hill

Frank's Lounge (p154)
660 Fulton Street
(Map 13 B4)
DJ Bar

Zombie Hut (p154)
261 Smith Street
(Map 13 B4)
Cocktail Lounge

Gowanus Yacht Club (p155)
323 Smith Street
(Map 13 B4)
Bar

Brooklyn Heights

**Lunatarium
@ DUMBOLUNA** (p154)
10 Jay Street
(Map 13 A3)
Club

Greenpoint

Warsaw (p130)
261 Driggs Avenue
(Map 13 C1)
Bar/Music Venue

Park Slope

Buttermilk Bar (p156)
557 5th Avenue
(Map 13 C5)
Bar

Great Lakes (p155)
284 5th Avenue (Map 13 C4)
Bar

Williamsburg

Spuyten Duyvil (p156)
359 Metropolitan Avenue
(Map 13 C2)
Ale House

Larry Lawrence (p156)
295 Grand Street
(Map 13 C2)
Cocktail Lounge

Galapagos (p157)
70 North 6th Street
(Map 13 B2)
Club/Music Venue

Trash (p156)
256 Grand Street
(Map 13 C2)
Bar

Havens:
Parks & Gardens

Crown Heights

Brooklyn Botanic Garden (p176)
1000 Washington Avenue
(Map 13 D4)

Jamaica Bay

Jamaica Bay Wildlife Refuge (p176)
Crossbay Boulevard,
Broad Channel

Park Slope

Prospect Park (p175)
www.prospectpark.org
(Map 13 D5)

Hotels

Boerum Hill

Union Street B&B (p191) $–$$
405 Union Street (Map 13 B4)

Park Slope

**Bed & Breakfast
on the Park** (p191) $$
113 Prospect Park West
(Map 13 C5)

Queens

Art & Architecture

Noguchi Sculpture Museum (p177)
32–37 Vernon Boulevard,
Long Island City
Art Gallery/Garden

P.S.1 (p109)
22–5 Jackson Avenue
Art Gallery

Sports Arenas

Shea Stadium (p131)
123-01 Roosevelt Avenue
Queens/Flushing Meadows
Baseball Stadium

Bronx

Shopping

Borgatti's Ravioli & Noodle Company (p167)
632 East 187th Street
Food

Egidio Pastry Shop (p167)
622 East 187th Street
Food

Sports Arenas

Yankee Stadium (p131)
161st Street & River Avenue
Baseball Stadium

Havens:
Parks & Gardens

Wave Hill (p175)
675 West 252nd Street
Garden

New Jersey

Performance

New Jersey Performing Arts Center (NJPAC) (p131)
1 Center Street, Newark
Performing Arts Center

Sports Arenas

Giants Stadium (p131)
50 State Route 120 (off map)
East Rutherford, New Jersey
Football and Soccer Stadium

Restaurants

Recommended places to eat, including cafés, tea rooms, and delicatessens

American

Alias (p28) $$
76 Clinton Street (Map 4 G4)
Downtown/Lower East Side

Amy Ruth's (p163) $
113 West 116th Street
(Map 11 D5)
212 280 8779
Above Central Park/Harlem

Annie's (p47) $
1381 3rd Avenue (Map 8 F1)
Upper East Side

Blue Smoke (p41) $$
116 East 27th Street (Map 6 F4)
Midtown/Gramercy

Butta'Cup Lounge (p54) $$
271 Adelphi Street (Map 13 C3)
Brooklyn/Fort Green

Crif Dogs (p36) $
113 St. Mark's Place (Map 4 F3)
Downtown/East Village

Florent (p38) $$
69 Gansevoort Street
(Map 3 A2)
*Downtown/Meatpacking
District*

Four Seasons (p38) $$$
99 East 52nd Street (Map 7 D5)
www.fourseasons
restaurant.com
Midtown/Theater District

Gramercy Tavern (p38)
42 East 20th Street (Map 4 E1)
212 477 0777
Midtown/Gramercy

The Grocery (p52) $$
288 Smith Street (Map 13 B4)
Brooklyn/Carroll Gardens

Jackson Diner (p167)
37 74th Street
Queens/Jackson Heights

Jane (p26) $$
100 West Houston Street
(Map 3 D4)
Downtown/West Village

Mercer Kitchen (p25) $$
99 Prince Street (Map 3 D4)
Downtown/SoHo

**Nathan's Famous
Hotdogs** (p166) $
Corner of Surf &
Stillwell avenues
Brooklyn/Coney Island

New Leaf Café (p51) $$
Fort Tryon Park, One Margaret
Corbin Drive (off map)
*Above Central Park/Fort Tryon
& Inwood*

Ouest (p49) $$$
2315 Broadway (Map 9 B5)
Upper West Side

Paul's Palace (p31) $
131 2nd Avenue (Map 4 E3)
Downtown/East Village

**Peter Luger
Steak House** (p55) $$$
178 Broadway (Map 13 B2)
Brooklyn/Williamsburg

Relish (p55) $$
225 Wythe Avenue (Map 13 D2)
Brooklyn/Williamsburg

Serendipity 3 (p47) $
225 East 60th Street
(Map 8 F4)
Upper East Side

Tavern on the Green (p38)
Central Park West bet 66th and
67th streets (Map 7 C3)
212 873 3200
www.tavernonthegreen.com
Upper West Side

**Top of the Tower @ Beekman
Tower Hotel** (p172)
3 Mitchell Place at 49th Street
& 1st Avenue (Map 6 G1)
Midtown/Turtle Bay

Union Square Café (p39) $$$
21 East 16th Street (Map 3 D1)
Midtown/Gramercy

WD-50 (p28) $$$
50 Clinton Street (Map 4 G4)
Downtown/Lower East Side

Asian

Daily Chow (p30) $
2 East 2nd Street (Map 4 E3)
Downtown/East Village

March (p47) $$$
405 East 58th Street (Map 8 G4)
Upper East Side

Austrian

Wallse (p37) $$$
344 West 11th St. (Map 3 A3)
Downtown/West Village

Bakeries

*See also Cafés, Delis, and
Tea Rooms*

Bonsignour (p72) $
35 Jane Street (Map 3 B2)
*Downtown/Meatpacking
District*

Egidio Pastry Shop (p167) $
622 East 187th Street
Bronx

Ess-a-Bagel (p44) $
831 3rd Avenue (Map 6 F1)
Midtown/Murray Hill

City Bakery (p39) $
3 West 18th Street
(Map 3 C1)
Midtown/Chelsea

Cukiernia (p165) $
223 Bedford Avenue
(Map 13 B2)
Brooklyn/Williamsburg

Dean & DeLuca (pp13, 65) $
560 Broadway (Map 3 D4)
Downtown/SoHo

Magnolia Bakery (p71) $
401 Bleecker Street
(Map 3 B3)
Downtown/West Village

Belgian

Pommes Frites (p36) $
123 2nd Avenue (Map 4 E3)
Downtown/East Village

Breakfast/Brunch

Deborah (p13) $
43 Carmine Street
(Map 3 C4)
Downtown/West Village

Florent (p13, 38) $
69 Gansevoort Street
(Map 3 A2)
Downtown/West Village

Norma's (p46) $$
Le Parker Meridien Hotel, 118
W. 57th Street (Map 7 D5)
Midtown/Theater District

Paris Commune (p13)
411 Bleecker Street (Map 3 B3)
Downtown/West Village

British

Park Slope Chip Shop (p53) $
383 5th Avenue (Map 13 C4)
Brooklyn/Park Slope

Tea & Sympathy (p31)
108 Greenwich Ave. (Map 3 C2)
www.teaandsympathy
newyork.com
Downtown/West Village

Cafés

*See also Bakeries, Delis, and
Tea Rooms*

Bonsignour (p72)
35 Jane Street (Map 3 B2)
*Downtown/Meatpacking
District*

Connecticut Muffin (p164) $
115 Montague Street
(Map 13 A4)
Brooklyn/Brooklyn Heights

DT–UT (p162) $
41 Avenue B (Map 4 G2)
Downtown/East Village

Egidio Pastry Shop (p167) $
622 East 187th Street
Bronx

**Housing Works Used Book $
Café** (p15)
126 Crosby Street (Map 3 D5)
Downtown/Little Italy

Joe (p31) $
141 Waverly Place
212 924 6750 (Map 3 C3)
Downtown/West Village

Mud Spot (p31) $
307 East 9th Street (Map 4 E2)
www.themudtruck.com
Downtown/East Village

Mud Truck (p31) $
14th Street and Broadway
(Map 3 D2)
www.themudtruck.com
Downtown/West Village

Rue B (p162) $
188 Avenue B (Map 4 G2)
Downtown/East Village

Verb Café (p165) $
218 Bedford Avenue
(Map 13 C2)
www.verbcafe.com
Brooklyn/Williamsburg

Via Quadronno (p31)
25 East 73rd Street
212 650 9880
(Map 8 F2)
Upper East Side

Caribbean

El Malecón II (p50) $
764 Amsterdam Avenue
(9 B3)
Upper West Side

Chinese

66 (p24) $$$
241 Church Street
(Map 1 D1)
Downtown/Tribeca

Fried Dumpling (p36)
99 Allen Street (Map 4 F4)
Downtown/Lower East Side

HSF (p160) $$
46 Bowery (Map 2 E1)
Downtown/Chinatown

Golden Unicorn (p25) $
18 East Broadway
(Map 2 F1)
Downtown/Chinatown

**Grand Sichuan
International** (p39) $
229 9th Avenue (Map 5 C5)
Midtown/Chelsea

Great NY Noodle Town (p160) $
Bowery at Bayard Street
(Map 2 E1)
Downtown/Chinatown

Peking Duck House (p25) $$
28 Mott Street
(Map 2 E1)
Downtown/Chinatown

Cuban

Cafe Habana (p27) $
229 Elizabeth Street
(Map 4 E4)
Downtown/Little Italy

Delis/Sandwich Shops

*See also Bakeries, Cafés, and
Tea Rooms*

2nd Avenue Deli (p33) $$
156 2nd Avenue (Map 4 E2)
Downtown/East Village

Amish Fine Food Market (p160)
17 Battery Place (Map 1 D5)
Downtown/Lower Manhattan

BB Sandwich Bar (p36) $
120 West 3rd Street (Map 3 C3)
Downtown/West Village

Cosi (p160) $
55 Broad Street (Map 1 D4)
Downtown/Lower Manhattan

Dean & DeLuca (pp13, 65) $
560 Broadway (Map 3 D4)
Downtown/SoHo

Pret a Manger (p160) $
60 Broad Street (Map 1 D4)
Downtown/Lower Manhattan

Sandwich Planet (p43) $
534 9th Avenue (Map 5 C2)
Midtown/Hell's Kitchen

Zabar's (p85) $
2245 Broadway (Map 7 B1)
Upper West Side

Eastern European

Café Arbat (p166) $
306 Brighton Beach Avenue
Brooklyn/Coney Island

Café Glechik (p166) $
3159 Coney Island Avenue
Brooklyn/Coney Island

European

Artisanal (p42) $$
2 Park Avenue (Map 6 F4)
Midtown/Gramercy

**Blue Ribbon
Bakery** (p33) $–$$$
33 Downing Street (Map 3 C4)
Downtown/West Village

Four Seasons (p38) $$$
99 East 52nd Street
212 754 9494
www.fourseasons
restaurant.com (Map 7 D5)
Midtown/Theater District

Montrachet (p24) $$$
239 West Broadway
(Map 1 C1)
Downtown/Tribeca

Picholine (p50) $$$
35 West 64th Street
(Map 7 C3)
Upper West Side

French

Aix (p51) $$$
2398 Broadway (Map 9 B4)
Upper West Side

Balthazar (p25) $$
80 Spring Street (Map 3 D5)
Downtown/SoHo

Chanterelle (p38) $$$
2 Harrison Street (Map 1 C1)
212 966 6960
www.chanterellenyc.com
Downtown/Tribeca

L'Ecole (p26) $/$$
462 Broadway (Map 3 D5)
Downtown/SoHo

The Elephant (p27) $$
58 East 1st Street (Map 4 F4)
Downtown/East Village

LouLou (p53) $$
222 DeKalb Avenue
(Map 13 C3)
Brooklyn/Fort Green

Mercer Kitchen (p25) $$
99 Prince Street (Map 3 D4)
Downtown/SoHo

Pastis (p161) $$
9 9th Avenue (Map 3 A2)
212 929 4844
www.pastisny.com
*Downtown/Meatpacking
District*

Le Tableau (p29) $$
511 East 5th Street (Map 4 F3)
Downtown/East Village

Tartine (p38) $$
253 West 11th Street
(Map 3 B2)
Downtown/West Village

Greek

Pylos (p30) $$
128 East 7th Street (Map 4 F3)
Downtown/East Village

Symposium (p51) $$
544 West 113th Street
(Map 11 B5)
Above Central Park

Ice Cream Parlors

**Brooklyn Ice Cream
Factory** (p164) $
Fulton Ferry Landing
(Map 13 A4)
Brooklyn/Brooklyn Heights

**Chinatown Ice Cream
Factory** (p160) $
65 Bayard Street (Map 2 E1)
Downtown/Chinatown

Cones (p36) $
272 Bleecker Street (3 C3)
Downtown/West Village

Indian

Tabla (p40) $$$
11 Madison Avenue (Map 6 E5)
Midtown/Flatiron

Tamarind (p41) $$$
41-43 East 22nd Street
(Map 6 F5)
Midtown/Flatiron

International

Biltmore Room (p40) $$$
290 8th Avenue (Map 5 C5)
Midtown/Chelsea

Red Cat (p39) $$
227 10th Avenue
(Map 5 B5)
Midtown/Chelsea

The River Café (p52) $$$
1 Water Street (Map 13 A3)
Brooklyn/Brooklyn Heights

Town (p46) $$$
Chambers Hotel, 15 West 56th
Street (Map 8 E5)
Midtown/Theater District

Italian

Acappella (p24) $$$
1 Hudson Street
(Map 1 C2)
Downtown/Tribeca

Acqua Pazza (p45) $$$
36 West 52nd Street
(Map 8 E5)
Midtown/Theater District

Restaurants

Italian *continued*

Al Di La (p53)　　　　$$
248 5th Avenue (Map 13 C4)
Brooklyn/Park Slope

Babbo (p34)　　　　$$$
110 Waverly Place (Map 3 C3)
Downtown/West Village

Bamonte's (p55)　　　　$$
32 Withers Street (Map 13 C1)
Brooklyn/Williamsburg

Convivium Osteria (p53)　　$$
68 5th Avenue (Map 13 C4)
Brooklyn/Park Slope

'inoteca (p28)　　　　$$
98 Rivington Street (Map 4 F4)
Downtown/Lower East Side

i Trulli (p42)　　　　$$
122 East 27th Street
(Map 6 F4)
Midtown/Gramercy

Mezzaluna (p47)　　　　$$
1295 3rd Avenue (Map 8 F2)
Upper East Side

Noodle Pudding (p51)　　$$
38 Henry Street (Map 13 A3)
Brooklyn/Brooklyn Heights

**Otto Enoteca and
Pizzeria** (p34)　　　　$$
1 5th Avenue (Map 3 D3)
Downtown/West Village

Pepe Rosso's (p36)
149 Sullivan Street
(Map 3 C4)
Downtown/West Village

Via Quadronno (p31)
25 East 73rd Street (Map 8 F2)
www.viaquadronno.com
Upper East Side

Japanese

Blue Ribbon Sushi (p33)　$$
119 Sullivan Street
(Map 3 C4)
Downtown/SoHo

Cube 63 (p28)　　　　$$
63 Clinton Street
(Map 4 G4)
Downtown/Lower East Side

Geisha (p46)　　　　$$$
33 East 61st Street (Map 8 E4)
Upper East Side

Genki Sushi (p44)　　　$
9 East 46th Street (Map 6 E1)
Midtown/Theater District

Nobu (p38)　　　　$$$
105 Hudson Street (Map 1 C2)
212 219 0500
www.myriadrestaurant
group.com
Downtown/Tribeca

Sobaya (p32)　　　$/$$
229 East 9th Street (Map 4 E2)
Downtown/East Village

Sumile (p38)　　　　$$$
154 West 13th Street (Map 3 C2)
Downtown/West Village

Sushi of Gari (p49)　　$$$
402 East 78th Street (Map 8 G1)
Upper East Side

Tomoe Sushi (p33)　　$$
172 Thompson Street (Map 3 C4)
Downtown/SoHo

Korean

Cho Dang Gol (p43)　　$$
55 West 35th Street (Map 6 E3)
Midtown/Murray Hill

Mandoo Bar (p42)　　　$
2 West 32nd Street (Map 6 E4)
Midtown/Flatiron

Mexican

Dos Caminos (p41)　　$$
373 Park Ave. South (Map 6 F5)
Midtown/Gramercy

Itzocan Café (p162)
438 East 9th Street (Map 4 F2)
Downtown/East Village

Mi Nidito (p43)　　　$$
852 8th Avenue (Map 5 C1)
Midtown/Theater District

La Palapa Rockola (p34)　$$
359 6th Avenue (Map 3 C3)
Downtown/West Village

Middle Eastern

Mamoun's (p36)
119 MacDougal St. (Map 3 C3)
Downtown/West Village

Yaffa Cafe (p30)　　　$
97 St. Mark's Place (Map 4 F3)
Downtown/East Village

North African

Cafe Gitane (p27)　　　$
242 Mott Street (Map 4 E4)
Downtown/Little Italy

Le Souk (p29)　　　$$
47 Avenue B (Map 4 G3)
Downtown/East Village

Pizzerias

Anna Maria's (p165)　　$
179 Bedford Avenue
718 559 4550 (Map 13 C2)
Brooklyn/Williamsburg

DiFara Pizzeria (p54)　　$
1424 Avenue J
Brooklyn/Midwood

Joe's Pizza (p19)　　　$
233 Bleecker Street
212 366 1182 (Map 3 C4)
Downtown/West Village

**John's of Bleecker
Street** (p35)　　　　$
278 Bleecker Street
(Map 3 C3)
Downtown/West Village

Polish

S & B Polish Restaurant (p165)
194 Bedford Avenue
718 963 1536 (Map 13 C2)
Brooklyn/Williamsburg

Theresa's (p164)
80 Montague Street
718 797 3996 (Map 13 A4)
Brooklyn/Brooklyn Heights

Seafood

Atlantic Grill (p48)　　$$
1341 3rd Avenue (Map 8 F1)
Upper East Side

Mary's Fish Camp (p37)　$$
64 Charles Street
(Map 3 B3)
Downtown/West Village

Mermaid Inn (p31)　　$$
96 2nd Avenue
(Map 4 E3)
Downtown/East Village

South African

i-Shebeen Madiba (p54)　$$
195 DeKalb Avenue (Map 13 C3)
Brooklyn/Fort Green

South American

**Churrascaria
Plataforma** (p44)　　$$
316 West 49th Street (Map 5 C1)
Midtown/Theater District

Spanish

Bolo (p40)　　　　$$$
23 East 22nd Street
(Map 6 E5)
Midtown/Flatiron

Swedish

Aquavit (p45)　　　$$$
13 West 54th Street
(Map 8 E5)
Midtown/Theater District

Tea Rooms

*See also Bakeries, Cafés, and
Delis*

Lady Mendl's Tea Room (p31)
56 Irving Place
(Map 4 E1)
www.innatirving.com
Midtown/Gramercy

Palm Court Tea Room (p31)
Plaza Hotel, 768 5th Avenue
(Map 8 E4)
Midtown/Theater District

Rotunda at the Pierre (p174)
The Pierre Hotel, 2 East 61st
Street (Map 8 E4)
Upper East Side

Tea & Sympathy (p31)
108 Greenwich Avenue
(Map 3 C2)
www.teaandsympathy
newyork.com
Downtown/West Village

Teany (p70)
90 Rivington Street
(Map 4 F4)
Downtown/Lower East Side

Wild Lily Tea Room (p171)
511-a West 22nd Street
(Map 5 B5)
Midtown/Chelsea

Thai

The Elephant (p27) $$
58 East 1st Street
(Map 4 F4)
Downtown/East Village

Joya (p52) $
215 Court Street
(Map 13 B4)
Brooklyn/Carroll Gardens

Planet Thailand (p55) $
133 North 7th Street
(Map 13 C2)
Brooklyn/Williamsburg

Turkish

Bereket (p27) $
187 East Houston Street
(Map 4 F4)
Downtown/Lower East Side

Pasha (p50) $$
70 W. 71st Street
(Map 7 C2
Upper West Side

Ukrainian

Vaselka (p19) $
144 2nd Avenue
(Map 4 E2)
Downtown/East Village

Vegetarian

Angelica Kitchen (p32) $
300 East 12th Street
(Map 4 E2)
Downtown/East Village

Bliss Café (p165)
191 Bedford Avenue
718 599 2547 (Map 13 C2)
Brooklyn/Williamsburg

Candle 79 (p48) $$
154 East 79th Street
(Map 8 F1)
Upper East Side

NY Dosas (p37) $
West 4th Street & Sullivan
Street (Map 3 C3)
Downtown/West Village

Vietnamese

Bao (p29) $
111 Avenue C (Map 4 G3)
Downtown/East Village

Shopping

Books

Heights Books (p164)
109 Montague Street
(Map 13 A4)
Brooklyn/Brooklyn Heights

**Spoonbill & Sugartown
Booksellers** (pp88, 165)
218 Bedford Avenue
(Map 13 B2)
Brooklyn/Williamsburg

The Strand (p77)
828 Broadway (Map 4 D2)
Downtown/East Village

Department Stores

Barney's New York (p82)
660 Madison Avenue
(Map 8 E4)
Upper East Side

Bergdorf Goodman (p81)
754 5th Avenue (Map 8 E4)
Midtown/Theater District

Bloomingdale's (p76)
1000 3rd Avenue (Map 8 F4)
212 705 2000
www.bloomingdales.com
Upper East Side

Henri Bendels (p76)
712 5th Avenue at 56th Street
(Map 8 E5)
212 247 1100
Midtown/Theater District

Jeffrey (p74)
449 West 14th Street (Map 3 A2)
*Downtown/Meatpacking
District*

Macy's (p76)
151 West 34th Street
(Map 5 D3)
www.macys.com
Midtown/Chelsea

Pearl River Mart (p61)
477 Broadway (Map 3 D5)
Downtown/SoHo

Saks 5th Avenue (p76)
611 5th Avenue
(Map 3 D1)
212 753 4000
www.saksfifthavenue.com
Midtown/Flatiron

Takashimaya (p79)
693 5th Avenue (Map 8 E5)
Midtown/Theater District

Fashion

Alexander McQueen (p161)
417 West 14th Street
(Map 3 A2)
www.alexandermcqueen.com
*Downtown/Meatpacking
District*

Banana Republic (p70)
1136 Madison Avenue between
84th and 85th streets
212 570 2465
www.bananarepublic.com
Upper East Side/Yorkville

Barney's CO-OP (p62)
116 Wooster Street (Map 3 D4)
Downtown/SoHo

Brooklyn Industries (p165)
162 Bedford Ave. (Map 13 C2)
www.brooklynindustries.com
Brooklyn/Williamsburg

Butter (p87)
389 Atlantic Avenue (Map 13 B4)
Brooklyn/Boerum Hill

Calypso (p67)
280 Mott Street (Map 4 E4)
Downtown/Nolita

Century 21 (p60)
22 Cortland Street (Map 1 D3)
Downtown/Lower Manhattan

Costume National (p63)
108 Wooster Street (Map 3 D4)
Downtown/SoHo

Diane B (p83)
1414 3rd Avenue (Map 8 F2)
Upper East Side

Gap (p70)
60 West 34th Street
(Map 5 D3)
212 760 1268
www.gap.com
Midtown/Chelsea

Helmut Lang (p62)
80 Greene Street (Map 3 D5)
Downtown/SoHo

**Hotel Venus by
Patricia Field** (p60)
382 W. Broadway (Map 3 D5)
Downtown/SoHo

INA (p67)
21 Prince Street (Map 4 E4)
Downtown/Little Italy

Intermix (p84)
210 Columbus Avenue
(Map 7 C3)
Upper West Side

Isa (p89)
88 North 6th Street (Map 13 B2)
Brooklyn/Williamsburg

J. Crew (p70)
347 Madison Ave. (Map 6 E3)
212 949 0570
www.jcrew.com
Midtown/Theater District

Keiko (p61)
62 Greene Street (Map 3 D5)
Downtown/SoHo

Kirna Zabete (p63)
96 Greene Street (Map 3 D4)
Downtown/SoHo

Marc by Marc Jacobs (p72)
403–405 Bleecker Street
(Map 3 D4)
Downtown/West Village

Marc Jacobs (p64)
163 Mercer Street
(Map 3 D4)
Downtown/West Village

Mayle (p68)
242 Elizabeth Street
(Map 4 E4)
Downtown/Little Italy

Metaphors (p165)
195 Bedford Avenue
(Map 13 C2)
Brooklyn/Williamsburg

Mini Minimarket (p88)
218 Bedford Avenue
(Map 13 B2)
Brooklyn/Williamsburg

Miu Miu (p63)
100 Prince Street (Map 3 D4)
Downtown/SoHo

Prada (p64)
575 Broadway (Map 3 D4)
Downtown/SoHo

Sahil Sari Palace (p167)
37–55 74th Street
Queens/Jackson Heights

Index by Type

Shopping

Fashion *continued*

Jazz Record Center (p78)
236 West 26th Street,
8th floor (Map 5 C5)
Midtown/Chelsea

St. Mark's Sounds (p78)
16 St. Mark's Place (Map 4 E3)
Downtown/East Village

Subterranean Records (p71)
5 Cornelia Street (Map 3 C3)
Downtown/West Village

Shoes & Accessories

ALife Rivington Club (p69)
158 Rivington Street (Map 4 F4)
Downtown/Lower East Side

Bond 07 By Selima (p68)
7 Bond Street (Map 3 D3)
Downtown/Nolita

Christian Louboutin (p83)
941 Madison Avenue
(Map 8 E2)
Upper East Side

Flight 001 (p72)
96 Greenwich Avenue
(Map 3 B2)
Downtown/West Village

Jimmy Choo (p78)
645 5th Avenue (Map 8 E5)
Midtown/Theater District

Kate Spade Travel (p60)
59 Thompson Street
(Map 3 C5)
Downtown/SoHo

Liliblue (p83)
955 Madison Avenue (Map 8 E2)
Upper East Side

Manolo Blahnik (p78)
31 West 54th Street
(Map 8 E5)
Midtown/Theater District

Niketown (p80)
6 East 57th Street (Map 8 E5)
Midtown/Theater District

Rafe (p68)
1 Bleecker Street (Map 4 E4)
Downtown/Nolita

Sporting Goods

Blades Board & Skate (p84)
120 West 72nd St. (Map 7 B2)
Upper West Side

Paragon Sporting Goods (p76)
867 Broadway (Map 3 D1)
Midtown/Gramercy

Super Runners (p85)
360 Amsterdam Avenue
(Map 7 B1)
Upper West Side

Stationery

Kate's Paperie (p66)
561 Broadway (Map 3 D4)
Downtown/SoHo

Thrift Stores

Beacon's Closet (p89)
88 North 11th Street
(Map 13 B1)
Brooklyn/Williamsburg

**Housing Works
Thrift Shop** (p85)
306 Columbus Avenue
(Map 7 C2)
Upper West Side

Art & Architecture

Art Galleries

Asia Society (p103)
725 Park Avenue at 70th Street
(Map 8 F2)
Upper East Side

Deitch Projects (p96)
18 Wooster Street
(Map 3 D5)
212 941 9475
Downtown/SoHo

Forbes Magazine Gallery (p98)
60 5th Avenue at West 12th
Street (Map 3 D2)
Downtown/West Village

Gagosian (p96)
555 West 24th Street
(Map 5 B5)
www.gagosian.com
Downtown/Chelsea

**International Center of
Photography** (p100)
1133 Ave. of the America
(Map 5 D2)
Midtown/Theater District

Leo Koenig (p96)
249 Centre Street (Map 2 E2)
212 334 9255
Downtown/Chinatown

Mary Boone (p96)
541 West 24th Street
(Map 5 B5)
www.maryboone.com
Downtown/Chelsea

Momenta Art (p108)
72 Berry Street
(Map 13 B1)
www.momentaart.org
Brooklyn/Williamsburg

Pace Wildenstein (p96)
534 West 25th Street
(Map 5 B5)
www.pacewildenstein.com
Downtown/Chelsea

Pierogi 2000 (p108)
177 North 9th Street
(Map 13 B1)
www.pierogi2000.com
Brooklyn/Williamsburg

P.S.1 (p109)
22–5 Jackson Avenue
www.ps1.org
Queens

**Williamsburg Art & Historical
Center** (p108)
135 Broadway at Bedford
Avenue (Map 13 B2)
718 486 7372
Brooklyn/lWilliamsburg

Historic Buildings

Block Beautiful (p98)
East 19th Street, between
Irving Place & 3rd Avenue
(Map 4 E1)
Midtown/Gramercy

**Jefferson Market
Courthouse** (p98)
425 6th Avenue
(Map 3 C2)
Downtown/West Village

Prospect Park West (p107)
between Union and 15th
streets (Map 13 C5)
Brooklyn/Park Slope

U.S. Customs House (p94)
1 Bowling Green (Map 1 D5)
Downtown/Lower Manhattan

Woolworth Building (p96)
233 Broadway at Barclay Street
(Map 1 D2)
Downtown/Lower Manhattan

Installations

Broken Kilometer (p96)
393 West Broadway
(Map 3 D5)
Downtown/SoHo

Earth Room (p96)
141 Wooster Street
(Map 3 D4)
Downtown/SoHo

Modern Architecture

*See also Museums:
Guggenheim and The Whitney*

Chanin Building (p99)
122 East 42nd Street at
Lexington Avenue
(Map 6 F2)
Midtown/Murray Hill

Chrysler Building (p99)
405 Lexington Avenue
(Map 6 F2)
Midtown/Murray Hill

Daily News Building (p99)
220 East 42nd Street
(Map 6 G2)
Midtown/Murray Hill

General Electric Building (p99)
570 Lexington Avenue at 51st
Street (Map 6 F1)
Midtown/Murray Hill

Ground Zero (p95)
(Map 1 C3)
Downtown/Lower Manhattan

Japan Gallery (p105)
1210 Lexington Avenue
(Map 10 F5)
Upper East Side

Skyscraper Museum (p95)
39 Battery Place
(Map 1 D5)
Downtown/Lower Manhattan

**Williamsburg Savings Bank
Building** (p109)
1 Hanson Place, corner of
Flatbush and Atlantic avenues
(Map 13 C4)
Brooklyn/Boerum Hill

Art & Architecture

Museums

Brooklyn Historical Society (p109)
128 Pierrepont Street
(Map 13.B4)
Brooklyn/Boerum Hill

Brooklyn Museum of Art (p108)
200 Eastern Parkway (13 D4)
Brooklyn/Crown Heights

The Cloisters (p106)
Fort Tryon Park (off map)
Above Central Park/Fort Tryon & Inwood

Cooper-Hewitt National Design Museum (p105)
2 East 91st Street
(Map 10 E4)
Upper East Side/Yorkville

Frick Collection (p102)
1 East 70th Street (Map 8 E2)
Upper East Side

Guggenheim Museum (p104)
1071 5th Avenue at 89th Street
(Map 10 E4)
Upper East Side/Yorkville

The Jewish Museum (p105)
1109 5th Avenue at 92nd Street (Map 10 E4)
Upper East Side/Yorkville

Lower East Side Tenement Museum (p97)
90 & 97 Orchard Street
(Map 4 F5)
Downtown/Lower East Side

Merchant's House Museum (p97)
29 East 4th Street (Map 4 E3)
Downtown/Nolita

Metropolitan Museum of Art (p103)
1000 5th Avenue (Map 8 E1)
Upper East Side

El Museo del Barrio (p107)
1230 5th Avenue at 104th Street (Map 10 E2)
Upper East Side/Spanish Harlem

Museum at the Fashion Institute of Technology (p98)
7th Avenue at 27th Street
(Map 5 D4)
Midtown/Chelsea

Museum of Chinese in the Americas (p160)
70 Mulberry Street, 2nd Floor
(Map 2 E1)
212 619 4785
Downtown/Chinatown

Museum of Modern Art (p101)
11 West 53rd Street (Map 8 E5)
Midtown/Theater District

Museum of Television and Radio (p103)
25 West 52nd Street
(Map 8 E5)
Midtown/Theater District

Rose Museum at Carnegie Hall (p100)
154 West 57th Street, 2nd Floor
(Map 7 D5)
Midtown/Theater District

Skyscraper Museum (p95)
39 Battery Place (Map 1 D5)
Downtown/Lower Manhattan

Studio Museum in Harlem (p107)
144 West 125th Street
(Map 11 D3)
Above Central Park/Harlem

Whitney Museum of American Art (p101)
945 Madison Avenue
(Map 8 E2)
Upper East Side

Whitney Museum of American Art at Altria (p100)
120 Park Avenue at 42nd Street (Map 6 F2)
Midtown/Murray Hill

Religious Buildings

Cathedral Church of St. John the Divine (p174)
1047 Amsterdam Avenue at 112th Street (Map 9 B1)
Upper West Side

Mahayana Buddhist Temple (p160)
133 Canal Street (Map 2 E1)
Downtown/Chinatown

St. Paul's Chapel (p94)
209 Broadway between Fulton & Vesey streets
(Map 1 D3)
Downtown/Lower Manhattan

Walking Tours

Big Apple Jazz Tours (p163)
www.bigapplejazz.com
718 606 8442
Above Central Park/Harlem

Harlem Spirituals (p163)
www.harlemspirituals.com
212 391 0900
Above Central Park/Harlem

Radical Walking Tours (p163)
718 492 0069
Above Central Park/Harlem

Performance

Ballrooms

Rainbow Room (p123)
30 Rockefeller Plaza, 65th Floor (Map 6 E1)
Midtown/Theater District

Swing 46 (p123)
349 West 46th Street
(Map 5 C1)
Midtown/Theater District

Cabaret

Don't Tell Mama (p123)
343 West 46th Street
(Map 5 C1)
Midtown/Theater District

Duplex (p116)
61 Christopher Street
(Map 3 B3)
Downtown/West Village

Galapagos (p157)
70 North 6th Street
(Map 13 B2)
Brooklyn/Williamsburg

Combined Arts

92nd Street Y (p125)
1395 Lexington Avenue
(Map 10 F4)
Upper East Side/Yorkville

Apollo Theater (p128)
253 West 125th Street
(Map 11 D3)
Above Central Park/Harlem

City Center (p123)
131 West 55th Street (Map 7 D5)
Midtown/Theater District

The Florence Gould Hall (p124)
55 East 59th Street (Map 8 F4)
Upper East Side

The Kitchen (p120)
512 West 19th Street (Map 3 A1)
Midtown/Chelsea

Makor (p127)
35 West 67th Street (Map 7 C3)
Upper West Side

P.S.122 (p120)
150 1st Avenue (Map 4 F2)
Downtown/East Village

Symphony Space (p127)
2537 Broadway (Map 9 B3)
Upper West Side

Comedy

The Comedy Cellar (p115)
117 MacDougal Street
(Map 3 C3)
Downtown/West Village

The Comic Strip (p125)
1568 2nd Avenue
(Map 8 G1)
Upper East Side

Gotham Comedy Club (p121)
34 West 22nd Street
(Map 6 E5)
Midtown/Flatiron

Stand-Up NY (p127)
236 West 78th Street
(Map 7 B2)
Upper West Side

Upright Citizen's Brigade (p121)
307 West 26th Street (Map 5 C5)
Midtown/Chelsea

Concert Halls

See also Music Venues

Barge Music (p130)
Fulton Ferry Landing (Map 13 A3)
Brooklyn/Brooklyn Heights

Brooklyn Academy of Music (p129)
30 Lafayette Avenue
(Map 13 B4)
Brooklyn/Fort Green

Carnegie Hall (p125)
881 7th Avenue at 57th Street
(Map 7 D5)
Midtown/Theater District

Lincoln Center for the Performing Arts (p126)
Straddling Broadway and
Amsterdam between 62nd and
66th streets (Map 7 B3)
Upper West Side

Merkin Concert Hall (p125)
129 West 67th Street
(Map 7 B3)
Upper West Side

New Jersey Performing Arts Center (p131)
One Center Street
New Jersey/Newark

Dance

The Joyce Theater (p120)
175 8th Avenue (Map 3 B1)
Midtown/Chelsea

Film Theaters

Film Forum (p114)
209 West Houston Street
(Map 3 C4)
Downtown/SoHo

Landmark's Sunshine Theater (p118)
143 East Houston Street
(Map 4 F4)
Downtown/East Village

Jazz & Blues

55 Bar (p116)
55 Christopher Street
(Map 3 B3)
Downtown/West Village

B.B. King Blues Club (p122)
237 West 42nd Street
(Map 5 C2)
Midtown/Theater District

Blue Note (p115)
131 West 3rd Street
(Map 3 C3)
Downtown/West Village

Lenox Lounge (p129)
288 Lenox Avenue between
124th & 125th streets
(Map 11 D3)
Above Central Park/Harlem

Smoke (p127)
2751 Broadway (Map 9 B2)
Upper West Side

Village Vanguard (p116)
178 7th Avenue South
(Map 3 B2)
Downtown/West Village

Music Venues

Apollo Theater (p128)
253 West 125th Street
(Map 11 D3)
Above Central Park/Harlem

Arlene's Grocery (p117)
95 Stanton Street (Map 4 F4)
Downtown/Lower East Side

Bowery Ballroom (p117)
6 Delancey Street (Map 4 E5)
Downtown/Lower East Side

CBGB (p118)
315 Bowery (Map 4 E4)
Downtown/East Village

C-Note (p119)
157 Avenue C (Map 4 G2)
Downtown/East Village

Galapagos (p157)
70 North 6th Street
(Map 13 B2)
Brooklyn/Williamsburg

Hammerstein Ballroom (p121)
311 West 34th Street (Map 5 C3)
Midtown/Chelsea

Kavehaz (p121)
37 West 26th Street
(Map 6 E5)
Midtown/Flatiron

Knitting Factory (p114)
74 Leonard Street (Map 1 D1)
Downtown/Tribeca

Mercury Lounge (p116)
217 East Houston Street
(Map 4 F4)
Downtown/Lower East Side

Rodeo Bar (p122)
375 3rd Avenue (Map 6 F5)
Midtown/Gramercy

S.O.B.'s (p114)
204 Varick Street (Map 3 C4)
Downtown/SoHo

The Soul Cafe (p122)
444 West 42nd St. (Map 5 B2)
Midtown/Hell's Kitchen

Tonic (p117)
107 Norfolk Street (Map 4 G4)
Downtown/Lower East Side

Warsaw (p130)
261 Driggs Avenue (Map 13 C1)
Brooklyn/Greenpoint

Performing Arts

Brooklyn Academy of Music (p129)
30 Lafayette Avenue
(Map 13 C4)
Brooklyn/Fort Green

Lincoln Center for the Performing Arts (p126)
Straddling Broadway and
Amsterdam between 62nd and
66th streets (Map 7 B3)
Upper West Side

New Jersey Performing Arts Center (p131)
1 Center Street, Newark
New Jersey

Poetry

Bowery Poetry Club (p118)
308 Bowery (Map 4 E4)
Downtown/East Village

Cornelia Street Cafe (p115)
29 Cornelia Street (Map 3 C3)
Downtown/West Village

Nuyorican Poets Cafe (p119)
236 East 3rd Street (Map 4 G3)
Downtown/East Village

Sports Arenas

Giants Stadium (p131)
50 State Route 120,
East Rutherford (special
buses from the Port Authority
Terminal at 8th Ave. & 41st St.)
www.giants.com
New Jersey

Madison Square Garden (pp17 & 131)
Map 6 E5
Midtown/Flatiron

Shea Stadium (p131)
123 Roosevelt Avenue,
Flushing (7 IRT Flushing Line
Subway from Times Sq., 5th
Ave., and Grand Central)
www.mets.com
Queens/Flushing Meadows

Yankee Stadium (p131)
161st Street & River Avenue
(4, B, D subway trains from
Manhattan), www.yankees.com
Bronx

Theater

The Public Theater (p119)
425 Lafayette Street (Map 4 E3)
Downtown/Nolita

Roundabout Theatre Company at the American Airlines Theatre (p122)
227 West 42nd Street
(Map 5 C2)
Midtown/Theater District

TV Studios

Ed Sullivan Theater (p124)
1697 Broadway,
at 52nd Street (Map 7 D5)
Midtown/Theater District

NBC Studios (p124)
Between 5th Avenue & 7th
Avenue from 47th to 51st
streets (Map 6 E1)
Midtown/Theater District

Bars & Clubs

Ale Houses

Blind Tiger Ale House (p147)
518 Hudson Street
(Map 3 B3)
Downtown/West Village

The Ginger Man (p151)
11 East 36th Street (Map 6 E3)
Midtown/Murray Hill

McSorley's Old Ale House (p142)
15 East 7th Street (Map 4 E3)
Downtown/East Village

Spuyten Duyvil (p156)
359 Metropolitan Ave. (13 C2)
Brooklyn/Williamsburg

Bars & Clubs

Ale Houses continued

Swift Hibernian Lounge (p142)
34 East 4th Street (Map 4 E3)
Downtown/East Village

Vol de Nuit (p146)
148 West 4th Street (Map 3 C3)
Downtown/West Village

White Horse Tavern (p147)
567 Hudson Street (Map 3 B3)
Downtown/West Village

Bars

2A (p141)
25 Avenue A (Map 4 F3)
Downtown/East Village

Antarctica (p136)
287 Hudson Street (Map 3 C5)
Downtown/SoHo

Arlene's Grocery (p117)
95 Stanton Street (Map 4 F4)
Downtown/Lower East Side

Baraonda (p153)
1439 2nd Avenue (Map 8 G2)
Upper East Side

Barramundi (p140)
147 Ludlow Street (Map 4 F4)
Downtown/Lower East Side

Bar Veloce (p144)
175 2nd Avenue (Map 4 E2)
Downtown/East Village

B-Bar & Grill (p143)
40 East 4th Street (Map 4 E3)
Downtown/Nolita

Boat Basin Café (p155)
West 79th St. at Henry Hudson
Parkway (Map 7 A1)
Upper West Side

Bungalow 8 (p150)
515 West 27th Street (Map 5 B4)
Midtown/Chelsea

Buttermilk Bar (p156)
557 5th Avenue (Map 13 C5)
Brooklyn/Park Slope

**Cabin Club at Pine
Tree Lodge** (p148)
326 East 35th St. (Map 6 G3)
Midtown/Murray Hill

Campbell Apartment (p151)
15 Vanderbilt Ave., Southwest
Balcony, Grand Central
Terminal (Map 6 F2)
Midtown/Murray Hill

Chez es Saada (p141)
42 East 1st Street (Map 4 F4)
Downtown/East Village

Chumley's (p146)
86 Bedford Street (Map 3 B3)
Downtown/West Village

Cubbyhole (p148)
281 West 12th Street (Map 3 B2)
*Downtown/Meatpacking
District or West Village*

Galapagos (p157)
70 North 6th Street (Map 13 B2)
Brooklyn/Williamsburg

Glass (p150)
287 10th Avenue (Map 5 B5)
Midtown/Chelsea

Gowanus Yacht Club (p155)
323 Smith Street (Map 13 B4)
Brooklyn/Boerum Hill

Great Lakes (p155)
284 5th Avenue (Map 13 C4)
Brooklyn/Park Slope

High Bar (p155)
2 Lexington Avenue (Map 6 F5)
Midtown/Gramercy

Hiro (p150)
366 West 17th Street
(Map 3 A1)
Midtown/Chelsea

KGB (p142)
85 East 4th Street (Map 4 E3)
Downtown/East Village

Korova Milk Bar (p145)
200 Avenue A (Map 4 F2)
Downtown/East Village

Library Bar (p148)
Hudson Hotel, 356 West 58th
Street (Map 7 B4)
Upper West Side

Mica Bar (p148)
252 East 51st Street (Map 6 F1)
Midtown/Turtle Bay

ñ (p138)
33 Crosby Street (Map 3 D5)
Downtown/Little Italy

Nevada Smith's (p142)
74 3rd Avenue (Map 4 E2)
Downtown/East Village

Parkside Lounge (p141)
317 E. Houston St. (Map 4 G4)
Downtown/East Village

Plunge Bar (p155)
18 9th Avenue (Map 3 A1)
Midtown/Chelsea

Pussycat Lounge (p136)
96 Greenwich Street (Map 1 D4)
Downtown/Lower Manhattan

Rhône (p148)
63 Gansevoort Street (Map 3 A2)
*Downtown/Meatpacking
District*

Ruby's (p155)
Coney Island Boardwalk
(F, D, Q subway trains to Coney
Island/Stillwell Avenue)
Brooklyn

Rudy's Bar & Grill (p148)
627 9th Avenue (Map 5 C1)
Midtown/Hell's Kitchen

Rue B (p145)
188 Avenue B (Map 4 G2)
Downtown/East Village

Russian Vodka Room (p153)
265 West 52nd Street
(Map 7 C1)
Midtown/Theater District

Serena (p149)
Chelsea Hotel, 222 West 23rd
Street (Map 5 C5)
Midtown/Chelsea

Single Room Occupancy (p152)
360 West 53rd Street (Map 7 C5)
Midtown/Theater District

Sky Bar (p155)
17 West 32nd Street (Map 6 E4)
Midtown/Flatiron

Slipper Room (p141)
167 Orchard Street (Map 4 F4)
Downtown/Lower East Side

Stonewall (p147)
53 Christopher Street (Map 3 B3)
Downtown/West Village

Trash (p156)
256 Grand Street (Map 13 C2)
Brooklyn/Williamsburg

**Welcome to the
Johnson's** (p140)
123 Rivington Street (Map 4 F4)
Downtown/Lower East Side

Winnie's (p136)
104 Bayard Street (Map 2 E1)
Downtown/Chinatown

Clubs

Avalon (p149)
47 West 20th Street (Map 3 C1)
Midtown/Chelsea

Cielo (p148)
18 Little West 12th Street
(Map 3 A2)
*Downtown/Meatpacking
District*

Copacabana (p151)
560 West 34th Street (Map 5 B3)
Midtown/Chelsea

Eugene (p149)
27 West 24th Street (Map 6 E5)
Midtown/Flatiron

Galapagos (p157)
70 North 6th Street (Map 13 B2)
Brooklyn/Williamsburg

Jimmy's Uptown (p154)
2207 Adam Clayton Powell, Jr.
Blvd. (Map 11 D3)
Above Central Park/Harlem

**Lunatarium
@ DUMBOLUNA** (p154)
10 Jay Street (Map 13 A3)
Brooklyn/Brooklyn Heights

Roxy (p149)
515 West 18th Street
(Map 3 A1)
Midtown/Chelsea

Spirit (p150)
530 West 27th Street
(Map 5 B4)
Midtown/Chelsea

Volume (p156)
Wythe Avenue at North 13th
Street (Map 13 C2)
Brooklyn/Williamsburg

Cocktail Lounges

Angel's Share (p142)
8 Stuyvesant Street (Map 4 E2)
Downtown/East Village

Ava Lounge (p152)
210 West 55th Street
(Map 7 D5)
Midtown/Theater District

Beauty Bar (p144)
231 East 14th Street
(Map 4 E2)
Downtown/East Village

Bemelmans Bar (p153)
Carlyle Hotel, 35 East 76th
Street (Map 8 E1)
Upper East Side

Lansky Lounge (p139)
104 Norfolk Street (Map 4 G4)
Downtown/Lower East Side

Larry Lawrence (p156)
295 Grand Street (Map 13 C2)
Brooklyn/Williamsburg

Métrazur (p152)
East Balcony, Grand Central
Terminal (Map 6 F2)
Midtown/Murray Hill

Pravda (p139)
281 Lafayette Street (Map 4 E4)
Downtown/Nolita

Temple Bar (p138)
332 Lafayette Street (Map 4 E4)
Downtown/Nolita

THOM's Bar (p137)
60 Thompson Street
(Map 3 C5)
Downtown/SoHo

**Top of the Tower @ Beekman
Tower Hotel** (p172)
3 Mitchell Place at 49th Street
& 1st Avenue (Map 6 G1)
Midtown/Turtle Bay

Zombie Hut (p154)
261 Smith Street (Map 13 B4)
Brooklyn/Boerum Hill

DJ Bars

Beauty Bar (p144)
231 East 14th Street (Map 4 E2)
Downtown/East Village

Flûte (p152)
205 West 54th Street (Map 7 D5)
Midtown/Theater District

Frank's Lounge (p154)
660 Fulton Street (Map 13 B4)
Brooklyn/Boerum Hill

Lansky Lounge (p139)
104 Norfolk Street (Map 4 G4)
Downtown/Lower East Side

Lotus (p144)
409 West 14th Street
(Map 3 A2)
*Downtown/Meatpacking
District*

Sullivan Room (p146)
218 Sullivan Street (Map 3 C3)
Downtown/West Village

Uncle Ming's (p146)
225 Avenue B, 2nd Floor
(Map 4 G2)
Downtown/East Village

Warsaw (p130)
261 Driggs Avenue (Map 13 C1)
Brooklyn/Greenpoint

Hotels

Expensive

60 Thompson (p182)
60 Thompson Street
(Map 3 C5)
Downtown/SoHo

Carlyle (p183)
Madison Avenue at 76th Street
Upper East Side

Four Seasons (p188)
57 East 57th Street (Map 8 E5)
Midtown/Theater District

The Lowell (p189)
28 East 63rd Street (Map 8 F4)
Upper East Side

The Mark (p189)
25 East 77th Street (Map 8 F1)
Upper East Side

Mercer Hotel (p182)
147 Mercer Street (Map 3 D4)
Downtown/SoHo

Morgans (p187)
237 Madison Avenue
(Map 6 E3)
Midtown/Murray Hill

The Peninsula (p186)
700 5th Avenue at
55th Street (Map 8 E5)
Midtown/Theater District

The Pierre (p189)
5th Avenue at 61st Street (Map
8 E4)
Upper East Side

Plaza (p183)
5th Avenue at Central Park
South (Map 8 E4)
Midtown/Theater District

Soho House New York (p184)
29–35 9th Avenue
(Map 3 A2)
*Downtown/Meatpacking
District*

The Stanhope (p190)
995 5th Avenue at 81st Street
(Map 8 E1)
Upper East Side

St. Regis (p186)
2 East 55th Street (Map 8 E5)
Midtown/Theater District

Tribeca Grand Hotel (p183)
2 Avenue of the Americas
(Map 3 C5)
Downtown/SoHo

Moderate

1871 House (p188)
East 62nd Street (Map 8 F4)
Upper East Side

Abingdon Guest House (p183)
13 8th Avenue (Map 3 B2)
*Downtown/Meatpacking
District*

**Bed & Breakfast
on the Park** (p191)
113 Prospect Park West
(Map 13 C5)
Brooklyn/Park Slope

Bevy's SoHo Loft (p182)
70 Mercer Street (Map 3 D5)
Downtown/SoHo

Bryant Park Hotel (p186)
40 West 40th Street (Map 6 E2)
Midtown/Theater District

Hotel Chelsea (p183)
222 West 23rd Street
(Map 5 C5)
Midtown/Chelsea

Hotel Wales (p191)
1295 Madison Avenue
(Map 10 E4)
Upper East Side/Yorkville

Hudson Hotel (p187)
356 West 58th Street
(Map 7 C4)
Upper West Side

Maritime Hotel (p185)
363 West 16th Street (Map 3 A1)
Midtown/Chelsea

Melrose (p189)
140 East 63rd Street
(Map 8 F4)
Upper East Side

Royalton (p186)
44 West 44th Street
(Map 6 E2)
Midtown/Theater District

Cheap

Chelsea Inn (p185)
46 West 17th Street (Map 3 C1)
Midtown/Flatiron

Chelsea Lodge (p185)
318 West 20th Street
(Map 3 B1)
Midtown/Chelsea

**The Harlem
Flophouse** (p190)
242 West 123rd Street
(Map 11 D4)
Above Central Park/Harlem

SoHo Grand Hotel (p182)
310 West Broadway (Map 3 D5)
Downtown/SoHo

Union Street B&B (p191)
405 Union Street (Map 13 B4)
Brooklyn/Boerum Hill

**Washington Square
Hotel** (p183)
103 Waverly Place
(Map 3 D3)
Downtown/West Village

**W New York,
Union Square** (p185)
201 Park Avenue South
(Map 3 D1)
Midtown/Gramercy

Travel Information

From pedicab to stretch limo, and with bikes, blades, bus, taxi, and train in between, many modes of transportation are available in New York. The city is easy to orient yourself in – a grid of roads covers much of Manhattan, with streets (west–east) and avenues (south–north) numbered in order. Don't bother hiring a car, or you will spend half your time stuck in traffic or looking for a parking space. Use the subway and walk whenever possible.

Arrival

Whether it's your first or hundredth time coming into New York, the approach by air, sea or road should inspire you with glimpses of the Statue of Liberty, Brooklyn Bridge, and a familiar spread of skyscrapers. Once you've arrived at one of the airports or major train or boat terminals, there are various options for getting into the heart of the city.

Note that because of security precautions, left luggage facilities have been suspended in all stations.

John F. Kennedy Airport

Also known simply as JFK (for the former U.S. president), this is the biggest of the three main airports and is used primarily for international and Los Angeles flights. Once you're cleared customs, choose either a yellow cab ($45 flat rate to Manhattan), express bus, the Air Train, or subway. Don't accept unsolicited taxi rides.

Private car services such as **Carmel** offer competitive pricing that's a little cheaper than yellow cabs, but you need to call them for a pick-up. **Super Shuttle** offers shared van rides. Allow 45–60 minutes for car and express bus services to and from Manhattan.

The AirTrain (**www.panynj.gov/ airtrain**) connects the terminals and takes you to Jamaica Station, from where you can take a LIRR (Long Island Rail Road) train to Penn Station. It's also possible to take a shuttle bus to the Howard Beach subway stop, from where you can take the A train on the subway to midtown (about an hour).

Newark International

Taxis from Newark can be pricey. To save money, take the **Newark Airport Express Bus** or shared **Super Shuttle** van, or the monorail to Newark Penn Station, which connects with New York's Penn Station and the PATH trains. Allow 45–60 minutes.

LaGuardia Airport

If you're heading to the Columbia or the Upper West Side, you can take the M60 bus for a mere metrocard swipe *(see below)*. Otherwise, share a **Super Shuttle** van or take a private car or **New York Airport Bus**. Yellow cabs offer a shared taxi ride option to keep fares lower. Allow 20–40 minutes.

Penn Station

Located close to Madison Garden, between 32nd and 33rd streets and 7th and 8th avenues, this train hub serves New Jersey Transit and Amtrak trains. It also connects with many subway lines.

Grand Central Station

This station serves Metro-North trains and many subway lines. The main entrance is on 42nd Street, between Vanderbilt and Lexington avenues. Even if you don't need to take a train, you should come to view the beautifully refurbished main terminal. Free tours are offered on Wednesday afternoons by the Municipal Arts Society (212 935 3960).

Port Authority

The Port lies between 8th and 9th avenues, from 40th to 42nd streets. It serves numerous bus lines and offers a gateway to all points in the Continental U.S., Canada, and Mexico.

Getting Around

The subway may be crowded in rush hours, but it's usually the fastest mode of transportation. New York is a pedestrian-friendly area too.

Subway Trains & Buses

The **MTA** (Metropolitan Transit Authority) is responsible for the 24-hour system of city buses and subways. The **metrocard** ticket works for both. You can purchase a set amount of rides or unlimited day, week, and month metrocards, which are cost-efficient for frequent trips (prices are listed on the website). Machines take credit cards and cash; note that booth attendants don't accept large bills.

One swipe ($2) allows you to enter the subway system for an unlimited time and distance, often with a free bus transfer. Buses take metrocards or exact change of $2 in quarters.

After midnight, trains are less frequent and some express lines run local, making many stops. Keep in mind that nights and weekends are the prime time for track work, so pay attention to notices and anounce-ments on service suspension or re-routing. After midnight, buses stop anywhere on the route upon request, even if it's not an official stop.

Taxis

Yellow cabs are the official New York taxis. The meter starts at $2.50 with $0.40 increments for every 1/5 of a mile, or after 2 minutes if you're stuck in traffic. There's a $1 weekday peak hour surcharge from 4–8pm; the night surcharge (after 8pm) is $0.50.

Taxi drivers have a reputation for being reckless or rude, but most are friendly. The white light in the middle of the sign on top of the car signals that it's ready for hire; if the whole sign is lit, then it's off duty. Most yellow cabs are limited to four passengers.

Other Options

It's pricier than a cab, but the human-powered pedicab is fun and can often dodge through traffic jams. Some drivers are also licensed tour guides.

PATH trains connect the 33rd Street and 6th Avenue, and World Trade Center stops with Hoboken, Jersey City and Newark for $1.50 – a useful service for getting to the NJPAC *(see p131)*.

Ferry services operate around the Manhattan coast and offer crossings to New Jersey. Special summer services on **New York Waterway** also connect downtown piers with a super beach at Sandy Hook, New Jersey.

New York has a network of scenic cycle paths, the best of which stick to the periphery of Manhattan or park-land in the outer boroughs. Cycles can be rented from Metro Bicycles (**www.metrobicycles.com**) and A Bicycle Shop (212 691 6149).

Tours

Big Apple Greeters are trained volunteers who take tourists on free, personalized walking tours for an insider's view of neighborhoods. Guides are also trained to give tours to the disabled (212 669 8159; **www.bigapplegreeter.org**).

By water, Circle Line (212 563 3200; **www.circleline42.com**) offers tours circumnavigating Manhattan, or shorter ones sailing in the Harbor or just up the Hudson or East rivers.

Helicopters

Besides getting you to the airport or the Hamptons, helicopters are a fun way to get a bird's eye view of the city. Various tour themes and lengths are available from **Liberty Helicopter**.

Walking & Eco Tours

Notable walking tours include Big Onion (**www.bigonion.com**) and I'll Take Manhattan Tours (732 270 5559). New York City Audubon (**www.nycas.org**) has a naturalist slant, offering tours of the parks or out on the water. You can also paddle a kayak in the Hudson for free at the Downtown Boathouse (**www.downtownboathouse.org**). In Harlem, there are three excellent cultural tours *(see pp163 & 226)*.

Directory

Amtrak Rail
800 USA RAIL; www.amtrak.com

Carmel Car Service
212 666 6666
www.carmelcarservice.com

Grand Central Station
www.grandcentralterminal.com

Greyhound Bus
800 229 9424
www.greyhound.com

JFK Airport
718 244 4444
www.kennedyairport.com

LaGuardia
www.laguardiaairport.com

Liberty Helicopter
212 967 6464
www.libertyhelicoptors.com

MTA
Subway/Bus/LIRR/Metro-North info
www.mta.nyc.ny.us

Newark Airport Express Bus
www.olympiabus.com

Newark International
973 961 6000
www.newarkairport.com

New Jersey Transit
973 762 5100; www.njtransit.com

New York Airport Bus Service
www.nyairportservice.com

New York Waterway
800 53 FERRY

NY/NJ Port Authority
For airports, bridges, tunnels, bus and train stations
212 564 8484
www.panynj.gov

PATH
800 234 7284

Super Shuttle
212 258 3826
www.supershuttle.com

Practical Information

Whether you need to find a decent public restroom, an accessible subway stop or a WiFi hotspot for your laptop, knowing the basics in any new place is useful. While this section offers practical help with some basic questions, remember that in spite of an alleged gruff exterior, New Yorkers are generally happy to offer guidance to the uninitiated. The key to getting information from a native is not to be shy and to ask for what you need directly.

Disabled Organizations

Since September 2002, the City of New York has committed to ensure that all 158,738 street corners are ramped for wheelchair accessibility. Work isn't fully completed yet, but many corners have been tackled.

Most MTA buses are equipped with lifts for wheelchairs, but only a select few subway stations are accessible. Reduced fare options are available for public transportation.

For subway maps in Braille call 718 330 3322. Hands On! is an organization providing sign language interpretation for films, theater productions, and museum exhibits. Hospital Audiences, Inc. offers an audio service for blind theatergoers and museum visitors.

• Hands On!
212 740 3087; TTY use relay 711

• Hospital Audiences, Inc.
888 424 4685; TTY 212 575 7673

Emergencies and Health

There are several good **emergency rooms** *(see Directory)*. You can also find details of all types of New York hospitals at **www.citidex.com**. The site lists walk-in centers, which are good for less urgent ailments. All of the 24/7 pharmacies belong to one of the three big chains: **CVS**, Rite-Aid, and Duane Reade. Remember that health insurance is essential.

Gay and Lesbian Travelers

A great place for up-to-date information is **The Lesbian, Gay, Bisexual & Transgender Community Center**. This is open daily from 9am–11pm and welcomes drop-in visitors. *The New York Times* has been recognizing same-sex unions in its Sunday "Society" pages since 2002.

Listings/What's On

Time Out New York is an informative weekly, with a bias towards Manhattan. The bi-weekly, free *L* magazine (**www.lmagazine.com**) focuses on events in Brooklyn and below 23rd Street in Manhattan; it can be found in the orange boxes on the streets, usually near another good freebie, the *Village Voice* (**www.villagevoice.com**). The *New York Magazine* features more mainstream events. The Friday *Weekend Guide* section to *The New York Times* (**www.nytimes.com**) highlights cultural events.

Opening Hours

Most **shops** are open by 9am, and regular closing time is 5–6pm, and later on Thursday. Many shops are open daily, including Sundays and holidays. However, some establishments choose to close on Mondays for a break. The same goes for most sightseeing attractions – including **galleries** and **museums**.

Hip clothing stores and record shops downtown tend to stay open until at least 8pm on a regular basis. Record shops may be open until midnight or even 1am. Some shops with late closing hours may open at 11am. **Restaurants** billed as "late-night" usually serve until 1 or 2am; standard serving hours are until 10:30–11pm. **Bars** tend to close between midnight and 1am during the week, staying open until around 3 or 4am on Friday and Saturday nights.

Money

A credit card (or two or three) is essential in New York, especially for booking a hotel room or if you want to hire a car. Visa, MasterCard, Amex, and Diners Club are accepted by the majority of businesses. Traveler's checks are also widely used. Indeed, many businesses accept payment in traveler's checks instead of cash, but the checks must be in denominations of U.S. dollars. Traveler's checks in U.S. dollars can be exchanged for cash at most banks in New York, but other currencies are difficult to exchange.

Before traveling, check with your bank to see if you can use your debit card in the U.S. In many New York stores, you will be asked to key in your debit card PIN rather than sign your name. This isn't the case in restaurants, however.

Phones and Communications

Check coverage with your cellphone provider before traveling, or hire a phone. Note that U.S. companies charge you to make and receive calls.

Verizon payphones on the streets charge 50 cents for an unlimited time on any local call. Some public phones charge only a quarter for a local call, but time is limited. Note that you must dial the full code 1 212 for any number within the 212 area code.

There are many Internet cafés. If you have a wireless laptop, then look for the free WiFi hotspots. Starbucks coffee shops have WiFi, but you pay for the T-Mobile connection. Free wireless connectivity can be found in Bryant Park and many of the small parks found downtown, including City Hall and Bowling Green Park. Check **www.wififreespot.com/ny/html** for updates of new areas. Many libraries have free Internet connectivity too.

Sales Tax

A sales tax of 8.5% is added to most things that you purchase, including to restaurant and bar bills.

Security & ID

Since 9/11/01, more attention is paid to security in public areas. Unattended bags and packages are treated with suspicion and removed.

Stay aware of who is around you when you're gazing up at skyscrapers (a dead giveaway that you're a tourist).

Take some form of photo ID if you plan to go bar- or club- hopping (the minimum age allowed is 21). Even if

you're sporting a walker and grey hair, many nightclub bouncers won't let you in without ID.

Tipping

The general rule of thumb is that you tip **restaurant serving staff** 15%–20% of the bill. (Salaries in the industry are very low, so most staff really do rely on tips). If you're mathematically challenged, then double the listed tax which will give a 17% tip. **Beauticians** and **taxi drivers** should receive a 15–20% tip, although many people offer drivers just over 10%. **Bartenders** usually receive a dollar per drink. For hotel **room service**, offer a 15% tip, unless a service fee is included in the bill; hotel **porters** get $1–2 per bag.

Tourist Information

The New York Convention & Visitors Bureau operates a visitor information center on Seventh Avenue and updates the official NYC tourist web site. Also try **www.ny.com** and **www.visit newyork.com**. Many locals use **www.newyorkmetro.com** to find things to do, eat, and buy. For up-to-date local news, weather and information, try **www.ny1.com**.

Washroom Facilities

There's a noted lack of public facilities in New York, which results in many a crossed leg. Natives are known to dash into hotel lobbies or a local Starbucks to find the nearest "rest" facilities. To work out where the good public wash-rooms are before you venture out, check **www.thebathroomdiaries.com**.

Directory

24/7 Pharmacies
CVS 1396 2nd Ave. (& other locations)
212 249 5062
www.cvs.com

Duane Reade
24 East 14th St. (& other locations)
212 989 3632
www.duanereade.com

Cellphone Rental
212 832 7143
www.roberts-rent-a-phone.com

Crime Victims Hotline
212 577 7777

Directory Enquiries
Dial 1 (area code) 411
or 1 (area code) 555 1212

Doctors on Call
212 737 2333 (24/7 service)

Emergencies
911

Emergency Rooms
St. Vincent's Hospital
West 11th Street at 7th Avenue
212 604 7997

Bellevue Hospital Center
462 First Avenue
212 252 9457

Urgent Care Center NY Hospital
525 East 68th Street
212 746 0795

Government Info & Services
311 (non-emergencies)

The Lesbian, Gay, Bisexual & Transgender Community Center
208 West 13th Street,
212 620 7310
www.gaycenter.org

National Organization on Disability
www.nod.org

Tourist Info
810 7th Avenue
212 484 1200
www.nycvisit.com

General Index

General Index

Acknowledgments

Contributors

Dahlia Devkota's love of travel has taken her to many parts of the globe, from Nepal to Cuba. As well as writing for travel publications, she has been Beauty Editor at W fashion magazine, covering beauty and fitness trends, and spas around the world. For this guide, she wrote the Shopping chapter.

Rachel F. Freeman, native New Yorker and committed foodie and nightowl, loves finding the spice in food, people, and destinations. She's lived in Scotland and Poland and has written for publications including *The Unofficial Guidebook to New York City* and *Voyage* magazine. She wrote the **Hotels**, **Havens**, **Performance**, **Streetlife**, and **Practical** chapters of this guide, as well as part of the **Restaurants** chapter.

Jonathan Schultz, a New England native, co-authored DK's *Top 10 Boston* guide. Despite a profound love for his adopted home of Brooklyn, Jonathan remains an ardent Boston Red Sox fan. For this guide, he wrote the **Art & Architecture**, **Bars & Clubs**, **Seasonal**, and **Top Choices** chapters, as well as part of **Restaurants**.

Andrew Holigan combines commercial travel-based photography and art photography. Since the 1980s he has lived and worked in New York, London, Sydney, and Melbourne. His works have been exhibited at galleries in the UK, and he has also worked on [guides to the *USA* and *France*.

Susannah Sayler is a New York-based photographer and artist. She has worked on more than 20 guidebooks, as well as *Metropolis* and *Planet* magazines. While shooting for this guide, Sayler reported that she had discovered many great spots that she hadn't known about, despite having lived in New York for eight years!

Produced by Blue Island Publishing
www.blueisland.co.uk
Editorial Director Rosalyn Thiro
Art Director Stephen Bere
Editor Michael Ellis
Editorial Assistant Allen Stone
Proofreader Jane Simmonds
Picture Researcher Chrissy McIntryre

Published by DK
Publishing Managers Jane Ewart, Vicki Ingle and Anna Streiffert
Senior Editor Christine Stroyan
Senior Designer Marisa Renzullo
Cartographic Editor Casper Morris
DTP Designer Jason Little
Production Coordinator Rita Sinha

...RAPHY PERMISSIONS

...blishers would like to thank all the museums, ...ls, restaurants, bars, clubs, shops, galleries and ...her sights for their assistance and kind permission to photograph at their establishments.

Placement Key: t = top; tc = top centre; tca = top centre above; tcb = top centre below; tl = top left; tr = top right; c = centre; ca = centre above; cl = centre left; cla = centre left above; clc = centre left centre; cr = centre right; crb = centre right below; crc = centre right centre; b = bottom; bl = bottom left; br = bottom right; l = left; r = right.

The publishers would like to thank the following companies and picture libraries for permission to reproduce their photographs:

66: 22tc, 24tl; 1871 HOUSE: 188br

ASIA SOCIETY: Frank Oudeman 103bl

BLISS SOHO: 170ca/cbl/cbr; BROKEN KILOMETER, Walter De Maria's: 96cl; BROOKLYN ACADEMY OF MUSIC: 129br; BROOKLYN BOTANICAL GARDENS: 5b, 10bl; BROOKLYN HISTORICAL SOCIETY: 109tl; BROOKLYN MUSEUM OF ART: Adam Husted 108tl, tc; BUNGALOW: 150cla

CAMPBELL APARTMENT: 151br; CHELSEA LODGE: 185cl; CITY CENTER: 123br; CORBIS: Viviane Moore 10tr, Adam Woolfit 11bl, Bettmann 11cr

RICHARD DABB: 15br; DK IMAGES: David King/Tim Knox 14tr, 163br; David King 17cl, 103tr; Michael Moran 15 bl; Guggenheim 92–3dps, 104t; Studio Museum Harlem 107cl; Trinity Church 160tl

EARTH ROOM: Walter De Maria 96br

FOUR SEASONS: 178–9dps, 181tc, 188tl; THE FRICK COLLECTION, John Bigelow Tayler: 102tr, bl, br

GETTY IMAGES: Mitchell Funk 1c, 6–7c

LOTUS: 144br; LUNATARIUM: 154cl

NORMAN MCGRATH: 172bl; MERCER HOTEL: 180bl, 182crb; MUSEUM OF MODERN ART: 101tr

NEW JERSEY PERFORMING ARTS CENTER: 131tl, tr

RAINBOW ROOM: 123crb

SKYSCRAPER MUSEUM: 95bl; SOHO GRAND HOTEL: 182cl; SOHO HOUSE: 180tc, 184tr
THE SPA AT THE MANDARIN ORIENTAL: 172tl; THE STANHOPE: 190tl; THE STRAND BOOKSTORE: 77bl

WHITNEY MUSEUM OF AMERICAN ART AT ALTRIA: 100cl; WHITNEY MUSEUM OF MODERN ART: 10blc, 101bl

JACKET IMAGES:
Front: Alamy Images/CheapShots (cr & spine)/Ralph Henning (clc); Corbis/Lester Lefkowitz (crc); DK Images/Dave King (cr); Getty Images/Mitchell Funk (background).

Back: Corbis/Lester Lefkowitz (tr); Getty Images/Mitchell Funk (c).

The Manhattan Subway

The Metropolitan Transit Authority subway service operates 24 hours a day. On this map, **bold** identification letters or numbers below station names indicate that trains always operate between 6am and midnight. A light letter or number shows that the train does not run at all times or skips a station. Following the destruction of the World Trade Center, Cortlandt Street Station is temporarily closed.

For more information call (718) 330 1234 or visit www.mta.nyc.us/nyct/subway/index.